have interacted an[...] mercialization has affected all of them in virtually the same ways. His analysis of the influence of radio and the recording industry is particularly revealing.

A most appealing feature of the book is the attention given individual songwriters and performers. Malone's lively and informed appreciation of the music and musicians he describes will delight all those who love the distinctive sounds of southern music.

BILL C. MALONE teaches in the history department of Tulane University. He is the author of several books and articles on the grass roots music of America.

NEW PERSPECTIVES ON THE SOUTH

Charles P. Roland, General Editor

SOUTHERN MUSIC

AMERICAN MUSIC

BILL C. MALONE

THE UNIVERSITY PRESS OF KENTUCKY

Library of Congress Cataloging in Publication Data

Malone, Bill C
    Southern music / American music.

    (New perspectives on the South)
    Bibliography: p.
    Includes index.
    1. Folk music, American–Southern States–History
and criticism. I. Title. II. Series.
ML3551.M27   781.7'75   79–4005
ISBN 0–8131–0300–2

Editorial and Sales Offices: Lexington, Kentucky 40506

TO MY WIFE BOBBIE

CONTENTS

Illustrations follow page 98.

EDITOR'S PREFACE

MUSIC is the South's most spontaneous and distinctive form of artistic expression. Music for dancing, music for marching, music for praising the Lord, music for commemorating heroic, tragic, or romantic episodes in the lives of the people, music for communicating love, joy, or sorrow, music for soothing the pain of toil and oppression–these and a dozen other themes come to mind. Not that the themes themselves are peculiar to the South; they are to be found in the music of any society. But the music of the South, like everything else there, is an outgrowth of the regional experience, and because this experience has been exceptionally dramatic, poignant, and colorful (in a word, elemental), southern music is exceptionally dramatic, poignant, and colorful. It is elemental. And it has an almost irresistible appeal.

Though the dominant sources of southern music are British and African, Mr. Malone makes clear that it has grown out of a rich variety of national and ethnic traditions, including those of most of the nations of Europe. All underwent changes, subtle and gross, in the southern environment. Ironically, much of the distinctiveness of southern music comes from the region's long juxtaposition of the white and black races and from its widespread rural poverty and isolation. Aesthetically unsophisticated and, by the usual standards, deprived, poor southerners responded by preserving and developing a folk tradition of ballads and spirituals, of blues and jazz, and of hillbilly, country, and gospel music. Finally, strains from all of these types blended to help create rock, the nearest thing there is, perhaps, to an ecumenical art form. Yet, even as southern music became nationalized and, to a degree, internationalized, it continued to demonstrate a remarkable capacity for renewing itself at the source.

In producing this excellent study, Mr. Malone draws upon a knowledge and understanding of southern music gained through performing it as well as through listening to it and reading, talking, and thinking about it. By describing the relationship between southern music and the broader aspects of the region's history and culture, and by showing the effects of southern music on the music of the nation and the world, he makes his work highly suitable for a volume of "New Perspectives on the South." The series is designed to give a fresh and comprehensive view of the South's history, as seen in the light of the striking developments since World War II in the affairs of the region. Each volume is expected to be a complete essay representing both a synthesis of the best scholarship on the subject and an interpretive analysis derived from the author's own reflections. Seventeen volumes are in preparation; twenty or more are in prospect.

CHARLES P. ROLAND

Introduction

IN HIS references to "the infinite variety of Southern mythology," George B. Tindall suggests that many southern myths have become casualties of the historians' endless speculations about the region or of the region's own flirtations with progress and social change.[1] The lazy South bows to the booster South; the genteel South wars with the violent South; and the rural South recedes before the urban-industrial South. Although the focus alters with every interpretation, one romantic notion persists—that of the South as a land of music. Conjure up almost any image of the South, whether Mississippi Delta cotton fields and toiling slaves, East Texas pine barrens and poor whites, Birmingham factories and industrial laborers, or Atlanta office buildings and aggressive executives, and music will be an essential accompaniment to the conception. Hoedown fiddlers, Cajun accordionists, gospel singers, barrelhouse piano players, blues guitarists, honky-tonk balladeers, hillbilly string bands, jazz combos, and hard rock bands predominate.

The music myth is one that has real substance. Music has been one of the great natural resources of the South and one of its most valuable exports. At least since the 1830s, when the blackface minstrels began their exploitation of southern musical forms and images, and increasingly after the 1870s, when Nashville's Fisk Jubilee Singers became the first of a long and continuous line of southerners to take their music north, the world has been growing ever more aware of the South's musical wealth. Like all of the South's natural resources, the region's music was long mined, exploited, and plundered for the enrichment of outsiders. With rare exceptions (such as Bessie Smith, Louis Armstrong, and Jimmie Rodgers), southern musicians themselves have only recently begun to reap rewards for their talents. Today, a Ray Charles, a Johnny Cash, or a Marshall Tucker Band can fill any auditorium in the United States. Southern performers of all varieties command fabulous salaries, and many of them make frequent appearances at the White House, especially now that a fellow southerner is the chief resident there.

The South has exerted a powerful influence on the whole of American music in two important ways: passively it has provided a source of images or symbols, both positive and negative, which have fueled the imagination of musicians and songwriters; actively it has contributed entertainers and styles that have done much to shape the entire realm of America's popular music. Since the days of Charleston's Saint Cecilia Society in the eighteenth century, some southerners have strived to build an appreciation for the fine arts in their region, and they are finally beginning to achieve some success in our own time. Similarly, a multitude of southern-born singers and musicians—such as Johnny Mercer, Kate Smith, Mary Martin, Tex Beneke, and Dinah Shore—have adapted with great success to the mainstream popular music forms of the nation. A book on such musicians would be a massive one. But this is not that book. I have concentrated neither on "high-art" music (operatic, symphonic, and so forth) nor on "mainstream pop" music (that which is geared toward the commercial demands of the mass market and is essentially classless, regionless, and raceless). The chief focus of this book is on the folk music of the South and upon the popular forms that emerged from it.

Early southerners, of course, were no different from other Americans in their indebtedness to folk traditions. All American folk music grew from European and African roots, but, as David Potter has argued, "the culture of the folk survived in the South long after it succumbed to the onslaught of urban-industrial culture elsewhere."[2] In the South it assumed a rich and varied texture, in part because here more than anywhere else in the United States there was a long and vital interrelationship between our two greatest folk music traditions, the African and the British. Southern folk music also acquired a special character because it developed in a society long known for its limitations: a social context of poverty, slavery, suffering, deprivation, religious fundamentalism, and cultural isolation. Southerners turned naturally toward music because it was an integral aspect of their cultural inheritance, and because it provided a means of release and a form of self-expression which required neither power, status, nor affluence. The result was the creation of a body of songs, dances, instrumental pieces, and musical styles—joyous, somber, and tragic—which simultaneously entertained, enriched, and enshrined the musicians and the folk culture in which they existed, and bequeathed a legacy the whole world has come to enjoy.

1

Folk Origins
of Southern Music

THE FOLK MUSIC reservoir of the South was fashioned principally by the confluence of two mighty cultural streams, the British and the African. Yet if one looks for purity in the music of the South, the search will be in vain. Besides influencing each other, these two great cultural traditions also drew sustenance from, and contributed to, other subcultural elements such as the folkways of the Germans of the Southern Piedmont, the Cajuns of Southwest Louisiana, and the Mexicans of South Texas. Furthermore, the songs and styles of English, Irish, Scotch-Irish, Scottish, and Welsh settlers intermingled so rapidly and frequently on the southern frontier that not even the best-trained folklorists today can distinguish conclusively among them or determine their exact origins. The composite quality of this music, in fact, made it "more British than anything one can find in Great Britain."[1]

The acculturation of the African to the white man's ways began on board the slave ships, and although no one can date precisely the exact moment at which black and white southerners began to exchange musical ideas at the folk level, Dena Epstein has argued in her superbly documented *Sinful Tunes and Spirituals* that the process probably began about the middle of the seventeenth century, when slaves and indentured servants mingled on the farms and plantations of colonial Virginia, Maryland, and the Carolinas.[2] Racial prejudice, then and since, did not deter cultural borrowing: slaves absorbed much of the master's music while also retaining some of their African inheritance. And the debt owed by white musicians to black sources is of course enormous. But the potential for musical interchange existed from such an early date in the South's history that it is not only difficult to calculate the degree of borrowing on either side, but also next to impossible to determine the "racial" origin of a large percentage of southern folk songs and styles. In fact, one can posit the existence of a folk pool shared by both blacks and whites, a common reservoir of songs known in one form or another by the poorer rural classes, regardless of race. As long as poor whites and blacks shared a milieu that was rural, agricultural, and southern, and one in which blacks were forced to adjust their lives to the needs of the dominant white population, the cultures of the two groups, while remaining distinctive, often overlapped. Much that has been termed "soul" in our own day is not so much the product of a peculiar racial experience as it is of a more general rural southern inheritance. A taste for cornbread, black-eyed peas, and collard greens is not the exclusive province of any one race; it once was a class prefer-ence that cut across racial lines. Similarly, inclinations in music were not rigidly segregated in the antebellum period. A ballad tradition existed among both blacks and whites, and black singers sometimes sang their own versions of the venerable British ballads. Even well into the twentieth century some black singers, such as Henry Thomas, John Hurt, and Mance Lipscomb (appropriately called songsters), clung to a repertory that was older and more diverse than those of most blues singers. They sang ballads, love songs, and pop tunes as well as blues numbers and demonstrated an acquaintance with a wide range of musical genres.

The religious music of southern blacks and whites also drew from common sources. The degree to which the Christian message replaced the religious world view of the Africans is still a much debated question,[3] but slaves received religious instruction from their masters by the mid-seventeenth century and the Church of England had begun its missionary work in the American mainland colonies as early as 1701. Along with the teachings of Christ came the English tradition of hymnody, a body of music which de-veloped out of psalmody (the singing of the psalms of David with a faithfulness to the English text, and with a minimum of melodic variation). White people, of course, had the greatest access to such music, but songs from the English hymnbooks were being taught to the slaves at least as early as the 1750s. Older blacks still know and cherish the old and stately hymns which they often call "Dr. Watts's hymns" because of their similarity to the compositions of Isaac Watts, the eighteenth-century English composer who made the first significant departure from psalmody by creating new songs with less literal reliance on scriptures and greater melodic diversity. Black choirs can still sing these old songs, and they not only revere a song like "Amazing Grace" as strongly as white singers, they can perform it in varying styles palatable to both black and white audiences.

Although slaves received formal instruction in the Christian religion at a rather early date, and even sat occasionally in segregated sections of the white churches, their first major exposure to the religious music of the poorer whites came in the camp meetings of the Second Great Awakening after 1800. More precisely, the camp meetings were arenas in which poor black and white southerners could learn both songs and styles from each other. In these emotional ecumenical gatherings where Presbyterian, Methodist, and Baptist evangelists thundered their mixed but amazingly compatible messages of hope, songs floated freely through the forest clearings from one group to another. The old hymns were supplemented by the addition of choruses or were replaced by new, spirited songs specifically designed for quick comprehension and mass performance.[4] Most of the songs were soon forgotten, but others were published in printed hymnals or absorbed into the folk culture where they became the common property of southern blacks and whites.

Many of the camp meeting songs, along with other types of religious song material, circulated in the South accompanied by a form of musical notation that was long cherished by rural southerners. The shape-note method, introduced in about 1800 in New England, was a simplified form of musical instruction in which four musical syllables, "fa, sol, la, mi," were designated by shapes whose position on the musical staff indicated their pitch (three shapes had to be repeated to make a complete scale). The itinerant singing-school teachers of the nineteenth century took their shape-note method from New England into Pennsylvania and then into the Shenandoah Valley where the first great concentration of southern shape-note activity occurred. At the little community of Singer's Glen, near Harrisonburg, Virginia, Joseph Funk printed in 1816 his first songbook, *Choral-Music* (in German), and began educating students and siring offspring who would eventually contribute mightily to the circulation of the shape-note method throughout the southern backcountry and as far west as East Texas.[5] The shape-note composers and songbook compilers adjusted readily to the seven-note "do re mi" system, but the most popular of all the southern-produced books, and one long revered in many southern homes as second only to the Bible, was Benjamin F. White's *Sacred Harp* (1844), a book that adhered to the four-note style and which is still the chief manual for many southern singers today. B. F. White and other shape-note teachers and writers ministered largely to the needs of white people, but the method, and the hymnals that conveyed it, also moved into the homes of some blacks. George Pullen Jackson described the black shape-note singers in 1933, and Joe Dan Boyd noted the surviving remnants of the tradition as late as the 1970s.[6] The paperback gospel songbooks of the twentieth century, which contained both the oldest hymns of Protestantism and the newest compositions, were color-blind; songbooks with compositions by both blacks and whites could once be found in great profusion in homes and rural churches throughout the South. Through this means, and through radio transmission after 1920, the gospel composers circulated their songs, on the whole oblivious to racial considerations. As a result, songs such as "I'll Fly Away" and "Turn Your Radio On," both by Albert Brumley, the popular Oklahoma-born white composer, could become fixtures in the repertories of black singers. On the other hand, white gospel singers may not always be aware that such songs as "Precious Lord" and "Peace in the Valley" were written by the black composer, Thomas Dorsey, or that such standards as "Stand by Me" and "Take Your Burdens to the Lord" came from the pen of the Philadelphia African Methodist Episcopal minister, Charles H. Tindley.

There was also once a string band tradition that encompassed both blacks and whites. The cultures of West Africa possessed a wide array of string instruments, including one-string instruments, which were both plucked and bowed (one can still find an occasional one-string instrument in the deep South today). The Negro's proficiency with the guitar has been well recognized since at least the turn of the century, and he seems to have mastered the instrument long before the southern white man. In the most inaccessible regions of the South, the guitar appears to have been a rather late acquisition among white folk musicians, coming to the Appalachians after the 1880s and to the Cajun bayou country of Louisiana even later. Folklorist David Evans has speculated that the so-called Hawaiian guitar (laid flat across the musician's lap and fretted with a steel bar) may have been inspired by American Negro sailors who introduced their bottleneck style of guitar playing into the Hawaiian Islands at the end of the nineteenth century.[7]

The banjo has long been recognized as an instrument of African origin, and Dena Epstein has documented its association with American Negroes as early as 1754. The addition of the fifth, or drone, string is often attributed to a white southerner, Joel Walker Sweeney, a popular minstrel entertainer from Appomattox, Virginia, although there is no clear proof of this assumption, and some evidence against it.[8] The banjo did attain national popularity through the performances of the touring white minstrel bands. Presumably these men adopted the instrument from black sources, but whether their styles of performance reflected black instrumental patterns is open to question. Regardless of its origin, the five-string banjo was by 1920 presumed to be the exclusive property of white musicians, first popular with stage entertainers, and then with southern folk performers.

No instrument has been more readily identified with southern whites than the fiddle. Since the fiddle was small and compact enough to be carried in a saddlebag, as the southern frontier advanced westward the fiddle moved with it. The fiddler could generally be heard anywhere a crowd gathered: at county court days, political rallies, militia musters, race days, county fairs, holidays, house-raisings and similar work/social functions, and of course at fiddle contests, which have been held in the South since at least the 1740s. The fiddle tunes constituted America's largest and most important body of folk music preserved and transmitted without benefit of written scores, and many of the tunes are still performed by country musicians today (although in styles that their European forebears would scarcely recognize). Included among them were old British dance tunes such as "Soldier's Joy," indigenous tunes of anonymous origin such as "Hell among the Yearlings," songs commemorating historical events such as "The Eighth of January" (about the Battle of New Orleans), and songs learned from the popular stage or from sheet music such as "Arkansas Traveler" or "Over the Waves."

Aside from public gatherings, the country dance was the natural habitat for the fiddle's versatility. The country dance was the most important social diversion among rural southerners, and it continued to be so almost to the 1930s. Although such dances were occasionally held in a more public social setting such as a tavern or a dance hall, the most typical locus was the private farm home. After a family sent out the word that a dance was scheduled for a particular evening, farm folk came by horse and wagon from all over the countryside and gathered in a room that had been stripped bare of furniture. In some cases, two rooms were prepared for the dancers, and a fiddler sat or stood in the doorway between the two rooms. A fiddler was one of the most prized members of a community. Quite often he had no accompanist; occasionally, though, he teamed with a musician playing a parlor organ, French harp, banjo, or guitar. As late as the twenties, in some parts of the Appalachian South a fiddle and banjo were considered to be a band. Elsewhere, a fiddle and guitar formed the most popular combination, and it was this combination that anticipated the larger and more diverse country music bands of the present.

The fiddle has been a fixture in white country music for such a long time that it has been all but forgotten that the instrument was once as popular among blacks as among whites. Newspapers, travel accounts, memoirs, plantation records, runaway slave narratives, and the WPA interviews with ex-slaves abound with references to slave fiddlers. The black fiddlers often played merely for the edification of their fellow quarters-dwellers, but they were also in demand for the social festivities sponsored by the planters. Plantation balls and barbecues and town functions featured both individual fiddlers and entire orchestras composed of slaves. To what extent modern country fiddling is indebted to the techniques or styles of slave musicians, or to the tunes played by slaves, is unknown, but the degree of mutual borrowing between blacks and whites may have been very large. Black fiddlers are not unknown today (and a few of them, such as Gatemouth Brown, Papa John Creech, and Butch Cage, are important concert attractions), but their numbers are now minuscule compared to the hordes of white country fiddlers.

The decline of the black fiddling tradition cannot be explained conclusively. Its demise, along with the virtual disappearance of the string band and the ballad traditions among blacks, coincided with the transition of blacks from slavery to freedom and the emergence of racial segregation. Emancipation brought new forms of discrimination and oppression to blacks, but it also permitted a self-expression that was not available under slavery. Post–Civil War blacks eagerly sought forms of musical assertion that were uniquely their own, and they experimented with all types of instruments. The Negro musician's stylistic inclinations were particularly shaped by his contacts with the city. As his immersion in the urban experience deepened, his ties to his rural past weakened. The younger black musicians generally rebelled against that which was reminiscent of the slave past. The fiddle not only evoked "old plantation days," it was also identified with the presumed enemy of the Negro, the southern poor white.

The musical interchange among the lower social strata of the South, black and white, Anglo-Saxon and Celtic, British and continental European, did not represent solely a folk process. Nor did a cultural vacuum exist. The southern folk, of whatever description, heard music from both popular and cultivated sources, and such music was sometimes absorbed or reshaped by them. We have little information concerning the extent to which the southern lower classes were exposed to the fine arts during the colonial period or even during the nineteenth century. There were as yet virtually no schools where the children of the poor might receive formal education, and only rarely did such a child gain admission to an academy of music. The opportunities for the poor to have heard actual concerts or recitals of high-art music during the colonial era would have been rare. The difficulties of travel and the veneer of social elitism associated with the music are factors that naturally inhibited attendance at these events.

The music audience in the South, as elsewhere in the United States, was very early divided between people who clung to the idea of music as a formal, academic art which could only be appreciated by an educated elite, and people who thought that music was an informal, emotionally perceived expression of the masses. High-art music, defined in such terms, was not only aesthetically elitist, it was also inherently class-conscious. Musical preference was a means, as it often is today, of social and economic distancing from one's neighbors. The southern colonial upper classes did not yet possess a cultural sense of mission that encouraged the inculcation of musical appreciation among the lower classes. On the contrary Charleston's Saint Cecilia Society, founded in 1762, the first organized group of music devotees in the South, rigorously limited its membership to 120 men, each of whom paid dues of twenty-five pounds a year. The society, which sponsored concerts and recitals and which organized its own troupe of instrumentalists, was primarily a socially exclusive club of gentlemen. There is no reason to believe that the "lower orders" ever heard any of the concerts sponsored by the organization. Other concerts, such as those given by touring groups of French musicians at the end of the colonial period, were also oriented primarily to the upper classes. Social extravaganzas sponsored by the planters were probably exclusively upper-class affairs too, for the most part, but black house servants certainly heard the music performed at these functions, and slave musicians were encouraged to learn the varieties of music featured there. Lower-class whites normally were not invited to the plantation balls nor to the other gala social affairs conducted by the planters, but on a very special occasion, such as a wedding or a political barbecue, the social bars could come down, and the poor white neighbor or relative might be invited to partake of the festivities.

Music of high-art origin did insinuate itself into the consciousness of the southern folk, but it probably entered indirectly, that is, through popular performers who had somehow absorbed music from the cultivated tradition. The first incidence, of course, of the interrelationship between the cultivated and folk traditions may very well have been the cherished British ballads. No problem of folk scholarship has been more hotly debated than that of ballad origins,[9] and we do not really know whether such beloved old songs as "Sir Patrick Spens," "The Wife of Usher's Well," and "The Lass of Roch Royal" originated among the anonymous folk or were the creations of sophisticated writers who aimed them at a literate audience (they probably derived from both sources). Regardless of where they began, the ballads were adopted by the folk who reshaped and preserved them and then bequeathed them to their American descendants.

The folk dances of the southern United States, both black and white, clearly demonstrate the interplay between the cultivated and folk traditions. At least since the mid-nineteenth century, when minstrel performers popularized such folk forms as jigs and "patting juba," dance steps of presumed folk origin have persistently made their way into the realm of popular entertainment. We are generally conscious of the origins of such dances as the Charleston, the Black Bottom, and the Bunny Hug, but we may not be quite so aware that many of our "folk dances" were survivals or imitations of formal or even courtly dances. The Negro cakewalk, so important in the development of ragtime music, may have begun as a burlesque of the formal plantation dances witnessed by the slaves (although the white masters may not always have recognized the satire). Square dancing, strongly identified with frontier America, appears to have been a survival of the early-nineteenth-century upper-class fascination with cotillion dancing. Cotillions were popular with upper-class Englishmen who adopted them from continental European sources. The terminology of square dancing —promenade, allemande, sashay—betrays its French associations. Scarcely anyone recalls that well into the nineteenth century a hornpipe was a solo dance (probably the ancestor of the tap dance) featured by stage entertainers and nimble equestrian performers. The dance was brought to North America by French and English dancers in the eighteenth century. Rural southerners have forgotten the dance, but they have preserved some of its accompanying tunes. Virtually every country fiddler knows "Sailor's Hornpipe" (familiar to most people as the theme song of "Popeye, the Sailor Man"), "Rickett's Hornpipe," and "Durang's Hornpipe," but probably only a few of them know that John Durang, of Philadelphia, was America's greatest dancer of the early nineteenth century, and that the dance tune was written in honor of his exploits.

We still do not know precisely how such material found its way into the backcountry South, but enough circumstantial evidence is available to suggest the manner in which the process occurred. In the years following the War of 1812, several troupes of actors and musicians moved into the South carrying their various brands of culture and entertainment into the most remote regions. The dramatic companies of Noah Ludlow and Sol Smith (which were combined after 1834) made regular annual circuits from Louisville to Saint Louis to Memphis to New Orleans to Mobile and thence to Nashville. They, and other groups similar to them, typically offered songs and variety entertainment, in addition to their dramatic presentations which ran the gamut from farce and melodrama to Shakespeare. Noah Ludlow, for example, gave the first public performance of the famous song, "Hunters of Kentucky," in New Orleans in 1827.

The "serious" dramatic performers learned to give audiences what they wanted, especially since these actors had to compete with an expanding list of entertainers whose central aim was to amuse and not to elevate. Before the Civil War blackface minstrels, singing clowns, Punch and Judy shows (which often had accompanying fiddlers or other musicians), equestrian performances (which sometimes included men like John Bill Ricketts who danced hornpipes on the backs of galloping horses), showboats, and the omnipresent medicine shows roamed far and wide through the towns and villages of the South. These performing units, along with the scores of tent and vaudeville shows that toured the region after 1865, circulated songs, dances, performing styles, and comedy routines that were often preserved long after their original creators had been forgotten (actually, we do not always know the "original creators," since the material was often borrowed from folk sources).

The great humbug Phineas T. Barnum was the first promoter to realize that with the proper ballyhoo the American people could be encouraged to patronize the highest forms of art as well as the low. When Jenny Lind, the "Swedish Nightingale," visited the United States under Barnum's tutelage in 1850 (he guaranteed her $187,000), she encountered a tumultuous reception everywhere she visited, including such southern cities as Memphis and New Orleans. The size and enthusiasm of the crowds that responded to her presence suggest that the Jenny Lind mania was not confined to the upper classes. Ole Bull, the flamboyant Norwegian violinist, also attracted large and enthralled audiences during his southern tours of 1843–1844 and 1853. Whether the reception of such musicians indicates a genuine hunger for, or appreciation of, high culture among southerners is open to question, because in an era devoid of radio or television, audiences responded to whatever was available. They could alternate easily between a melodrama and a Shakespearean tragedy, a minstrel show and a concert by Jenny Lind.

The highly musical city of New Orleans may have been atypical of the rest of the South in the breadth of its cultural interests, but chroniclers of its music history argue that patronage of the opera was a community enterprise supported by people of all social classes. Operas were performed in the city as early as 1791, and at least three opera houses had flourished there before the Civil War, presenting productions by French, English, and Italian companies. Beginning in 1827, a New Orleans–based opera company presented well-received productions in such northern cities as Philadelphia, Boston, and New York. Many of these early operas were in the ballad or light opera vein, but several of the most famous operas of the world, such as *The Barber of Seville*, were presented in New Orleans before they were performed anywhere else in the United States. Opera has certainly become separated from the masses in New Orleans, as it has elsewhere in the United States, but at least two scholars of the New Orleans music scene, Ronald Davis and Henry Kmen, argue that attendance at opera performances in the antebellum era was much more socially diverse than it is today. According to Davis, "opera became an integral part of the city's life not for just the wealthy and elite, but for the humblest citizen as well." Street vendors and draymen hummed melodies from the latest productions, and Kmen believes that some of this music may have made its way into jazz.[10]

The preceding remarks have suggested that while attempts to separate music into categories reflecting social distinctions have generally succeeded, the various forms have often intermingled in unexpected ways. Even the most august "serious" music has occasionally been adopted and reshaped by folk communities, and devotees of classical music are well aware that some of the world's great music has a folk basis and that such composers as Liszt and Bartok used the folk music of peasant Europe for their own artistic purposes.

In the United States, high-art exponents have never been totally opposed to folk music; indeed, they have favored its utilization or exploitation as long as the proper, academically trained coterie of cultivated musicians is doing the utilizing and exploiting. And they have not necessarily opposed folk musicians as long as those musicians have adjusted their styles to the demands of the cultivated tradition. A "diamond in the rough," for instance, might be encouraged to cultivate his natural talents in a conservatory or under the direction of a master and to abandon his uneducated tastes for something more elevated and refined. Folk music in its natural state was seldom appreciated, and the folk performers of such music were almost totally ignored.

Nevertheless, cultivated musicians in the South did occasionally explore the folk resources of their region in order to appropriate them for artistic purposes. This exploration did not assume the proportions of a crusade until about the turn of the twentieth century, but there was at least one major manifestation of it before the Civil War. Louis Moreau Gottschalk, born in New Orleans in 1829, was the South's first great classical musician and composer, and the nation's first musical matinee idol. As a child prodigy, Gottschalk was given the best formal musical education available, studying under such European-born masters as François Letellier, the organist and choirmaster at the Saint Louis Cathedral in New Orleans, and then traveling to Europe at the age of twelve where he impressed his teachers (and Fréderic Chopin, who heard him in concert) with his ability. He won great acclaim in Europe before he became widely known in his own country, but, impressed by Jenny Lind's earlier success, he came back to the United States in 1853 and made a whirlwind concert tour of our major cities, including New Orleans. Like most crowd-pleasers who have appeared in American musical history, Gottschalk achieved fame with more than just splendid musicianship. Dramatic stage presence, dark good looks, and an exotic Latin charm all contributed to the charisma that earned Gottschalk his international reputation. He also learned to give his audiences what they wanted to hear: patriotic songs, classical arrangements of popular melodies, and genteel, sentimental airs (his own most enduring composition was "The Last Hope").

But Gottschalk was more than an entertainer; he was also a composer, and it was in his role as songwriter that he tapped, at least partially, the folk resources of the South. In compositions such as "Bamboula," "Le Bananier," and "La Savanne," written during his European sojourn in the late forties and early fifties, Gottschalk drew upon the Negro, Creole, and Caribbean resources of New Orleans music. Gottschalk's principal biographer, Vernon Loggins, points to his subject's childhood experiences in New Orleans as the primary factors that motivated such compositions: the drumbeats accompanying the slave dances at the Place Congo (now the site of the Municipal Auditorium); the rhythmic chants of the street vendors; and the lullabies and other snatches of tunes sung by his slave nurse, Sally.[11] Folk music of various kinds was certainly available to Gottschalk during his formative years, but so was the popular music of the traveling entertainers who often visited the city. Blackface minstrelsy was still in its early stages when Gottschalk sailed for France in 1841, but "Negro music" as conceived by white men was already the rage of both the United States and Europe by the time he returned to this country twelve years later. Although Loggins refers to "The Banjo" (1853) as Gottschalk's most enduring Negro composition, the piece seems more obviously modeled on Foster's "Camptown Races," just as "La Savanne" had earlier drawn upon the frontier dance tune, "Skip to My Lou."[12]

Gottschalk was thoroughly grounded in the European art tradition, but he was also a highly eclectic musician who scarcely could have avoided either consciously or unconsciously drawing upon the varied music forms that so vigorously interacted in the middle years of the nineteenth century. The peak of Gottschalk's artistic production came during the first great flourishing of popular culture in the United States.[13] The boundary between folk and popular culture, however, was so thin that it is next to impossible to determine the origin or "authenticity" of much of the music of the era. It was Gottschalk's sensitivity to the unique presentation of the varieties of music available (especially in New Orleans) and his ingenuity in translating these into his own compositions that demonstrated the potential that the southern folk tradition already held for musicians, classical and otherwise. Whatever the precise sources of his compositions, the imagery and rhythm captivated the popular imagination in a way that anticipated a continuing fascination with romantic southern themes.

2

National Discovery

THE SOUTH, both as a set of images and as a source of music ideas, exerted a powerful influence on American popular music long before the region developed musicians with national reputations. As a land of violent contrasts, with picturesque terrain and exotic peoples, the South proved irresistible to poets and songwriters who saw in its lazy rivers, wagon-rutted roads, and old folks at home endless material for art. Stephen Foster was not the first, nor has he been the last, American composer to seize upon the endlessly appealing romantic myth of the South.[1] American musicians, from the blackface minstrels of the 1830s to the rock singers of our own day, have persistently exploited southern images and have drawn upon southern-derived instrumental and vocal styles in order to shape and enhance their own careers.

The first dramatic evidence of the fascination exerted by the South on American performers came with the vogue for blackface entertainment after the 1830s. Blackface entertainers, of course, had been popular long before the rise of the minstrel show, but their acts did not typically include music until the Jacksonian era. The early minstrels were itinerant song-and-dance men who had traveled widely throughout the United States, and most of them had a strong familiarity with the South and an acquaintance with southern folkways. Thomas D. "Daddy" Rice, the creator of the "Jim Crow" character and the man who inaugurated the craze for blackface comedy in Louisville in 1829, was only one of several entertainers who had picked up themes in his rambles through Ohio and Mississippi river towns. Daniel Emmett, the composer of "Dixie" and one of the most popular of the minstrel men, told of the old circus people such as himself, whose thoughts had always turned toward "Dixie Land" when the icy blasts of winter ravaged the North.

The early minstrel men, then, were certainly familiar with the South, and they demonstrated through their stage garb and make-up that they were fascinated by one human resource of this region – the Negro. Nevertheless, it is extraordinarily difficult to determine how much of the minstrel musical material was derived from southerners. Considering the close identification blackface minstrelsy had with the South, it is remarkable how few prominent minstrel men before the Civil War were southerners. LeRoy Rice's *Monarchs of Minstrelsy* shows a heavy preponderance of New Yorkers and Pennsylvanians, and with an occasional exception such as Joel Walker Sweeney (the banjoist from Appomattox, Virginia, who toured with his own troupes in both England and the United States) the names of southerners are very rare.

It long has been assumed that blackface minstrelsy was a direct borrowing from plantation slave music, and there is probably some merit to the assumption. The banjo and the rhythm instruments – the tambourine and bones – probably were of slave and/or African origin. Some of the dance forms, such as the juba (the practice of hand clapping as a rhythmic accompaniment for dancing), may have originated with the plantation Negro, but even the juba was popularized in northern entertainment in the 1840s by the Negro stage dancer William Henry Lane, one of the great dancers of the antebellum period. Lane's career suggests that white minstrel men may have learned many of their techniques not directly from plantation folk sources, but from the commercial urban stage entertainers of their day or from urban blacks. We know, for example, that Daddy Rice received inspiration for the Jim Crow character from a black worker whom he saw in Louisville. Henry Kmen, in his study of New Orleans music, further alludes to the probable influence of urban blacks on antebellum popular music when he describes the immense popularity of a black street vendor named Old Cornmeal, who took his street routine onto the stages of New Orleans.[2] The itinerant song-and-dance men of the ante-bellum era were more likely to witness the scenes of southern towns and cities than they were the rural, and the folklore they appropriated, though perhaps rural in origin, came through urban contacts. Certain songs, rhythms, and dance steps definitely came from rural black sources, but, as Robert Toll, the most recent scholar of minstrelsy, has argued, the minstrels picked up material wherever they traveled in the United States.[3] Furthermore, folk styles so often interacted in America that it is difficult to determine the ethnic origin of a piece of folklore. Minstrel music was an amalgam of all the rural folk styles (Anglo-Saxon, Celtic, German, African) and urban popular forms to which the minstrels were exposed, plus the original creations they were busily producing.

By the time of the Civil War, minstrelsy had become such an overpowering factor in organized entertainment, here and abroad, that it had moved far beyond its folk roots and had spawned a large contingent of professional musicians and independent composers who had little or no relationship to rural folk America. Such songs as "Jordan Am a Hard Road to Travel," "Old Dan Tucker," and "Old Zip Coon" may have had folk origins, or they may have been the original brainchildren of such men as Dan Emmett and Stephen Foster, who merely imitated folk styles.

Foster, of course, was the most important (if not necessarily the most popular) product of the minstrel school of songwriters. Robert Toll has argued that minstrelsy as a whole presented to northerners a "non-threatening picture" of blacks, but Stephen Foster specifically must be given much of the credit for implanting the romantic image of the Old South in American popular culture.[4] Foster's conception of the South represented a victory of the imagination because he had little firsthand acquaintance with the region. He spent a short time in central Kentucky and took one trip down the Mississippi to New Orleans in 1852. We can be certain that he saw some of the great houses along the river, but he seems to have seen little else, and he did not acquaint himself with the lives of the plain people who lived inland from the river's banks.

Like Harriet Beecher Stowe, Foster painted descriptive pictures of southern characters and themes, but his music did not come from southern sources. According to his most recent biographer, William Austin, Foster's music came from the general and diverse body of influences available to most popular songwriters of his era. He absorbed some influence from German music, but more came from American hymnody and the international body of genteel popular music.[5] Much of his success (and again we are reminded of Harriet Beecher Stowe) came from his immersion in the sentimental tradition. People responded to his music not so much because it presented a realistic picture of southern blacks (which it did not), but because it reinforced the values of the family fireside and featured the stereotypical characters of nineteenth-century sentimental literature: the beautiful but doomed maiden, the dying child, the departed mother, the saintly old man.

Foster's reputation steadily grew in the years after the Civil War, but his real enshrinement as America's greatest popular composer came at the end of the nineteenth century when Dvořák in effect anointed him by applauding some of his songs, thus suggesting their affinity to high-art music.[6] Foster's songs seemed particularly appropriate for a late-nineteenth-century America that was trying to heal the wounds of the Civil War. The appeal of Foster's nostalgic songs cut across regional lines; Americans everywhere could identify with the themes of domestic sentiment and a pastoral society that now seemed to be succumbing to the inroads of industrial progress. The image of a stable and placid Old South was therefore emotionally satisfying, for different reasons, both to northerners and to southerners. Whatever the bases for its appeal, the image of an unchanging, exotic land with gentle manners and contented, nostalgic slaves has been a perennially enduring myth of American life.

Foster was but one of several minstrel-derived songwriters who contributed to the myth of the Old South. There were others, in fact, who may have been more popular than he, and whose compositions have more readily endured in folk tradition without the support accorded to Foster by the high-art establishment. Such writers as Septimus Winner ("Listen to the Mockingbird," "Whispering Hope"), Daniel Emmett ("Old Dan Tucker," "Jordan Am a Hard Road to Travel," "Dixie"), and Henry Clay Work ("Kingdom Coming," "Father, Dear Father," "Grandfather's Clock") produced songs that were cherished by nineteenth-century Americans who have orally bequeathed them to their twentieth-century descendants.

The writer who had the closest relationship to the South, though his characterizations of it never went beyond the romantic, was William Shakespeare Hays. A native of Louisville, Kentucky, and for a time a riverboat pilot on the Ohio River, Hays spent most of his life as a reporter for the *Louisville Courier-Journal*. He was also a prolific songwriter whose lyric themes were highly reminiscent of Stephen Foster. Hays was a gifted melodist and an effective composer of gentle, Victorian lyrics, and several of his songs have remained singable even though their messages seem alien to the twentieth century. He wrote an occasional comic song, but his general repertory was saturated with the sentimentality that typified so much of the popular music of the nineteenth century (including that of Foster). Sentimentality, in fact, often descended to bathos, as in the tale of the penniless orphan girl in "Nobody's Darling on Earth." Many of Hays's songs swelled with Victorian sentiment reinforcing the themes extolling domesticity —the passion of love devoid of eroticism. Such songs as "Molly, Darling," "I'll Remember You, Love, in My Prayers," and "We Parted by the Riverside" told of tender but broken love affairs that ended among scenes of pastoral charm. The moon was forever shining, dewdrops kissed the roses, and rivers murmured to the sea as lovers parted. Hays also wrote an occasional song of nostalgia: plaintive reminiscences of the departed village or farm, or evocations of a vanished way of life with which many could identify. One such song, perhaps the most enduring in the Hays repertory, was "Little Old Log Cabin in the Lane," still heard in country music today. The song was typical of the "faithful slave laments" often heard in minstrelsy in that it described the sadness of a poor old slave who surveyed the decay of his once-happy cabin as "ole massa and missus" slept nearby. Such lyrics could be used to defend the idea of a racially harmonious Old South or of the Negro's inability to adjust to freedom. But, like many of the songs that came out of minstrelsy, "Little Old Log Cabin" ceased to be merely a "darky song" and became a lament for the departed rural home.

The sentimental parlor songs of the nineteenth century, though generally northern in origin and aimed at an urban, middle-class audience, dealt often with romantic southern themes. Though they were immediately appealing to audiences everywhere, they found a natural, and seemingly permanent, home in the rural South. Such songs are rarely known in the North today, or are remembered with amusement as quaint relics of an unsophisticated era. Southerners, on the other hand, are more likely to cherish and preserve such "regional" songs as "Mid the Green Fields of Virginia," "My Little Home in Tennessee," or "Carry Me Back to Ole Virginny" (written by a black northerner, James Bland), as well as such weepers as "The Dying Girl's Message," "The Blind Child," "The Little Rosewood Casket," "The Letter Edged in Black," and "Baggage Coach Ahead."

Although minstrelsy may not have been of southern origin, the phenomenon made a great impact on the region, and it left a legacy that was felt in southern music well into the twentieth century. Minstrel troupes still visited southern cities as late as World War I, and by that time several of the organizations had made their headquarters in the South and were staffed with southern-born entertainers. Minstrel songs, styles, dances, jokes, and even the corking of the face, became almost permanent facets of southern folk and popular culture. The interflow between folk and popular music was often so continuous that it is sometimes difficult to determine the origin of a form, and in the development of minstrel popular entertainment there was a definite cycle of such interaction. The minstrels adopted material from folk sources and then adapted it to appeal to a more urban audience, feeding it back to the folk through the traveling shows. Nowhere was such material more deeply cherished, or longer preserved, than in the rural South.

Exhibiting a continuing tendency to retain those social phenomena which had lost favor in the industrializing North, rural southerners absorbed minstrel ideas and made them the bases for their own personal and localized musical expressions. Commercial black entertainment, for instance, is largely indebted to minstrelsy. The Negro's entrée to professional entertainment began when such all-black troupes as the Georgia Minstrels took their brand of minstrelsy to towns and cities all over the United States. The early black minstrel groups corked their faces, as custom demanded, and generally performed in a self-mocking manner that was degrading to their race. Nevertheless, these pioneer performers created the commercial route that later black entertainers would follow and modify, and the original black minstrels included some of the most gifted song-and-dance men American audiences had yet witnessed, performers such as Sam Lucas, Billy Kersands, and James Bland. Black entertainers carried the burden of minstrelsy with them into the twentieth century, and southern black performing groups still called themselves "minstrels" through the World War I period. It was these latter-day groups—such as Mahara's Minstrels, headed by the young W. C. Handy, and the Rabbit Foot Minstrels, led by the great blues singer Ma Rainey and including Bessie Smith—who played the "chittlin' circuit" of the South and finally forged independent forms of black musical expression.

White rural musicians, on the other hand, did not move into professional show business as early as southern blacks, but they did strongly display the lingering influences of minstrelsy, and early hillbilly music is filled with evidence of this indebtedness. The five-string banjo became a fixture of white rural instrumentation, particularly in the Southeast, and some minstrel-derived banjo styles remained common in country music until the introduction of the Scruggs style in the 1940s.

The major link between nineteenth-century minstrel music and modern country music was Uncle Dave Macon, an outstanding five-string banjoist and member of the Grand Old Opry from 1926 to 1952. Uncle Dave was born in McMinnville, Tennessee, in 1870 but was very early exposed to minstrel entertainers when his parents moved to Nashville and opened a theatrical boarding-house. He picked up banjo techniques and stage patter from the minstrel men, as well as numerous songs that would later appear in both his recordings and personal appearances: "Rise When the Rooster Crows," "Hold That Woodpile Down," "Rock about My Sara Jane," "Jordan Am a Hard Road to Travel."

Many of the more rousing minstrel tunes, those suited for comic, dance, or instrumental purposes, regularly found their way into country repertories. The early hillbilly string bands of radio and recording, such as the Skillet Lickers, Al Hopkins and the Buckle Busters, Charlie Poole and the North Carolina Ramblers, and the Fruit Jar Drinkers, often featured fiddle-and-banjo-dominated versions of old minstrel songs with the same rollicking spirit that must have characterized the original performances. The "rural skits" recorded by the Skillet Lickers on the Columbia label —comic dialogues interspersed with music—also reflected the influence of earlier minstrel routines. The comedy of minstrelsy, in fact, has been a constant in the history of country music. The blackface comics Jamup and Honey were still appearing regularly on the Grand Ole Opry and headlining a popular touring tent show through the World War II period. Musicians from Uncle Dave Macon to Lew Childre, Grandpa Jones, and Roy Clark—as well as stand-up comics such as Rod Brasfield and Benny Ford (the Duke of Paducah)—have persistently delved into minstrel-derived humor to bolster their routines; today the syndicated television show "Hee Haw" still dispenses a considerable amount of minstrel-like material, including a variation of "patting juba."

The sentimental songs of minstrelsy, such as "Sweet Allalee," "Away Down upon the Old Plantation," "Listen to the Mockingbird" (a virtuoso fiddle piece), and "Yellow Rose of Texas," also appeared with great frequency in the repertories of country musicians. The minstrel performers had drawn so heavily through the years on the folk cultural resources of the South that it was only fitting that much of that material should be returned to its rightful home.

While serious doubts can be entertained about the legitimate southern, folk, or Negro content of minstrel music, no one can deny the authenticity of another musical form that came out of the South after the Civil War—the spiritual. Although spirituals, unlike minstrel tunes, were introduced to the world at large by bona fide southerners (the Fisk Jubilee Singers), they were first circulated in printed form by northerners—the teachers and missionaries who came south during and after the Civil War to work among the freedmen. Moreover as in the case of minstrelsy, the perception and reception of this music were affected by external (that is, northern) images of both the Negro and the South. While the minstrels exploited the Negro's supposed hedonism for its entertainment potential, the advocates of the spirituals either stressed the innate religiousness of the blacks or recoiled against their sensuality by trying to suppress dancing and "sinful music" among them. It was felt that this hedonism should be replaced with the decorum and propriety of middle-class evangelical Protestantism. Northern observers were generally impressed or intrigued by black spiritual singing, but, as Epstein has observed, "very few were able to dissociate themselves from European norms of musical performance and to evaluate Afro-American music on its own terms."[7] Too often the freedmen were encouraged to replace their own songs with the "more dignified" hymns of the evangelical churches, or they were urged to adopt the more sedate and conventional performing styles of their benefactors.

Individual spirituals began to appear in northern magazines as early as 1861 ("Go Down, Moses" was the first to be printed), but the first significant collection of spirituals, *Slave Songs of the United States*, came in 1867. Although it is now recognized as one of the seminal works of American folk scholarship, the book was generally ignored in the music periodicals of the day and there was no immediate explosion of interest in the spirituals, either by musicians or by the public. When the Fisk Jubilee Singers took their versions of the Negro spirituals north in 1871, they sparked the first real national flurry of interest in southern-derived folk songs. These young black singers were genuine products of folk communities, even though their performing styles were far from representative of folk tradition. Nevertheless, the vogue they inspired for the spirituals would not diminish until well into the twentieth century. The young singers also encouraged a major excursion by high-art musicians into the realm of southern folk culture. The choir was organized in 1867 by George White, the white treasurer of Fisk University, in order to raise money for the Nashville school. It was believed that the singers would be particularly effective among middle-class white Americans interested in the "cultural uplift" of the black race. The young black students would demonstrate both the potential and the passivity of ex-slaves, and, incidentally, reinforce the already well-rooted assumption that music was at least one thing at which blacks excelled.

Students who went to Fisk, or to other southern schools that were products of northern religious philanthropy, certainly did not go there to be reminded of the humiliation of their slave origins. They hoped they were on their way to the world of the middle class. Understandably, then, the Fisk Jubilee Singers did not at first feature the performance of slave-derived religious music. But after audiences at Oberlin and elsewhere in the North made clear their desire to hear such music, the Fisk Jubilee Singers made the spirituals the nucleus of their repertory. They sang to the enthusiastic acclaim of genteel audiences all over the North and then made a highly successful tour of Europe in 1872, the first of several such trips. Though their subject matter was indigenous and rooted in black folk experience, their style of performance came directly out of the European cultivated tradition. On recordings made in 1913 of a later version of the Fisk Jubilee Singers, the singing is in a restrained, highly polished manner, with none of the swinging, uninhibited, emotional style associated with the southern, downhome black churches. Nevertheless, they made the world conscious of the spirituals, and they initiated the first real excursion by high-art music advocates into the folk resources of the South.

The vogue for the spirituals, and the subsequent fascination with other types of southern-derived folk music, should be considered, at least in part, as a facet of the larger quest for a national music. This quest, of course, was not new but had been pursued at least since the days of Lowell Mason, who had sought to create a music that would represent America's distinctiveness while also winning the respect of the world. Implicit in this search was the belief that a true national music must embody native American material—that is, that it must rest upon an indigenous folk basis. During the last decade of the nineteenth century, and increasingly in the years immediately following World War I when nationalism was at a peak, high-art music advocates vigorously debated the merits of various folk traditions. Some people, of course, denied the existence of any type of indigenous folk music in the United States, while others stressed the usefulness of Indian, black, and Anglo-Saxon themes, or even commercial materials (such as ragtime or jazz), as the raw stuff from which a fine, finished, American musical product could be built. The black spirituals (but not the raw secular or downhome gospel material of southern blacks) obviously appealed to some musicians because they were both beautiful and presumably of American origin.

The composer who did most to promote the high-art potential of the spirituals was the Czech composer, Antonin Dvořák, who came to the United States in 1892. Settling down in a New York apartment, and on a farm in Iowa during the summers, Dvořák began producing a number of musical works said to be based on American themes. Although Dvořák was an ardent and outspoken advocate of the utilization of Negro themes,[8] there is still some question about whether or not he actually used Negro melodies himself. The appealing theme of the symphony *From the New World*, "Goin' Home," certainly sounds like a spiritual, but it seems to have no analogue in Negro music. Dvořák had been inspired to create "folklike" melodies, but, like Stephen Foster before him, he exhibited a larger indebtedness to the cultivated musical traditions of the world.

In the years following Dvořák's American sojourn, singers, musicians, and composers often dipped into the spiritual bag. Instrumental and vocal concerts of spirituals were often given well into the 1920s, and performance of them was the springboard for the careers of such great American singers as Paul Robeson and Marian Anderson. At least one of these singers was a southerner— the Georgia-born Roland Hayes, who built a very successful first career singing spirituals and then moved on to another career as one of America's leading opera singers. The composers who dealt with the spirituals were usually white men who arranged the material to fit the tastes of white middle-class concertgoers. But a few black composers, such as Harry Burleigh and Nathaniel Dett, specialized in the spirituals, and William Grant Still, from Mississippi, wrote symphonies based on spirituals or adaptations of them.

Despite the rage for the spirituals, many musicians and composers rejected them as ingredients for a national music. The spirituals, so the argument ran, did not spring from the majority of Americans and therefore could not represent the soul of American experience. And one of the leading scholars of southern religious folk music, George Pullen Jackson, denied the originality of the spirituals and asserted that they were borrowed from older white religious music.[9] Missionaries for a national American music clearly must look elsewhere for a folk basis for the high-art form they wished to create.

Considering the American social context at the turn of the twentieth century, it is not surprising that an Anglo-Saxon school of folk music should emerge. The decisive turn toward imperialism taken by the United States in the years immediately preceding and following the Spanish-American War set off a renewed emphasis on the mission of America's "Anglo-Saxon" people. This missionary impulse to spread the American Way to the unenlightened peoples of the world was accompanied by the disquieting concern that the Anglo-Saxon core of our culture was disintegrating or being dangerously diluted under the impact of urban industrialism and immigration.

Such fears, at least among scholars, partly explain the resurgent interest in folklore at the end of the nineteenth century, a phenomenon marked by the founding of the American Folklore Society in 1888 and by the collecting of the British popular ballads by the Harvard scholar, Francis James Child. A sense of urgency accompanied the collecting and classifying of folklore in this country, as if the scholars had only a short time to work before the folk tradition succumbed to the processes of modernization. Folklore was not only equated with peasant pastoralism, but in this country the best of that folklore was presumed to be of Anglo-Saxon origin. Our Anglo-Saxon rural peasantry was disappearing —through urban migration, adjustment to industrial occupations, increasing literacy, and intermarriage with outsiders, and this would also mean the disappearance of our folklore. Burdened by these biases, then, early folk song scholarship in the United States was destined to be overlaid with a heavy strain of romanticism. It was difficult to see the folk as they actually were when one gazed through the misty lens of this myth-tinged scholarship.

When looking for survivals or remnants of the Anglo-Saxon past, it was inevitable that the gaze would be directed south. It had long been assumed that in a nation characterized by ceaseless change the South was a land of stability and a repository of traditional values. And the region was already being referred to as the most Anglo-Saxon part of the country. The publication of John A. Lomax's *Cowboy Songs and Other Frontier Ballads* in 1910 sparked a great surge of interest in folk songs of all kinds, and, in fact, inspired a search for folk material in all regions of the nation. We now know that the cowboy culture was a composite of many racial and cultural groups, and that Mexicans and Negroes made invaluable contributions to its creation. But in 1910 the vision of the man on horseback was more apt to be a close approximation of the character earlier portrayed in the dime novels or in Owen Wister's *The Virginian*. In short, he was a modern Anglo-Saxon knight. It was fortuitous that the cowboy's commemoration in popular culture should come when it did, at the moment when Americans needed such a symbol to counter their anxieties concerning the disappearance of rugged individualism in modern mass society.

If the cowboy symbolized what the American would like to have been, the southern mountaineer was, it was felt, a living reminder of what he once was. Isolated from the currents of social and economic change, the mountaineer remained our "contemporary ancestor," a self-reliant frontiersman who clung to Elizabethan ways. Mary Noailles Murfree (writing under the pseudonym of Charles Craddock) made a powerful contribution to the romantic myth of the mountains with her short stories and novels of the 1880s, but the most decisive entry of the mountaineer into American popular culture came with the novels of John Fox, Jr., written before World War I. By the time the folklorists began venturing into the mountain regions in the early twentieth century, Americans were already predisposed to think of mountain people as quaint relics of a bygone era or as conservators of an archaic tradition. That they should be singing songs that no one else remembered was not surprising to anyone.

The mountaineers were of special interest to the teachers in the mountain settlement schools. These Protestant missionaries, predominantly women, had come south in the years after the Civil War to educate mountain children, or to bring "cultural uplift" to them, replacing the rough edges of mountain culture with something closely approximating the New England middle-class ideal. The settlement ladies' interpretation of the fine arts was much influenced by their northern genteel upbringing, and their concept of folk music was naturally shaped and limited by their high-art or literary orientations. They were clearly not prepared either to understand or to appreciate the rural music that enveloped them in their adopted mountain surroundings. Furthermore, many of the mountain families who sent their children to the settlement schools were eager to have their sons and daughters exposed to that finer world outside; they and their children were sometimes embarrassed by their culture and were actively seeking "improvement."

Still, some of the settlement schools did come to conceive of themselves as "folk schools" where the mountain people would be encouraged to preserve their own culture; consequently, students were encouraged to learn the traditional ballads, folk songs, and dances. The teachers, however, were biased in favor of the oldest and rarest British songs and generally hostile to the newer songs which had long been moving into the mountaineers' repertory; these "newer" songs included, among others, those in the gospel and parlor song categories. Moreover, like the academic folklorists of their day, the settlement teachers had a rather static view of folklore, and in the moral fervor of their mission they rejected songs they considered "unsuitable," such as "Frankie and Johnny" or "The Birmingham Jail."

One of the settlement women, Olive Dame Campbell, wife of John C. Campbell (director of the Southern Highland Division of the Russell Sage Foundation), contributed directly to the arousing of national attention to the folk music of Appalachia. She wrote Cecil Sharp, an English folk dance authority, and encouraged him to come to the southern mountains where he would find a body of folk songs larger than that in his own country. Sharp spent a total of about twelve months in the hills from 1916 to 1918, talking to local song informants and, with the assistance of Maud Karpeles, transcribing in his notebooks both words and melodies of traditional songs, many of which were included in his seminal book, *English Folk Songs from the Southern Appalachians* (1932). Sharp suggested in his commentary that folk singing in the mountains was far from being an archaic practice confined to a few old-timers. Such singing was common among both young and old and was a vigorous, living force indeed.

Sharp confirmed, therefore, much of what the literary romancers had long been saying about the Southern Appalachians. The region was indeed a land of preserved ancient values, and it was a cultural outpost of England. Other students would follow Sharp's example, and in ensuing decades they explored the resources of several folk communities in the United States, mountain and lowland.

Sharp's contributions to the broadening of understanding of

America's cultural history were many and positive, but his conservative, academic approach to folk music created a false impression about the breadth and scope of southern music which later scholars have never really overcome. Sharp came to the United States to find "English" songs, and, like most literary folksong scholars of his day, he was much influenced by the scholarship of Francis James Child. Child, in his *English and Scottish Popular Ballads*, had selected 305 ballads and their variants, a corpus of material presumed to be literary in origin and the most valuable surviving examples of the British tradition. Folk scholars have since eagerly sought specimens of the Child canon extant in oral tradition, and they have generally described their collected ballads or variants by the numbers ascribed to them in the Child volumes (as in the case of "Barbara Allen," Child 84). Sharp was understandably quite pleased to find such songs still being sung in the mountains, but he was not nearly so delighted with the other varieties of music that he heard. Consequently Sharp's book did not present to its readers the total picture of folk music preferences in the southern mountains (it omitted religious music, for example), while it did reinforce the prevailing romantic ideas about the mountains as the isolated repository of old English ways.

Largely inspired by Sharp's scholarship, a host of folk-song enthusiasts descended upon the Appalachians: not just scholars, but amateur collectors, seekers after local color, and musicians and composers searching for concert material. The decade of the twenties witnessed a vigorous exploitation of mountain folk music by concert performers, men and women who "interpreted" the music for their sophisticated urban audiences. Elaine Wyman and Howard Brockway, for example, compiled in 1920 a book called *Kentucky Folk Songs*. They had originally collected such songs in order to use them in their song recitals. Some of the folk-song performers of the period specialized in costume recitals, wearing clothing of the time period or ethnic group from which the music was derived. Grace Wood Jess, from Kentucky, gave concerts all over the United States, dressing like a slave, a plantation mistress, a Creole belle, a Mexican maiden, or whatever the occasion or song dictated. Ethel Park Richardson, a long-time radio performer of folk songs and the compiler of *American Mountain Songs* (1927), sometimes dressed like a mountain lady and churned butter or shelled peas as she sang. Oscar Fox, a former ranch boy from Burnet, Texas, who had studied classical piano in Germany, arranged the cowboy songs he found in John Lomax's collection (such as "Rounded Up in Glory") and presented them to his concert audiences. He was sometimes assisted by Woodward Maurice Ritter from Murvaul, Texas, appropriately attired in cowboy regalia, who would one day be known to country and western fans as "Tex."

The most active and probably the most successful costume recitalist was Edna Thomas of New Orleans. Thomas had performed classical and semiclassical compositions in New York during the World War I period, but she began concentrating more heavily on folk material in the twenties. Dressed usually in the costume of a gracious plantation lady, she carried southern folk songs to genteel audiences in the United States and Europe. Such audiences had never heard these songs before and would not have listened to them at that time had the songs not been presented in a cultivated, semiclassical style.

Edna Thomas and her folksinging colleagues of the twenties were the first of that breed of entertainers who would eventually be termed "urban folk singers." Thomas, Elaine Wyman, Grace Wood Jess, and such later singers as Richard Dyer-Bennett, Theodore Bikel, Bob Dylan, Judy Collins, and Joan Baez were not folksingers at all, but interpreters of folk traditions with which they had only remote connections. Their material was taken from the folk, but whether presented in a concert recital hall, a university setting, or a coffeehouse, it was performed for a nonfolk audience and in styles compatible with either cultivated or popular tastes. The audiences who heard either the Fisk Jubilee Singers or Edna Thomas sing came away with a broader perception of the kinds of songs available to southern folk, but they received no inkling of "how" the folk sounded.

The research of Cecil Sharp and of the folklorists who followed him quickened the interests of those who believed that "Anglo-Saxon" folk music should be the basis of a national American music. No matter that the music of the mountains was a composite of the heterogeneous groupings of people who had settled the Appalachians (English, Scotch-Irish, Irish, Welsh, Germans, Indians, and even a few blacks) and was therefore anything but purely Anglo-Saxon; no matter that the mountains had never been the totally isolated sanctuary of Elizabethan folkways so celebrated in romance: it seemed important for the Anglo-Saxon theorists to believe that they had found at least one bastion of racial purity in a society increasingly given over to racial and ethnic diversity, religious pluralism, and cultural amalgamation. Henry Shapiro argues, in fact, that to many Americans beset by unsettling changes in the twenties, mountaineers "now appeared as the conservators of the essential culture of America" and "Appalachia seemed to provide a benchmark against which to measure how far the nation had come from its essential self."[10]

The music the Anglo-Saxon nationalists extracted from the Appalachian repertory was that which best reflected the romantic view of mountain life, marked by social conservativism, fierce individualism, simplicity, and morality (a general set of characteristics that many Americans like to ascribe to themselves). And the songs chosen for concert adaptation usually included the oldest and most pastoral items in the Appalachian songbag. The emphasis on such material was not false; it was merely incomplete. Mountaineers did preserve much British folklore, including some of the well-respected Child ballads, and they had created their own store of songs reflecting their pioneer inheritance. But newer songs and styles had been gradually moving into the mountains for at least a hundred years before Sharp came to the United States.

Mountain boys had seen service in all of America's wars and had therefore increasingly come in contact with the outside world. By 1917, too, the industrial revolution had touched the mountains, and highways and railroads were beginning to penetrate even the most isolated hollows, and the timber, coal, and textile interests were blasting the image of a wilderness paradise as they robbed the land of its resources. Long before the radio and recording industries accelerated the process of social awareness, new songs, styles, and instruments had moved into the mountains, and mountain musicians had created their own songs to deal with the changing socioeconomic realities of their region. Mountain singers knew and loved the old "lonesome songs" such as "Little Matty Groves" and "The Wife of Usher's Well," but they were equally fond of the more recent sentimental songs of pop origin such as "Bury Me beneath the Willow," "Kitty Wells," and "Little Rosewood Casket." They saw no contradictions between these two types of songs, even if the academic folklorists abhorred the sentimental tunes and generally refused them admission to their printed collections.

The Anglo-Saxon theorists recognized the growing encroachments of industrialization—that is one reason their campaign was accompanied by a sense of urgency—and they could see little value in the newer songs. In fact, a dual purpose often characterized the folk-song ventures of both the Anglo-Saxonists and the academic folklorists: the need to preserve the old songs and to combat their strongest competitors, the hillbilly songs (folk songs disseminated for commercial purposes via radio and recordings).

The chief proponent of the Anglo-Saxon folk-song school was John Powell, a Virginian and one of the South's leading classical musicians. In addition to being a composer and prominent classical pianist, Powell lectured, wrote articles, and sponsored associations and festivals designed to promote the preservation of the folk music of the South. He certainly was no monomaniac on the subject of mountain music, for he had made piano arrangements of Negro spirituals before he ventured into the field of Anglo-Saxon balladry, and he submitted an article to the first issue of the *Southern Folklore Quarterly* in which he noted the survival of ancient British songs in southern locales outside the mountains.[11] But in the twenties, Powell was a dedicated evangelist of Anglo-Saxon balladry and its suitability for classical artistic expression.

Powell, David Guion, and Lamar Stringfellow were the three most active classical arrangers of southern folk music. Guion, a composer and pianist from Ballinger, Texas, was more catholic in his approach to folk music than most of his academically trained fellows. His arrangements included Negro tunes, fiddle tunes such as "Turkey in the Straw," and cowboy melodies such as "Home on the Range." Lamar Stringfellow was from North Carolina and was the director of the North Carolina Symphony Orchestra, the first state-sponsored orchestra in the nation. His most important work drawing upon southern folk music was his Pulitzer Prize–winning *Suite from the Southern Mountains*, composed in 1930.

Powell was often associated with Annabel Morris Buchanan (born in Texas) in the campaign to promote an appreciation for folk music in the South. Together they founded the White Top

Mountain Folk Festival in Virginia in 1931. This was not the first festival in the South, but it seems to have been the first collaboration by high-art music people in the direction and control of such an event. It might be interpreted, therefore, as a phase of the cultural mission of the southern upper class to teach and elevate the masses. Annabel Buchanan was director of the folk music section of the Federated Women's Music Clubs of America and was herself a "serious" musician. She and Powell occasionally wrote articles that conveyed their theories of folk music and revealed their ideas about the proper cultural and moral implications of such music.

Buchanan and Powell were more tolerant toward the folk as people than were most high-art advocates. That is, they encouraged the singing of old songs by the folk themselves (rather than by cultivated singers who came from outside the tradition). But Buchanan and Powell tried to restrict the kinds of songs which made their way onto the festival stage. Their criterion for exclusion seemed to be not necessarily the age of a song (although that was extremely important), but rather its nature and tone. It semed, in fact, as if the cultural mission of the mountain settlement schools were being transferred to the festival setting. In an article in the *Southern Folklore Quarterly*, Buchanan described the songs that would never gain admittance to a White Top Festival: "products of the streets . . . the penitentiaries . . . the gutter." Songs from the paperback gospel hymnals, or a song like "Birmingham Jail," would "beg admittance to the White Top programs in vain." [12]

In rejecting certain types of music, the White Top Festival people were also rejecting major historical developments in the lives of the plain people of the South. The festival conception of southern folk society was still that of a static, racially homogeneous, pastoral, and isolated people. This projected idealization had some basis in fact; the South was overwhelmingly rural and its people tended to be socially more conservative than people in other parts of the United States. But change had come to the mountains, and to other parts of the South, with newer songs and styles persistently making their way into the repertories of the folk. Southern singers still occasionally sang ballads that were old when the first American settlements were made, but they also composed

and sang songs that reflected the commercial-urban-industrial order that was slowly supplanting agriculture in the South. The distorted White Top Festival point of view failed to recognize that
the folk music of the South was an organic reflection of the changes
in the world of the southern folk and that their music mirrored
their grappling with the emerging social forces which challenged
the whole of their existence.[13]

By the end of the twenties, then, the proponents of high-art
music had discovered two general types of southern folk music
and had mined them for artistic purposes: the Negro spirituals,
and the mountain ballads. But in each case, the form had been
heavily romanticized, and consequently the lives of their creators
were greatly distorted. The world at large, while enriched by these
borrowings, received a decidedly limited view of the cultures of
black and white southerners, and the total richness and diversity
of their music remained largely hidden from the majority of the
American public.

Meanwhile, these same black and white southerners had been
building their own forms and styles of music, for the most part
oblivious to what the high-art advocates did or believed. These
forms, disseminated to the American audience through commercial
means of exploitation, would one day become the bases for much
of America's popular music in the twentieth century.

3

Early Commercialization:
Ragtime, Blues, Jazz

WITH THE emergence of ragtime in the late 1890s, southern-born singers and styles first entered the realm of American popular culture. The ragtime craze, which did so much to make the popular music business a major industry in the United States, was only the first of several vital infusions made by southern-derived folk styles into mainstream popular music. But like the other forms that would continually follow it (such as blues, jazz, gospel, rhythm and blues, rock 'n' roll, and country), ragtime was destined to lose its unique regional and racial identities as it became absorbed in the national mainstream.

Ragtime was only one product of the Negro's search for individuality in music in the decades following emancipation, and the style reflected the rise of the city and the entrance of blacks and "ethnics" into American popular culture. To an even greater degree than blackface minstrelsy, ragtime represented the most serious threat that the genteel tradition of popular music had yet faced in the United States. With Scott Joplin and other blacks providing the initial impetus for making the music nationally popular, and Jewish firms such as Shapiro and Bernstein dominating the publishing business, it is no wonder that such an Anglo-Saxon nationalist as Henry Ford could later charge that Tin Pan Alley was a Jewish conspiracy to "africanize" America's music.

White men contributed to the making of ragtime at every stage of its evolution, but there is no denying the central role played by blacks during the formative years of the style. The roots of ragtime lay in Afro-American dance music, in the fiddle-and-banjo music of the plantations marked by the rhythmic accompaniment of foot stomping and hand clapping. In the latter decades of the nineteenth century, ragtime became intimately associated with the piano, an instrumental adaptation which constitutes a major innovation in American black music. The late nineteenth century was the great age of the piano in the United States, and blacks differed little from whites in their desire to purchase an instrument whose ownership was equated with respectability. Few blacks, however, could afford pianos, and as Eileen Southern has argued, many black musicians received their first introduction to keyboard instruments on the little parlor organs which their families bought on lifetime installment plans.[1] Other musicians learned by watching pianists in restaurants, saloons, honky-tonks, brothels, churches, or music stores. A few even managed to receive some formal musical instruction. Most of the ragtime pianists, however, were the itinerants who roamed through towns and cities from New Orleans to Chicago or to the East Coast, playing in the flimsy barrelhouses of the lumber camps, in the sporting houses of New Orleans, Memphis, and Saint Louis, and in saloons, gambling establishments, and bars everywhere. The instrument they played was new to the black folk experience, but the music to which it was adapted, and the styles that became identified with it, came out of the older traditions of black dance music. Although the piano was soon to become a valuable component of instrumental combos, the early pianists in effect had to be little "bands" themselves. Consequently, as the left hand beat out a percussive rhythm, the right played a syncopated melody.

Although he neither created the music nor coined the term "rag," Scott Joplin became most clearly associated with the developing art form, and he strove mightily, but with tragic frustration, to get the genre accepted as an example of "serious" music. Joplin was born into a family of self-taught musicians near Texarkana, Texas, in 1868. His father, a railroad worker, somehow managed to buy a piano, and Scott soon picked up the rudiments of a style. He received some training in classical music from an old German piano teacher, but his first real experience as a pianist came in the honky-tonks and brothels of the Mississippi Valley.

The most recent students of ragtime—Schafer and Riedel—describe Joplin and other early ragtime composers as folk collectors who absorbed the music they heard in the black communities and then organized it into "brief suites or anthologies which they called piano rags."[2] By the time he published his first rag, "Original Rags," in Sedalia, Missouri, in 1899, Joplin had already served about fourteen years of apprenticeship in the honky-tonks of Saint Louis, Chicago, and Sedalia. His most popular song, "Maple Leaf Rag," named for the Sedalia club where he often played, was published by John Stark, Joplin's partner until 1909. "Maple Leaf Rag" was one of the biggest sheet music sellers in popular music history, and along with other ragtime compositions that began pouring from the publishing houses, it helped to fuel the first great boom in the popular music industry.

The urban-industrial revolution of the late nineteenth century had created an audience hungry for musical innovation, and pianos were appearing in thousands of American homes, which now demanded sheet music in unprecedented quantities. The ragtime craze lured songwriters from all over the nation, and the syncopated rhythm was often fused in the nineties with the "coon song," a very popular type of song of minstrel origin which depicted the Negro as a razor-toting, watermelon-eating, chicken-stealing buffoon with a prodigious sexual appetite. The form became so pervasive in American show business that even a black writer (Ernest Hogan) could compose a song called "All Coons Look Alike to Me."

After 1900 the term "rag" began appearing in all kinds of songs, such as Irving Berlin's "Alexander's Ragtime Band," which had only the remotest relationship to original ragtime music. Joplin was frustrated by his inability to get his music accepted as serious art—his rag opera, *Treemonisha*, had only one performance in Harlem in 1915—and he died in a mental hospital in 1917. Still, he, Tom Turpin, James Scott, Eubie Blake, and other composers had made the nation ragtime-conscious, and in so doing they had "brought attention to black musicians, either as serious artists or as capable and inventive entertainers."[3] They had also demonstrated once again the persistent appeal of southern images to a nation moving rapidly toward the complexity of urban society.

But this time the image was not necessarily one of stability or security. Although one is struck today by the gentle or innocent sound of ragtime, in 1900 "respectable" patrons of cultivated music were scandalized by it, and its adherents found escape in a music that suggested the reputed gay charm and sensuality of "darky" and/or southern life.

The challenge to Anglo-Saxon supremacy and the genteel music tradition mounted by ragtime was further strengthened by another product of the folk South—the blues. The blues had been developing and maturing in the rural South since the Civil War, emerging from the tradition of field hollers, work shouts, and spirituals. Emancipation brought a new freedom to articulate grievances or desires, and it also permitted black music to develop in something other than a communal setting. Indeed Lawrence Levine argues that the blues were "the first almost completely personalized music that the Afro-Americans developed" and therefore "represented a major degree of acculturation to the individualized ethos of the larger society."[4] The blues musician was not merely a solo performer, however, who voiced his own private feelings; he was an entertainer who sought also to divert, amuse, and provide escape for his listeners. The blues no doubt arose out of a context of pain, poverty, and injustice (and many of the songs speak directly to these problems), but the general mood of the music was not exclusively sad or self-pitying: "Like the spirituals of the nineteenth century the blues was a cry for release, an ode to movement and mobility, a blend of despair and hope."[5]

As innovative as the blues might appear to be as a solo expression, the form continued to demonstrate its indebtedness to and interrelatedness with other and older Afro-American forms of folk music. The vocal mannerisms of the singers were not original to the new music, nor was the classic twelve-bar, three-line *aab* stanzaic formula of the blues. Even the most pervasive and group-oriented black musical trait, the call-and-response pattern, endured in the solo blues style as the singer interacted with his audience or carried on a dialogue with himself or with his instrument. During the concluding years of the nineteenth century and in the early years of the twentieth, black musicians achieved a mastery over the guitar that they had never exhibited during the days of slavery. In the hands of a skilled blues musician the guitar became, in effect, a second voice, punctuating the singer's remarks, or responding to them. The blues were both personal and communal. The individual singer might utter a very personal message, but it was one that his listeners could easily understand and share, and it drew upon the total body of black folk experience. In a sense, the improvising blues singer "composed" a song each time he performed, but the lyrics of his songs, as Samuel Charters maintains, were a distinctive language that had the "inflection and richness of the spoken language . . . the way people talked to each other on the street, the way men and women talked to each other."[6] The lyrics of blues songs floated freely from singer to singer and from one part of the South to another—and on to the ghettos of the North. The blues were the common possession of the Negro people.

Scholars may agree that the blues were rooted in the black experience and that the South was the general milieu in which the music developed, but there is no conclusive agreement concerning the precise geographical origins of the form. Several researchers, including Samuel Charters who wrote the first general study of the rural blues, postulate a genesis in the Mississippi Delta where a heavy concentration of Negro field workers built "a strongly developed tradition of rhymed work song material" in the context of almost total isolation from white society.[7] Jeff Todd Titon, the most recent student of the subject, suspects that polygenesis is a more likely explanation, but he agrees that "the tradition developed most fully in east Texas and the Mississippi River Delta region during the first decades of the twentieth century.[8]

Many of the most famous Mississippi bluesmen of commercial recording fame—performers such as Charley Patton, Sam Collins, Tommy Johnson, Son House, Skip James, and John Hurt—began their careers playing for plantation social functions such as fish fries, picnics, and Saturday night dances. They learned from each other and bequeathed much of their music to younger musicians who often heard them only on recordings. Strong vocal and instrumental similarities consequently do exist among Mississippi bluesmen, but the migration of musicians began so early after the Civil War, and the influence of other forms of music, such as ragtime, was so pervasive, that it is dangerous to make hard and fast judgments concerning musical style. While the style of Mississippi Delta singers was often "hard and unrelenting," melodically limited, and marked by growling tones which sometimes ascended into falsetto, John Hurt, one of the most beloved of the Delta singers, sang in a gentle, relaxed, and almost lyrical style.[9] Similarly, Mississippi bluesmen generally favored "harmonically ambiguous and polyrhythmic" guitar styles, but so did occasional musicians from other regions, such as Blind Lemon Jefferson and Blind Willie Johnson of Texas.[10] On the other hand, the use of devices to make the guitar simulate the voice—the sliding of bottlenecks, pocket knives, or metal objects along the strings, or pushing a string to one side of the fingerboard (called "choking" the string)—seems to have been more common among guitarists in Mississippi than elsewhere.

Texas blues, by and large, exhibited a greater stylistic variability than did the Mississippi blues, while also suggesting the greater cultural complexity of the Texas milieu (Alger "Texas" Alexander, however, confounds the generalizations because this highly respected Texas bluesman sang in a rough wail which suggested the field holler origins of the blues). Not only was the black population of Texas less concentrated than that of the Deep South, it evolved in proximity to a number of important musical traditions: the rural Anglo, the Cajun, the cowboy, the Mexican, and the Central European. Texas blues singers in eastern and southeastern Texas sang for parties and other rural social functions and in the barrelhouses found in the lumber camps. Singers who grew tired of singing for local functions might venture into a nearby town or county seat to sing on street corners or in bars, or for any crowd that might assemble, whether at a county fair, a political rally, a trades day, or a medicine show. Musicians also wandered into the bigger towns and cities of the region, such as Austin, Shreveport, Fort Worth, Dallas, and Houston, and several of the best of them were to be heard on phonograph recordings in the late twenties and early thirties.

Although the rural blues were widely known throughout the South to whites as well as blacks in the years before World War I, Americans elsewhere scarcely knew of the music, or vaguely conceived of it as "songs of the Southern underworld.[11] The blues in rawest form had to wait until the middle of the decade of the twenties to gain a national hearing. Like most manifestations of folk music, the southern blues moved into the American consciousness through a rather circuitous route. That is, they were first popularized by professional, nonfolk entertainers who arranged, or watered them down, for respectable, urban consumption.

The agents through whom the blues revolution was inaugurated were two southern black men, William C. Handy and Perry Bradford, both of whom had absorbed musical material from the grass roots but who aspired to better things. As he describes it in his autobiography, Handy's first encounter with the raw, rural blues was like a revelation in its impact upon him and was a turning point in his career.[12] One day in 1903, while he and his Knights of Pythias band were stopping in Tutweiler, Mississippi—right in the heart of the Delta country—Handy heard a Negro rural bluesman strum his guitar and wail that he was going to where "the Southern cross the dog" (a reference to a railroad junction). The tune eventually became the basis for Handy's own "Yellow Dog Blues," but it also inspired his larger campaign to seize upon the ingredients of the southern rural blues for his own artistic purposes.

Like Scott Joplin, Handy was a trained musician who, though born among the folk, sought to find his musical fortune in the city and in more elevated types of music. But, again like Joplin, he was an unconscious folklorist who absorbed and revitalized the musical styles he heard during his wanderings through the South and Midwest. When he made his fateful contact with the rural blues in 1903, Handy had thirty years behind him of varied experiences and varied exposures to virtually every kind of music available in the United States, from classical to ragtime. Born in Florence, Alabama, on November 16, 1873, the precocious Handy had to combat the prejudice of his father, who believed that stringed instruments were tools of the devil, and that of his first music teacher, who told him that professional musicians were wastrels and drunkards. But the irrepressible Handy could not be kept away from music, and he played cornet in a local band, sang first tenor in a quartet, toured with a small Alabama minstrel unit, played in a brass band, and in 1896 went to Chicago and joined W. A. Maharas Minstrels, a large organization which played everything from marches and overtures to Stephen Foster songs. This diverse background in popular music, along with a stint as an

English teacher and band leader at the Agricultural and Mechanical College in Huntsville, Alabama, where he encountered a strong prejudice against native American music, lent an eclecticism to his music that few musicians possessed.

After another short period with Mahara's Minstrels, Handy became director of a Knights of Pythias band in Clarksdale, Mississippi, in 1903. From this date until 1914 Handy became immersed in the blues, hearing the form often during appearances throughout the Delta, and then in Memphis where he relocated. When Handy moved there, Memphis was a hub of musical energy, and Beale Street had already become the fabled center of saloons and brothels where such bands as the one led by West Dukes played for the nightly enjoyment of the rural blacks who had been pouring into the city since emancipation. In 1909 Handy made his first contribution to the emerging blues genre when he wrote, upon the request of the Crump mayoralty campaign organization, a song called "Memphis Blues" ("Mr. Crump don't 'low no easy riders around here"). He sold the song for only fifty dollars, but it was immensely popular in the Memphis area and established his reputation as a songwriter. The tune was followed by other blues compositions, but the one that did most to make the nation blues-conscious was "St. Louis Blues," written in September 1914 while Handy was still in Memphis, but inspired by an 1893 visit to Targee Street in Saint Louis. "St. Louis Blues," with its half-blues, half-Latin beat, illustrates Handy's eclecticism well, and displays the sophistication lent to a rural-derived form by a professionally trained, urban-oriented musician.

Between 1914 and 1920, Americans at large gradually became introduced to the blues, but generally in a sophisticated form largely shorn of rural characteristics, both written and performed by people who knew the form only secondhand. In other words, the songs that gained popularity in these years were the composed vaudeville blues that were sung by torch and cabaret singers. W. C. Handy spawned imitators, white and black, who churned out songs for the emerging city blues singers. One such successful blues composer was Perry Bradford, born in Montgomery, Alabama, on February 14, 1895, but by 1919 domiciled in Harlem, where he produced musicals, played the piano, and wrote songs. Bradford fought valiantly in those years to gain national acceptance for

Negro music and Negro entertainers. When he moved to New York, he entered an active black show business scene in Harlem that was vigorously breaking away from the constricting influences of minstrelsy. Bob Cole and others were producing all-Negro revues, and the Johnson Brothers from Florida (J. Rosamond and James Weldon) were busily producing music (such as "Under the Bamboo Tree") which competed favorably with that written by the white composers of Tin Pan Alley. Bradford sought to move black music out of Harlem and into the national limelight, while also expanding the performing horizons of Negro singers. In 1919–1920 the most effective means of quick and augmented exposure appeared to be phonograph recording. Since heretofore black entertainers had been conspicuously absent from recordings, Bradford set out to correct the imbalance.

Bradford approached both Victor and Columbia and tried to persuade them to record Mamie Smith, a young singer from Ohio who had become well known in New York because of her singing in the 1919 production "Made in Harlem," an all-Negro revue. Those two companies rejected his requests, but the General Phonograph Company, owner of the Okeh label, recorded Mamie's singing of two Bradford compositions: "That Thing Called Love" and "You Can't Keep a Good Man Down." Neither song was a blues tune, but, according to Chris Albertson, they were the first examples of a black singer recorded in solo performance, and they were soon followed, on August 10, 1920, by Mamie's recording of another Bradford song, "Crazy Blues," the first vocal blues recording.[13] Significantly, Okeh had renamed the song—once called "Harlem Blues"—in order to attract white as well as black customers. Bradford had told the Okeh people that southern blacks would enthusiastically buy records by a member of their race, and that southern whites, who had heard such music all their lives, would buy them "like nobody's business."[14]

This record, as well as subsequent recordings by Mamie Smith, did sell well. Mamie, however, was a cabaret singer rather than a blues stylist, and many of the women who followed her, recording for other companies that quickly followed Okeh's lead, were "overnight converts from pop music who learned the form but lacked the feel of the blues idiom."[15] But America's black population was hungry for black music, and the recording industry, after decades of neglect, began to satisfy the demand. In the years following 1920 an extraordinarily wide array of black talent was recorded, on major labels such as Okeh, Victor, Brunswick, and Columbia; or on small labels such as Gennett and Paramount; and occasionally on black-owned labels such as Harry Pace's Black Swan.

The music recorded ranged from primitive blues renditions that echoed the field hollers or work shouts to sophisticated and complex jazz arrangements. Despite the heterogeneous nature and stylistic diversity of the material, black recordings for many years were categorized as "race records" in catalogs and brochures. The term *race* was used widely before 1920 to describe the emerging and self-conscious black population of the United States, so when militant newspapers such as the *Chicago Defender* advertised or endorsed "race recordings," they meant that such songs sprang from or represented the feelings of the Negro race. It became a matter of racial pride, and an example of incipient black nationalism, to support such musical expression. Pullman porters brought armloads of records south on their runs out of Chicago, and Negroes everywhere purchased records in great quantities. Phonographs were highly prized pieces of furniture in black tenant farmers' homes, and even those farmers who did not own phonographs often bought records and played them on their neighbors' machines.[16]

The recording of Mamie Smith's version of "Crazy Blues" in 1920 was a major milestone in the exploitation of folk music in the United States. She was neither southern, folk, nor rural, and "Crazy Blues" was a sophisticated imitation of the rural blues; nevertheless, her successful rendition inspired the recording of singers whose voices carried both the inflections and the feeling of the southern blues. The greatest was Bessie Smith, "the Empress of the Blues," who made her first records for Columbia under the direction of veteran talent scout Frank Walker on February 16, 1923.

Bessie was born in Chattanooga, Tennessee, about April 15, 1894, the youngest of seven children. Both of her parents died before she was nine years old, and by the time she reached that age she was singing for nickles and dimes on Ninth Street in Chattanooga to the guitar accompaniment of her brother Andrew.

About 1912 she became a member of a show that included her brother Clarence and the legendary blues singer Gertrude "Ma" Rainey. Only a few months later she joined another traveling troupe along with Ma and her husband, Will Rainey. Gradually she built an extensive popularity in the South, and in some of the northern ghettos, traveling with all-black troupes (some of which still carried the "minstrel" tag), and appearing in clubs and theaters everywhere. Many of the theaters, which included the 81 Theatre in Atlanta, the Frolic in Birmingham, the Bijou in Nashville, and the Palace in Memphis, were part of a black vaudeville chain organized in 1911, called the Theatre Owners Booking Association (TOBA). Because of the low pay and grinding performing schedule associated with it, black entertainers often referred to TOBA as "tough on black artists" (or "asses"). Bessie continued to play the southern circuits throughout her career, but by 1920 she had moved to Philadelphia and by 1923, when she made her first records, she had amassed a large following in most northern communities where blacks had congregated.

There had probably been no singer before Bessie Smith who so effectively communicated with the black masses, and none who achieved such a heroic stature among them. As her commercial appeal broadened, her repertory also expanded to encompass songs well outside the blues idiom, including the newest pop hits of the day. But she invested even the most sophisticated songs with the moaning, soulful quality of the downhome South. Although her personal life would have shocked many church members, her style was strongly suggestive of religious singing, and she, in turn, influenced the stylings of some later gospel singers including Mahalia Jackson. Bessie's reputation became such that many of America's greatest musicians, especially from the developing jazz field, became associated with her on recordings and in personal appearances. On the other hand, the careers of several fledgling musicians were enhanced by an association with the great Bessie. Fletcher Henderson, for example, began recording with her in 1923, and on January 14, 1925, the young Louis Armstrong participated in three recording sessions with Bessie, one of which included her great recording of "St. Louis Blues." Bessie's personal career, then, is closely intertwined with, and largely responsible for, the popularization of both the blues and jazz.

After the mid-twenties Bessie Smith was usually in command of her own touring shows, some of which were highly organized and elaborate operations such as the 1925 *Harlem Frolics*. These were shows which carried a large orchestra, a group of dancers, a stage crew, and stage equipment. Bessie, too, was highly conscious of her image and lived the blues queen role, dressing regally, spending money lavishly, and traveling in grand style. In the mid-twenties, for instance, she traveled in a private railroad car equipped with a kitchen and a bathroom. Bessie won both fame and fortune which lasted at least until the mid-thirties; but her personal life was often fraught with tragedy and pain, marital distress, drugs, and alcohol. She was only forty-three when she died on a lonely road near Clarksdale, Mississippi—the victim of an automobile accident—on the night of September 26, 1937. It was fitting that the "Empress of the Blues" should die in the region where the blues was born, and not many miles from where W. C. Handy first heard the form.

The commercial success enjoyed by Bessie Smith and other "classic blues" singers (women who sang with jazz accompaniment) awakened the recording industry to the existence of a large black audience that wanted to hear real blues music performed by its own people, and not the watered-down adaptations composed and arranged for white audiences. The rural blues, however, the music that provided the basis for the entire blues genre, experienced a relatively brief recording history. It was not recorded with any frequency until 1926, and it suffered a drastic decline after the onset of the Great Depression.

The rural or country blues, in contrast to the classic or city blues, was essentially a music performed by men to their own guitar accompaniment. In an excellent recent study of the early blues, Jeff Titon has described the rural material as downhome blues, because whether performed by a singer living in a southern city or in a northern ghetto, the music reflected, or reminded the listener of, the old southern rural home and the associations it brought to mind.[17] Titon argues that the first downhome singer on records was Daddy Stovepipe who recorded two songs on May 10, 1924, but the singer usually credited with the first recordings was an ex-minstrel entertainer, Papa Charlie Jackson, who recorded with his own guitar accompaniment in August of 1924. The downhome blues style flourished on recordings from about 1926 to 1930 during which period approximately two thousand titles were issued and the entire range of rural blues material (if not the total preference of the musicians) was recorded on the old 78-rpm discs. Echoes of unaccompanied nineteenth-century field hollers (Texas Alexander), the songster tradition (Ragtime Henry Thomas), Delta blues (Charley Patton), gospel blues (Blind Willie Johnson), hillbilly blues (Coley Jones), jug band blues (Cannon's Jug Stompers), and sophisticated blues (Lonnie Johnson) were only a few of the styles available to the record buyer.

The recording of Blind Lemon Jefferson in April 1926 was the catalyst which promoted the first major search for downhome talent by the phonograph companies. Jefferson was born in 1897 in Couchman, Texas, not far from Wortham, in the county of Freestone. Blind from birth, he was already singing on the streets of Wortham well before World War I and soon was a fixture at country dances throughout the county. In about 1917 he moved to Dallas where he remained for almost ten years, using that city as a base for his performances in north central Texas. Occasionally another musician worked with Jefferson, but usually the blind singer worked alone, often playing all night long for a dance. Jefferson was anything but personally attractive; he was enormously fat and, though totally blind, wore wire-rimmed glasses on the end of his nose; but he had an uncommon power over his listeners. Women fawned over him, and some of the most famous blues singers, such as Huddie Ledbetter (Leadbelly), Josh White, and Lightning Hopkins, later claimed to have had a close association with him. Long before he made his first records for Paramount (apparently after a Dallas record dealer, Sam Price, had suggested his name in a letter to the company), Jefferson had already built a regional reputation and had developed the individualistic style that would make him a popular recording performer on both the Paramount and the Okeh labels.

Jefferson sang in a freewheeling, wailing manner that set him apart both from his Texas contemporaries and from the Mississippi Delta singers. His guitar playing also contributed to his popularity, providing an expressive second voice which complemented rather than repeated the shouted lyrics. Blind Lemon was already virtually a legend among his fans and fellow bluesmen when he died of exposure on a Chicago street one wintry night in 1930. He was buried in a country cemetery near Wortham, Texas, in a grave which for many years bore no marker.

The downhome blues reminded the Negro of his humble, rural origins; jazz, in contrast, suggested the aura and liberation of the beckoning city. Jazz moved into the national consciousness as a southern-derived music, but its roots lay in many places: in Africa, in the Caribbean, in Europe, and in the United States. The songs in the jazz repertory came from a multitude of sources: folk music, religious music, minstrelsy, ragtime, blues, marches, and music of modern composers. But jazz was an instrumental style, and it developed when musicians welded these various musical forms into ensemble instrumental patterns.

Although jazz drew from many sources, nowhere were these diverse musical influences so concentrated as in New Orleans. Some interpreters of jazz point to its African origins and posit a rather simplistic progression from Africa to the Caribbean to New Orleans, where it was concentrated in the brothels of Storyville, the red-light district that flourished from 1897 to 1917. Then with the closing of Storyville by the Navy Department, jazz musicians took the music up the river and also to Chicago and ultimately to the rest of America. But New Orleans was peculiarly situated to receive music from many places in the world. It did have a close relationship to the Caribbean, but it also had lived under French and Spanish as well as American rule, and as a seaport it received visitors and experienced cultural and economic interchange from all over the world. Furthermore, like the great port cities of the East, New Orleans received large waves of Irish, German, and Italian immigrants in the nineteenth century. Throughout that century New Orleans was known for the breadth and variety of its music. We have already seen that light opera was performed there from the 1790s on, and grand opera after the 1830s. In addition balls and street parades were held constantly, and virtually all fraternal and benevolent organizations, black and white, had marching bands that were ready to march at the slightest provocation. One could hear their music in the parks on weekends, as well as a myriad of musical styles from street entertainers and vendors.

The jazz band borrowed its instruments, and many of its songs ("the bedrock of the New Orleans jazz repertoire"), from the marching street bands. But the street bands also, according to William J. Schafer, introduced the Afro-American impulse toward syncopation: "The process changed the plodding, walking march measure into a varied dance rhythm. The march beat shifted from the stiff 1-and-3 accent of military cadence to the springy 2-and-4 of Afro-American music."[18] The real transition to jazz came at the turn of the century when small groups of musicians, drawing upon the marching-band experience, began playing what was generally called ragtime for the hordes of partygoers caught up in the great national vogue for social dancing.

The ingredients that made jazz distinctive—syncopation, antiphony, improvisation, polyrhythm, the use of blue notes—came from black musicians drawing upon the Afro-American, and not solely the African, experience. Jazz did not develop in Africa; it developed in the United States when Americans of African descent drew upon their total experience to meld a new musical style out of a multitude of older ones. Several musicians, including the white bandleader Papa Jack Laine, speak of "ragging" tunes before 1900, but the performer who is commonly conceded to be the "first man of jazz" was Charles "Buddy" Bolden. Between 1895 and 1907 Bolden became "the key figure in the formation of classic jazz and his personal cornet style, one of a shouting, incredible power, established one of the two main jazz trumpet styles" (the other, that of Bunk Johnson, was characterized by a light touch and precise phrasing).[19] Bolden made no phonograph recordings and was not mentioned in the New Orleans newspapers until he was committed to a state mental institution in 1907; consequently, he had always been a shadowy figure in the history of early jazz until the appearance of Donald M. Marquis's myth-shattering and meticulously documented biography.[20]

Although he seems to have been little known to the white community, Bolden became a heroic figure to blacks through his performances in the local parks and in the string of bars and dance halls in the area intersected by South Rampart and Perdido streets. Encouraged by the enthusiasm of his listeners and by the fierce competition of other musicians, Bolden continually strived to create distinctive sounds and rhythms; it was this kind of creativity that sparked the transition to jazz. In the peak years of his activity, 1900–1905, Bolden built the most popular dance band in New Orleans and pioneered in the employment of the "classic" jazz ensemble: a front line of horns and a back line of string rhythm instruments. This great pioneer of jazz spent the last twenty-five years of his life in the state mental hospital in Jackson, Louisiana. His death on November 4, 1931, was scarcely noticed or mourned, and he now rests in an unmarked grave in New Orleans.

Like all early jazz musicians Bolden drew upon the total musical environment of New Orleans, and his performances took him all over the city and into a wide variety of entertainment formats. Only rarely, however, did he play in the one area that in the public mind has been most associated with the birth of jazz–Storyville. No facet of the jazz story has had a more tenacious or romantic hold on the popular imagination than that of its supposed Storyville origins. This notorious haven of legalized sex (named after Sidney Story, the alderman who suggested its creation, but described in the press as "the restricted district") abounded in bars, dance halls, and cabarets as well as bordellos, and in all of these music was a constant backdrop for the diversions of the flesh. Many fine musicians played in the Storyville establishments–including the great "professors" of the piano Clarence Williams, Tony Jackson, and Ferdinand "Jelly Roll" Morton, and such groups as the Olympia Band, Bunk Johnson's Superior Band, Freddie Keppard's Creole Band, Kid Ory's Brownskin Band, and Manuel Perez's Imperial Orchestra–and many of them departed for other cities once the district was closed down. Nevertheless, jazz began before the district was established by statute in 1897, and "the majority of black musicians of outstanding ability in New Orleans never worked so much as a single night" in the area. Al Rose, the most knowledgeable student of New Orleans jazz, placed the Storyville-jazz relationship in the proper perspective when he said that "jazz was not born in Storyville, nor was it even reared there. Storyville was just one part of the passing scene in which this great art form happened to thrive." [21]

The exodus of musicians from New Orleans began considerably earlier than 1917. Jazz (or what would later be called jazz) began moving north at the end of the nineteenth century on the excursion steamers to Memphis, Saint Louis, and other points on the Mississippi River. The showboat bands were not always really jazz groups, but they included such great jazz personalities as Baby Dodds, Pop Foster, Johnny St. Cyr, and Louis Armstrong. Furthermore, the Original Creole Band was already making vaudeville tours to points as far west and east as California and New York by 1912, and other Negro musicians were playing in obscure bars on the south side of Chicago by 1915.

Despite the vital contributions made by Negro musicians to the creation and shaping of jazz, it was white New Orleans musicians who introduced the form into the national consciousness, and it was they who first popularized the term "jazz." In June 1915 Tom Brown and his New Orleans band took a job at Lamb's Club in Chicago and were petulantly described by the local musicians' union as a "jazz" group, a term associated with whorehouse music. As might have been expected, the notorious connotation only made the public curious, and they attended the band's performances in great numbers. The band soon styled themselves as Brown's Dixieland Jass Band.

In 1916 another group of white performers moved from New Orleans to Chicago, playing first at Schiller's Cafe and then at the Del'Abe Cafe. At the latter gig they adopted the name of Dixieland Jass Band. After their move to New York in January 1917, the spelling was changed to "jazz," and the band made recording history. An initial record for Columbia was filed away and not immediately released, but on February 26, 1917, they recorded "Livery Stable Blues" and "Dixieland Jazz Band One-Step" for the Victor Talking Machine Company. The record experienced an extremely large sale; white imitators began to spring up everywhere, and the national vogue for jazz music was under way.

The jazz revolution, then, was ushered in by southern white musicians, and it would be another five years before the first black jazz records would be issued. Therefore, it was "dixieland," a style of music imitative of black music, that first captured the attention of the American public. H. O. Brunn, in *The Story of the Original Dixieland Jazz Band*, discusses the pervasive musicality of New Orleans and tells how Dominic James "Nick" LaRocca absorbed such music from infancy, but almost nowhere is a black musician mentioned. Certainly, none of the black New Orleans bands are cited as influences on LaRocca's or the other ODJB mem-

bers' styles. Virtually all other writers, however, described the
ODJB as a band imitative of black musicians, and Rudi Blesh calls
it a rather weak imitation.[22]

Almost immediately jazz, like rock 'n' roll about forty years
later, became the center of controversy, and the term came to be
applied to an entire decade. Many people saw it as an exciting
art form and as a healthy liberation of musical styles. Few high-
art people recognized any art in it, and many other Americans
thought they saw in it, and in the life-style it supposedly represented, a force potentially destructive not only of good music but
of decency itself. Even the *New Orleans Times-Picayune* said that
"jazz music is the indecent story syncopated and counterpointed"
and that "its musical value is nil." (Donald Marquis asserts that
there were no friendly accounts of jazz in the New Orleans newspapers until 1933).[23] It is not surprising that, given its rhythmic
abandon and Negro origins, jazz would soon be denounced by
Henry Ford's *Dearborn Independent* magazine as ruinous to public morals and as a Jewish conspiracy designed to debauch American music.[24]

Actual recordings of black jazz musicians did not come until
1923. Joseph "King" Oliver, born in New Orleans about 1885,
came to Chicago in 1917 or 1918 and played his cornet in several
bands before organizing his own Creole Jazz Band in 1920. After
a short sojourn in California he returned to the Lincoln Gardens
Cafe in Chicago where, in 1922, he added a second cornetist, the
youthful Louis Armstrong. The following year the band recorded
for both Paramount and Gennett, with the Gennett records being
the first to appear on the market. These records, along with others
released by the band on the Okeh and Columbia labels, were described by Blesh as "the first definitive records of the Negro's
classic jazz."[25] This music was immediately imitated as much as
was that of the earlier white dixieland recording groups. In fact,
Europeans began to be jazz-conscious almost as quickly as did
Americans. The Original Dixieland Jazz Band had gone to Great
Britain in March 1919 and played to standing-room-only crowds.
While jazz was winning international acclaim, back home it was
also making inroads into the "better music" audience, but in a
greatly diluted form. On February 12, 1924, Paul Whiteman held
his "Jazz Concert" at Aeolian Hall in New York. This concert of

"symphonic jazz," which featured George Gershwin's first public performance of *Rhaposody in Blue*, was designed to give jazz respectability and to break down the opposition of the "good music" people. Already, in a pattern that had been demonstrated earlier in the case of ragtime and blues and that would surface repeatedly in the twentieth century, a black-derived folk art was being taken over by whites and was moving away from its folk moorings.

But although jazz quickly expanded in style and popularity and often merged its identity with other forms of popular music, its classic style endured. By and large, its direction was shaped by black southern musicians, with some of the greatest coming from New Orleans: for example, Ferdinand "Jelly Roll" Morton, a pianist of great diversity and the first successful composer and arranger in jazz music; Johnny Dodds, a great clarinetist; and Daniel Louis Armstrong, the most beloved of all jazzmen and virtually a national institution at the time of his death in 1971.

Louis Armstrong was born in New Orleans in 1900 and was introduced to music at the Negro Waifs' Home for Boys, where he had been admitted at the age of thirteen after firing his stepfather's gun on the street New Year's Eve. Although he studied music and was the leader of the home's brass band, his real introduction to jazz came from the music he heard floating out of the Storyville establishments and from his membership in the Kid Ory and Fate Marable bands. He took his style to Chicago in 1922, and then to New York in 1924, as a member of Fletcher Henderson's band. After 1925, when he returned to Chicago, he usually led his own bands, including the Hot Five and Hot Seven groups with such preeminent musicians as Johnny Dodds, trombonist Kid Ory, banjoist Johnny St. Cyr, and pianist Lil Hardin Armstrong (his wife). Armstrong was the first "star" to emerge from the burgeoning throng of jazz musicians, and the first of them to forge a reputation as a great soloist and innovator. Americans also came to know Armstrong as much for his singing as for his trumpet playing. His gravel-voiced style was peculiarly effective, and his "scat singing" (the use of nonsense phrases to stimulate the sound of horns) influenced other jazz and pop singers. Through his personal appearances in this country and abroad (the first of many foreign tours came in 1932), as well as through a prolific outpouring of recordings which began with King Oliver in 1922, Armstrong became virtually the symbol of American jazz for people around the world.

It would take many books to document the further history of jazz or to record its many stylistic changes as it became an international phenomenon. Although the music lost its southern identity, many southerners (such as Fletcher Henderson, Lester Young, Nat "King" Cole, and Ella Fitzgerald) continued to play pivotal roles in its periodic reinvigoration or reshaping. In the years since jazz burst onto the national scene, its various forms, ranging from the traditional to the most progressive, have built identities somewhat apart from mainstream pop music and have attracted adherents who will neither listen to nor play any other kind of music. Still, jazz as a whole influenced virtually every other kind of American music, from country to classical. And the entire popular music industry profited from the jazz explosion after the twenties. Most mainstream pop performers showed the influence of jazz in one way or another, and in so doing they demonstrated the tendency of pop music to absorb and dilute all musical genres while also deregionalizing music styles.

4

Expanding Markets:
Hillbilly, Cajun, Gospel

THE DECADE of the twenties witnessed the first full-scale commercialization of southern rural folk music. Although the recording industry predated the broadcasting industry, the popularity of the radio forced the recording field to seek means of remaining commercially competitive. The introduction of electrical reproduction in 1925–1926 promoted better recording quality, and an effort was made, simultaneously, to reach a broader audience—an effort evidenced by the search for ethnic and folk performers.

Radio stations appeared in southern cities as early as 1922, and almost immediately they began featuring local live talent, including fiddlers, string bands, mandolin and guitar clubs, Hawaiian groups, yodelers, quartets, and blues singers. Such entertainers performed on an irregular basis, but a few stations, such as WBAP in Fort Worth, WSM in Nashville, and WSB in Atlanta, were offering regularly scheduled "barn dances" on a week-to-week basis by the mid-twenties. The barn dances were inspired by the rural dances of frontier America and were composed almost exclusively of string band music. The most famous of these radio shows, ultimately, was to be the WSM Barn Dance, inaugurated in 1925, and soon to be called the Grand Ole Opry. WSM used the talent found in Nashville and in the immediate surrounding area. The performers, according to Charles Wolfe, the chief historian of the Grand Ole Opry, were generally amateurs who had played only at home, but occasionally, like Uncle Dave Macon, they had had some experience on the southern vaudeville circuits, or had built at least minor reputations playing in medicine shows or entertaining at county fairs, political rallies, fiddle contests, or merely singing and hawking their song sheets wherever a crowd gathered.[1]

Commercial potential had never been totally absent from southern rural music, but the radio provided a means of immediate and widespread exposure far more advantageous than any medium yet created. Radio folk entertainers played for increasingly large audiences, built up a string of personal appearances within the listening range of the stations, and increased both the size and scope of their performing repertories. Newly composed songs inevitably, and successfully, competed with the traditional material, but folk styles of performance demonstrated a remarkable endurance.

The recording industry since its inception in 1888 had generally ignored rural folk music and had been preeminently a city-oriented phenomenon. An occasional folk song or dance tune had appeared on records, usually performed by a professional urban musician, but except for an occasional group like the Dinwiddie Colored Quartet virtually no bona fide example of rural music had been documented on either disc or cylinder recordings. Mamie Smith's recording of "Crazy Blues" in 1920, however, generated an interest in Negro music, and the subsequent discovery of a large black audience led to the desire to tap other previously neglected markets among the nation's ethnic and grass roots groups. Much of this music (Finnish, Irish, Polish, and so forth) was aimed at northern and big-city audiences, but the rural South was also found to have its enclaves of unassimilated ethnic elements, and their folk music forms were also recorded. Regrettably, most of this music still awaits documentation.

Mexican-Americans make up the largest minority group in Texas (larger even than the black population), and they have produced a vigorous and exciting body of music, described variously as chicana mexicana, nortena, or Tex-Mex, which is scarcely known except by the people who gave it birth. Commercially recorded for the first time in the late twenties, the music has always shared some of the stylistic traits of the music produced south of the border and is replete with corridos—narrative ballads that are often concerned with real or historical events—but it is largely derivative of the Chicano's Texas experience and of his interrelationship with other cultural groups in that cosmopolitan region south of Austin. Joe Nick Patoski asserts that the music is "wholly Texan and is considered foreign even in Monterrey."[2] The music has remained the chief cultural staple of working-class Chicanos but is often a symbol of racial pride for people at other socioeconomic levels. Anywhere Mexican migrants have gone—to the Pacific Northwest, the Great Lakes region, or Florida—nortena music has moved also.

While adhering to the Spanish language (or the South Texas version of it), the Tex-Mex musicians built up a peculiar composite of musical styles, drawing heavily upon the accordion and polka rhythms of their Texas-German neighbors. Today, such performers as Flaco Jimenez, Lydia Mendoza, and Little Joe Hernandez, while remaining heroes to their compatriots, have also begun to win some recognition within the larger Anglo population. Les Blank's splendid short-film documentary, "Chulas Fronteras," and Chris Strachwitz's ten-record collection of Tex-Mex music, ranging from 1928 to the seventies, are both indications of this growing interest in nortena music, but thus far little scholarship has been devoted to its historical origins or to the tracing of its commercial evolution.[3] The rediscovery of early Cajun music, in contrast, came as an outgrowth of the popular taste for such music which burgeoned after World War II (when Cajun songs began to appear on country music popularity charts), but nortena music remained isolated and obscure to all but its most devoted fans.

The commercial discovery of Cajun music came rather inauspiciously in 1928 when a singer and accordionist from Rayne, Louisiana, was recorded in New Orleans. Joe Falcon, accompanied by his guitar-playing wife, Cleoma Breaux, recorded a song called "Allons à Lafayette" (Let's Go to Lafayette), a reference to one of the principal cities in Acadian territory. Falcon was neither the best nor the most representative of the Cajun musicians, but his recordings were immensely popular among his Cajun countrymen, and Falcon contributed mightily to the popularization of the accordion in southwestern Louisiana. The fiddle, which had long been a fixture at fais-do-dos (the all-night country dances so beloved in Cajun territory), was temporarily submerged by the accordion's popularity and did not really reassert itself until the thirties. Cajun culture exerted a powerful impact on all the groups who came into southwestern Louisiana, whether Anglo, Spanish, German, or Negro, and, as Lauren C. Post notes, "the newcomers lost all contact with their original groups and had no feeling of belonging to any but the Acadian population."[4] As a result, several musicians have attained great prominence as Cajun entertainers who have little if any French blood: among them are Lawrence Walker, Dennis McGhee, Harry Choates, and the Negro accordionists Amade Ardoin and Clifton Chenier.

Despite the prominence on early Cajun recordings of the accordion (which went into its own decline in the thirties), the fiddle was never totally absent. While there was no single style of Cajun fiddling, the musican who would eventually do most to revitalize the instrument, and who would also play a central role in the thirties in both the popularization and modification of Cajun music, was Leo Soileau of Ville Platte, Louisiana. Soileau began his recording career in 1928, playing a duet with Mayuse Lafleur, a young accordionist who met his death from a stray bullet in a tavern brawl in October of that same year. Not only did Soileau contribute to enduring fiddle styles, he was also partly responsible for popularizing the high-pitched, wailing vocal style so typical of Cajun music.

Early Cajun recordings were probably limited in circulation to those areas inhabited by people of Cajun-French extraction or by people who had grown up in the Cajun culture: southwestern Louisiana, the Gulf Coast eastward to Mobile, and westward through Beaumont and Port Arthur to Houston. Although the world at large after World War II would become very much aware of Cajun music in its hybridized country-and-western form, or as zydeco, the blues-influenced dance music of the French-speaking Creole blacks, the music before 1930 was still very strongly rooted in the rural French culture which gave it birth (even if that music had borrowed heavily from German, Negro, and Anglo sources).[5] The music had not lost its identity, nor was it widely known outside the area of its origins.

In its competition with radio the recording industry also began to exploit other varieties of southern white rural music, much of which was recorded after it first gained exposure through the broadcasting medium. Much of the rural talent heard on WSB in Atlanta soon after the station began operating in 1922 made its way onto recordings later in the decade.

The first of such entertainers to record, and the one who did most to illustrate the commercial potential of what would soon be called hillbilly music, was Fiddling John Carson from Georgia. Although the Okeh talent scout, Ralph Peer, was intensely skeptical of the salability of the material he heard—he described Carson's singing as "pluperfect awful"—Fiddling John's recording of "The Old Hen Cackled and the Rooster's Going to Crow" and "Little Old Log Cabin in the Lane" sold several thousand copies. Peer had greatly miscalculated the tastes of the Georgia farmers and millworkers who had been hearing Carson at fiddle contests and political rallies for many years, and he apparently failed to realize that there were millions of working-class southerners who yearned to hear music performed by entertainers much like themselves. Despite Peer's personal predilections, Carson was a good singer, but he sang in a rather formal, hymn-singing style that seemed archaic to twentieth-century urbanites, and in a dialect that came straight out of the redneck South.

The rural singers who appeared on recordings in the wake of Carson's success represented a host of occupations: they were farmers, millworkers, railroad men, coal miners, cowboys, and even barbers, doctors, and lawyers. But they and the music they performed were destined to be labeled "hillbilly," a catch-all term that branded all southern white grass roots music as culturally inferior. Ralph Peer seems to have first applied the term to southern rural music in 1925 when he described Al Hopkins's string band as the Hillbillies, but given the social context of the twenties, it is not surprising that such a label would be popularly affixed to a rural-derived music coming out of the South. As George B. Tindall has shown, the image of the South as a "benighted" region —a land of backwardness, decadence, violence, superstition, and racism—gained greater strength in a decade characterized by national progress and social change.[6] The people who produced the Scopes monkey trial, the Ku Klux Klan, sharecropping, and prohibition had also produced hillbilly music.

The music thus began its commercial evolution laden with negative connotations that it has never really overcome; it was presumed by many to be the product of cultural degenerates and a projection of their demented values. The fact that the music was commercial also affected the reactions that people had to it. Hillbilly music, the creation of the folk, did not conform to the romanticized conceptions of folk music so prevalent in the twenties, and it certainly did not square with the self-images that many upper-class and "progressive-minded" southerners held of themselves and their region. If anything, the music seemed to represent the victory of the Snopesian South, the distasteful fusion of poor white music with the business civilization of the United States. The radio hillbillies seemed far different from the then-prevalent conception, held by both scholars and the public alike, of the folk as the isolated and unchanging descendants of Elizabethan settlers, and the music they performed could hardly be accepted as the remnants of medieval and pastoral balladry.

If some people rejected hillbilly music because of what they considered its crassness, others may have gravitated toward it because it represented to them an image of an older and simpler America, and an alternative to the frenetic dance music of the twenties. Henry Ford was not alone among Americans in deploring the rise of jazz and the subordination of the less complex and more restrained dance music of earlier, rural America. He struck a receptive chord in the hearts of many people when he sponsored a series of old-time fiddle contests after 1926 in several cities of the United States. If Americans yearned to hear the good old songs of the nineteenth century or earlier, they were most likely to hear them on the radio barn dances or on the hillbilly recordings. The barn dances tried hard to project an aura of wholesome, down-to-earth, family-style entertainment (listening to them was like looking at a Currier and Ives print, or going home to grandmother's farm for the Thanksgiving holidays), and radio program directors and advertisers often insisted that hillbilly performers affect rustic attire and rustic names (even though the performers might prefer a more urban get-up).

The old 78-rpm hillbilly records, issued between 1923 and 1930, are valuable repositories of song material that urban America had forgotten: variants of British ballads and lovesongs, frontier fiddle tunes and play-party songs, camp-meeting songs and tunes from the shape-note hymnals, and a very large body of songs that had begun their lives as pop songs in the nineteenth century (such as "Put My Little Shoes Away," "Over the Garden Wall," "The Fatal Wedding," and "I'll Twine mid the Ringlets," known today as "Wildwood Flower.") The lover of old-time sentimental songs had no need to despair about their disappearance, for he could hear such numbers, or ones similar to them, on hillbilly recordings (albeit with southern rural accents). In the newly composed songs found on hillbilly records one could also find a reaffirmation of traditional religion and conventional morality.

Country music, whether in its hillbilly form, or in its more recent sophisticated manifestations, has always been a music of social commentary. Blind Alfred Reed, for instance, voiced a concern felt by many conservative Americans in the twenties when he sang "Why do you bob your hair, girls?" A very popular type of song found on hillbilly records in the twenties was the event song, a type reminiscent of the broadside ballads that commented on topical events of the day. Such songs as "The Sinking of the Titanic," "The Wreck of the 1256," "The Fate of Edward Hickman," "Bruno Richard Hauptmann," and "The Death of Floyd Collins" invariably pointed the morals that could be drawn from tales of tragedy and disaster. Floyd Collins, according to the ballad of 1925, met his death in a sandstone cave because he had not followed the advice that his father often gave.

Hillbilly music, as the product of the rural South, conveyed the conflicting impulses and images of the region which gave it birth.[7] It was a welding of rural and urban influences; it was simultaneously southern and American; and its performers and audience were torn by opposing desires, clinging to a self-image of rustic simplicity while at the same time striving to be accepted in an urban, middle-class milieu. Consequently, the music has encompassed widely divergent strains. Hillbilly singers could alternately condemn and endorse demon rum (and some of the heaviest drinkers were the most ardent advocates, in song, of abstinence). Their songs could on the one hand defend law and order and on the other glorify outlaws such as Jesse James and Billy the Kid. They could on occasion applaud man's mastery over the machine, as in the classic "John Henry" (more popular among hillbillies than in black music), but they just as often lauded the machine itself, as in Uncle Dave Macon's paean of praise to the Ford automobile, "On the Dixie Bee Line"; and they could extol the virtues of the old home place, and the sense of security it represented, while conversely romanticizing the rambling men who refused to be tied down to such an existence. Country music's first two great influential acts, the Carter Family and Jimmie Rodgers, embodied the conflicting impulses of love of home and fascination with the wanderer both in their lives and in their repertories.

The Carters and Jimmie Rodgers were first recorded in the same short time span—during the first four days of August 1927 —by a Victor portable recording unit directed by Ralph Peer (who inexplicably has never been named to the Country Music Hall of Fame). A. P. Carter, his wife Sara, and A. P.'s sister-in-law Maybelle, came down from the mountains of southwestern Virginia to inaugurate a family career that would endure as such until 1943 and, in various separate manifestations, up to our own time (Maybelle, later called Mother Maybelle, performed with her daughters as part of her son-in-law Johnny Cash's traveling show until her death in 1978). The Carter Family built up a large following through their Victor, Columbia, and Decca recordings, as well as by personal appearances and transcribed broadcasts over the Mexican border station XERF.

Even though their reputation spread, the Carter Family never moved very far stylistically from their origins. They always sounded like a group singing for a small circle of friends gathered in a family parlor or at a church social, and the bulk of their songs came from the paperback hymnals or from the nineteenth-century song sheets. Even when they moved toward the inclusion of newly composed songs—as all hillbilly performers did—their choices still reflected the values, aspirations, and fears of the rural Protestant South and its longings for stability in a world succumbing to change. A. P. and Sara were divorced during much of their performing career, so when the Carter Family sang "Will the Circle Be Unbroken," one of their most enduring songs, they sang with an acute consciousness of family dissolution.

Jimmie Rodgers, on the other hand, had never enjoyed the advantages of a settled home life. Born near Meridian, Mississippi, in 1897, he lost his mother before he was four years old, and since his father's railroad work often took him away from home, the boy lived in a succession of relatives' homes. Rodgers became a railroad worker when he was fourteen years old and remained in that line of work until 1925, when a worsening case of tuberculosis forced his retirement. By late 1927 when he became a full-time professional musician, Rodgers had seen more of the world and had sampled a broader range of experiences than had the average rural southerner. His railroad work had taken him to Texas and the Southwest, and he had lived for a brief period in New Orleans. Before he made his first records for Victor, Rodgers had played in a dance band in Meridian, had toured as a black-face entertainer with a medicine show through the southern mountains, and had played briefly with a string band in Asheville, North Carolina.

While the Carter Family was a repository of nineteenth-century popular music, Rodgers was more responsive to the popular currents of his own day, and his recordings were important vehicles by which such forms as the yodel and dixieland and Hawaiian sounds moved into country music. Eclecticism was not his sole contribution to country music, however. Through his songs, his devil-may-care personality, and his early death at the age of thirty-six, Rodgers contributed to a mystique that has been enduringly popular in country music: that of the free, rambling, but star-crossed young man. There was nothing menacing in his personality, and certainly no tinge of the outlaw, but Rodgers projected the image of a man who had been everywhere and who had done everything. He was the worldly-wise rounder who loved the women and left them behind, but who also possessed a tender solicitude for children and mothers (as in "Sleep, Baby, Sleep" and "Mother, the Queen of My Heart"). Rodgers often sang about hoboes (as in "Waiting for a Train" and "Hobo Bill's Last Ride," rounders (as in "My Rough and Rowdy Ways"), and convicts (as in "Moonlight and Skies" and "Ninety Nine Year Blues," both written by a real convict, Raymond E. Hall, then serving in the Texas state prison).

Rodgers, in short, drew upon images that had been popular among southerners' British ancestors, and perhaps among poor and oppressed people everywhere. Although the rambling-man image had Old World origins, it gained a new validity during the Depression era among poor, confined, and isolated rural southerners who could find escape, if nothing else, in an identification with unfettered and footloose men. Hillbilly music, like the people who produced and nourished it, was typically ambivalent, idealizing home while exhibiting a fascination with the rambling man. Home was often extolled after it was abandoned, and the wandering life was sometimes glorified because it was unattainable. Ironically, but not surprisingly, Jimmie Rodgers's favorite song among his own recordings was "Daddy and Home."

Another expression of the white grass roots mind which underwent commercialization during the twenties was gospel music. White gospel music has always been closely related to the rural secular music of the South, with both phenomena drawing upon the folk resources of the region. The two, in short, were different expressions of the same mind and experienced a similar commercial evolution. The gospel music business, which is today a major facet of the nation's entertainment industry, developed out of two aspects of nineteenth-century American religious history—the shape-note singing schools and the evangelical revivals; but it drew much of its dynamism and much of its personnel from the Holiness-Pentecostal movement of the late nineteenth and early twentieth centuries. By 1900 a great stream of religious songs, fed by the big-city revivals of the era, flowed into American popular culture, and in the South such songs circulated invariably in shape-note form. On an average of twice a year several publishing houses printed paperback hymnals designed for church conventions and singing schools. The publishing houses were sometimes aligned with, or adjuncts of, religious denominations, but even the independent ones defined their goals in missionary terms: the evangelizing of the nation through the power of song.

The most effective of the houses, at least until the late thirties, was the Vaughan Publishing Company of Lawrenceburg, Tennessee. The founder of the company, James D. Vaughan, was a devout member of the Church of the Nazarene, one of the principal denominations of the Holiness movement in America. Vaughan never wavered in his commitment to the Holiness faith, and he was acutely perceptive in his ability to advertise his belief while also enhancing the commercial viability of his publishing concern. Vaughan and his gospel cohorts preached an otherworldly message, but they very astutely utilized the techniques of this world to popularize that vision. Vaughan's business was the selling of songbooks, and as a salesman he was an ingenious innovator. He appears to have been the first southern publisher to send quartets to churches and singing conventions to plug the Vaughan song-books. The members of the early quartets were employees of the company who presumably shared J. D. Vaughan's spiritual mis-sion. Their purpose was to advertise the songbooks and their contents, and not their own particular talent. In 1923 Vaughan opened station WOAN, one of the earliest commercial radio stations in Tennessee, as a medium for advertising his company's religious merchandise. And in 1922 one of the Vaughan quartets (there were as many as sixteen of them on the road during the decade) recorded for a Vaughan-owned label. Though the discs were not recorded in the South, "they were the first records designed for a specifically southern audience."[8]

The Vaughan Company was only one of several publishing houses that carried on the shape-note tradition. A. J. Showalter, a descendant of Joseph Funk of Singer's Glen, Virginia, and the composer of "Leaning on the Everlasting Arms," conducted such a business in Dalton, Georgia, and educated a long list of South-erners who in turn fanned out through the South holding their own music schools. R. E. Winsett published his widely circulated songbooks in Dayton, Tennessee. Eugene Bartlett worked through his Hartford Music Company in Hartford, Arkansas. The chief competition to Vaughan, however, came from J. R. Baxter, from Tennessee, and from Virgil O. Stamps, from Texas, who merged their concerns in 1926.

The Stamps-Baxter firm dominated much of the white gospel market until World War II, particularly in the region west of the Mississippi River. V. O. Stamps, the son of a sawmill operator and state legislator in Gilmer, Texas, sent out several quartets bearing the name of "Stamps" and often sang bass and acted as the genial master-of-ceremonies in one of the touring quartets. One of these quartets, the Stamps All-Star Quartet, which in-cluded V. O.'s brother Frank as bass singer, achieved a wide popu-larity and did much to establish a separate identity for the quartets apart from the publishing houses. In October 1927 the quartet made some recording for Victor under the direction of the ubiqui-tous Ralph Peer, apparently without the consent or foreknowledge of Virgil Stamps. Peer encouraged them to record some of the older, stately hymns, but one of their alternative, newer selections, "Give the World a Smile," was immediately popular; it became one of the best-loved songs in the Southwest, primarily because every Stamps-sponsored quartet used it as a theme song. "Give the World a Smile" featured a bass lead on the chorus, but was made distinctive by the use of an after-beat rhythm in which the other three quartet members made antiphonal, syncopated responses to the lead. The style, obviously borrowed from instrumental jazz, was likely the product of gospel pianists who had absorbed the technique from secular sources. The pianist for the Stamps All-Star Quartet, for instance, was Dwight Brock from Gadsden, Alabama, who has expressed an affinity for the stylings of such pop pianists as Little Jack Little and Whispering Jack Smith.

White gospel quartet music, then, drew considerable inspiration from the dominant secular music forms of the nation (the quartets, in fact, often sang popular songs or semiclassical numbers such as "The Lost Chord" during their concerts). The gospel singers learned much of their four-part harmony from the shape-note singing schools, but they also picked up elements from the barbershop quartets, the black gospel quartets, and the other popular quartets of their day. The publishing houses promoted competition among their quartets, and the singers adopted mannerisms and techniques that would contribute to their acceptance. Religious zeal either gave way to show business or made an accommodation to it.

By the end of the twenties the white gospel quartets had taken long strides away from both the publishing houses and the singing schools and had become more thoroughly immersed in the world of commercial competition, using the same methods of dissemination—radio, recording, and personal appearances—that were available to secular singers. As the nation descended into the depths of the Great Depression, the quartet business suffered drastically, but the messages of the gospel songs—and no music has been more cherished by southerners than such songs as "Precious Memories," "Farther Along," and "If I Could Hear My Mother Pray Again"—brought succor and relief to millions of Americans.

5

The Great Depression and New Technologies

THE Great Depression, while bringing temporary economic distress to the American entertainment industry, also wrought serious changes in the nature and structure of the various forms of commercialized southern folk music. The period from 1929 to 1941 was a transitional era characterized by the evolution and maturation of southern regional folk styles to more professionalized forms possessing greater national recognition and acceptance. The record industry severely curtailed its operations under the impact of hard times. Some of the smaller companies collapsed, while a few were consolidated with other companies. RCA Victor responded to the economic crisis by introducing a cheap, budget label called Bluebird which specialized in hillbilly and race recordings. In 1934 Decca came into existence with a thirty-five-cent record that proved so successful that it encouraged other companies to introduce cheaper subsidiary lines.

In the urge to economize, the record companies dropped from their rosters some of the folk talent that had shown little commercial appeal. The percentage of traditional songs on records declined during the thirties, a consequence of the urge to come up with fresh and commercially stimulating material as the singers gradually moved beyond their native, home audiences. The performers who began to record for the first time in the thirties were as likely to have learned their material from the recordings of the entertainers of the twenties as the latter were to have learned theirs from the folk sources of their communities. Therefore, many of the folk songs that did appear on recordings in the thirties, or in radio performances, were learned from earlier commercial sources.

While newer and younger personnel affected the nature and scope of southern grass roots music forms, the inexorable force of technological innovation probably did more to alter the whole tone of folk music in this country. The replacement of acoustical recording by electrical innovations in 1926 greatly improved the fidelity of recorded sound, and the introduction of electrical transcription in the mid-thirties expanded the radio audience potential for all entertainers. It is difficult to assess the impact of the microphone, for it encouraged the development of both "natural" and contrived styles. Singers could be heard, and could hear themselves, in front of large or noisy audiences, and they were also freer to experiment and improvise. Most crucial, however, in the modification of rural or folk-derived musical forms was the introduction of electrically-amplified instrumentation. Although musicians had long experimented with electronics, the first commercially successful employment of electric instruments came in the mid-thirties when guitarists, first in blues and jazz, and soon thereafter in country music, attached primitive electrical pickups to their instruments.

While the recording industry was forced to make serious adjustments in order to survive the depression, radio was in its great heyday. Radio was the cheapest form of entertainment available, and it brought both solace and security to anxiety-ridden Americans who sought escape in its programming. In the South, depending on the location, one could usually begin the day, or spend the noon hour, listening to a program of hillbilly, Cajun, blues, or gospel music. The radio entertainers generally built their personal appearance schedules on the strength of their radio broadcasts. The size and scope of the listening audience could be estimated by the nature of the correspondence received from fans—hence the hillbilly admonition, "Keep them cards and letters coming in."

The Mexican border stations, popularly called the X-stations because of their call letters, were powerful forces in the dissemination of hillbilly and gospel music throughout North America. These stations were owned by Mexican nationals but were often leased or managed by American businessmen who used them to promote their own products or those of other advertisers. The first of these entrepreneurs was the "goat gland man," Dr. J. R. Brinkley, who began the operation of XERA (later XERF) in 1932 in Villa Acuña, Mexico, just across the Rio Grande from Del Rio, Texas. Brinkley became a wealthy man by selling his medical books and advertising his scheme to promote male sexual rejuvenation through goat gland transplants. XERF, and other stations such as XEAW, XENT, XEPN, and XEG ("the Voice of North America"), aimed their transmitters toward the United States and blanketed North America with power that sometimes exceeded 100,000 watts.

Much of the material from their broadcasts became part of our national folklore. Long-winded announcers hawked the virtues of such patent medicines as Kolorbak and Black-Draught, as well as baby chicks, songbooks, prayer cloths, resurrection plants, and "autographed pictures of Jesus Christ that glow in the dark." Once-in-a-lifetime offers were always being advertised as scheduled to go off the air forever at midnight, but somehow generally reappeared the next night on another program. The X-station broadcasts could be heard occasionally in every region of the United States and in Canada, but it is difficult to know who listened to them. Late-night listeners, particularly people who kept their radios on while driving in order to stay awake, were most likely to hear these broadcasts, because the border stations were often the only ones on the air during these hours. Regardless of who they were, or what their motivations may have been, the listeners to the Mexican border stations could hear (usually by transcription) some of the most important acts in hillbilly and gospel music. The Carter Family, the Pickard Family, the Callahan Brothers, Jesse Rodgers (Jimmie's cousin), Cowboy Slim Rinehart, J. R. Hall (the Utah Cowboy, who was really from Texas), the Stamps Quartet, and the Chuck Wagon Gang were among the most prominent entertainers who could be heard on border radio. A little bit of the rural South, therefore, made its way into the nation at large through the medium of border radio programming.

The radio exploitation of folk music was, of course, accompanied by the expanded role of commercial advertising. Hillbilly music, for example, reached its first national audience through the sponsorship of certain products that became household words through their association with various hillbilly acts or shows. Crazy Water Crystals, produced in Mineral Wells, Texas, was the premier national advertiser of country music during the thirties. Although it was ballyhooed as a curative for a wide array of ailments, Crazy Water Crystals was essentially a laxative. Beginning first in Texas with the sponsorship of local radio shows, the Crazy Water Company soon branched out into cities throughout the Midwest, South, and East, aligning its product with all kinds of music shows, but especially those with a country flavor. In the two Carolinas and Georgia the company was particularly energetic in its recruitment and use of hillbilly talent. There was a Crazy Barn Dance each Saturday night in Charlotte, North Carolina, with a large roster of performers, and several of the hillbilly acts in the Southeast carried the term "crazy" in their titles—the Crazy Mountaineers, and the Crazy Hillbillies, for example.

The vogue for Crazy Water Crystals did not extend beyond the thirties, but some of the products that first gained national recognition through their association with hillbilly music are still very much a part of the American scene today. Alka-Seltzer, for example, was catapulted toward its status as a ubiquitous household commodity in 1933 when it began sponsoring a thirty-minute segment of the National Barn Dance. The collaboration between hillbilly music and various brand names worked to the benefit of both. The music repeatedly demonstrated its ability to sell products while simultaneously entering millions of homes through its association with popular brand names advertised on radio shows. The Grand Ole Opry, though a fixture on WSM in Nashville since 1925, might never have become an institution in American show business had it not attained in 1939 the sponsorship of the R. J. Reynolds Tobacco Company for thirty minutes each Saturday night on NBC. Hosted first by Roy Acuff, and later by Red Foley, the Grand Ole Opry along with pitches for Prince Albert Smoking Tobacco, moved into millions of American homes where it formerly had been barred admittance.

While hillbilly music gained a national forum in the thirties through radio exposure, race music had widened its geographic range and altered its basic forms through population movement. Migration, of course, slowed during the depression years, but the "great migration north," which had reached its peak during World War I and the early twenties, did not really ebb in any significant way until well after World War II. Much of the blues music of the post-1930 era was produced in the new black communities of the North by southern migrants, or by their children. The music might occasionally make reference to the old southern homes, and most certainly did evoke images of "down home," but it was qualitatively different from the music of the previous decade. Younger musicians especially, rebelled against a sound that seemed too reminiscent of the plantation or of rural slavery, so the rural blues, that is, the solo singer with his guitar, was rarely recorded after 1930. Instead, the music became more closely attuned to a generation living in the city, and more sophisticated in its arrangements and instrumental accompaniment.

Led by such musicians as Eddie Durham, Charlie Christian, and Aaron T-Bone Walker, blues performers everywhere after 1934 began electrifying their guitars. They also increased the size of their combos, adding pianos, saxophones or other horns, basses, and drums. By the end of the thirties, the term *race* was being replaced by a label more consonant with the city, *rhythm and blues*. Like race music before it, rhythm and blues served as an umbrella phrase for a large number of black styles that were often very different from each other; but, as the name implies, rhythm and blues was much more oriented toward dancing than country blues ever had been. It was urban, rhythmic, aggressive, electrified, and youth-oriented. And it projected an image of hipness that was far different from the rusticity to which hillbilly music still clung at the end of the thirties.

Black gospel music assumed a more independent identity apart from secular music than it had possessed in the twenties. To many black people there was a clear and unbridgeable chasm between "sinful" music and "spiritual" music, and some religious singers would not sing a secular song. Nevertheless, the gospel singers still exerted a powerful influence over their secular brethren. A very large percentage of Negro blues and pop singers obtained their first experience singing in church and many of them began their professional careers as members of gospel quartets or choral groups. Tony Heilbut, in *The Gospel Sound*, argues that many of the vocal techniques and stage mannerisms associated with blues and soul music actually began with the gospel singers.

Several gospel quartets were on the road during the thirties, some of which, with new personnel, are still active today. The Zion Harmonizers, the Fairfield Four, the Five Blind Boys, the Swan Silvertones, the Sensational Nightingales, the Charioteers, and the Dixie Hummingbirds were only a few of the black quartets that sang, chiefly in the southern states, in churches, auditoriums, and radio stations. Engaged in intense competition with each other, such singers as Archie Brownlow of the Five Blind Boys, R. H. Harris of the Fairfield Four, and Claude Jeter of the Swan Silvertones did not depend on beauty of voice alone, but also stressed vocal gymnastics that could drive an audience to distraction. To a much greater degree than in white gospel music, where singers tended to sing with physical restraint, black gospel music stressed theatrics, and its singers pulled out all the stops in trying to evoke a total audience response. Ascending into falsetto, growling a note, repeating a word over and over, or "worrying" it endlessly (bending it, prolonging it), sometimes unleashing an unearthly, almost primordial, scream, and accompanying their singing with some of the fanciest footwork seen outside of a dance hall, the gospel singers pioneered in the use of methods that would be commonplace decades later in the performances of such rhythm and blues and soul singers as Ray Charles, Sam Cooke, Aretha Franklin, and James Brown.

If one individual can be singled out as the father of black gospel music in the United States, it would surely be Thomas A. Dorsey, one of the great names in both southern and American music history. Dorsey was born in Villa Rica, Georgia, in 1899, the son of a Baptist minister. Like most young men of his time, Dorsey was attracted to the sounds of blues and jazz. He worked for a while with Ma Rainey, and as a pianist made records under the name of Georgia Tom and, along with Pinetop Smith, as part of the Hokum Boys. Even during his most secular phase, when he was recording such songs as "It's Tight like That," Dorsey never strayed very far from the faith of his childhood.

The compulsion to do the work of the Lord bore fruit in 1929 in Dorsey's decision to perform only religious music. He had moved to Chicago about 1916 where he and Sallie Martin founded the Gospel Singers Convention. This association became a source and training ground for quartets and choirs which fanned out into the black communities of the nation. Dorsey's chief inspiration as a composer came from the works of Charles Tindley, an African Methodist Episcopal minister in Philadelphia in the early years of the twentieth century. Tindley may have been unknown to most southerners, but his songs circulated widely among them and were deeply loved. Such songs as "We'll Understand It Better By and By," "Stand by Me," "Take Your Burden to the Lord," and "I'll Overcome Some Day" (the basis for the great protest song "We Shall Overcome") were cherished by white and black southerners alike.

Dorsey was the successor, if not the protégé, of Tindley, and his songs, having the advantages of modern media dissemination, were even more broadly circulated. His most famous song, "Precious Lord, Take My Hand," written in 1932, grew out of deep personal loss, the death of his wife and infant son, but it has become the possession of all the American people. The most compelling interpretations of "Precious Lord" have been those of such black singers as Mahalia Jackson, but the song has also been recorded and performed by white singers Red Foley, Ernie Ford, Elvis Presley, and others. Another of Dorsey's more famous songs, "Peace in the Valley," gained enormous commercial success through the recording of Kentucky-born Clyde Julian "Red" Foley, a very popular country singer in the years following World War II. Dorsey, therefore, deserves to be evaluated in terms of the total gospel picture, black and white, in the United States. His songs are known by an exceedingly wide spectrum of Americans; he has long been a member of the white-dominated National Gospel Singers Convention; and his compositions have appeared frequently in the southern gospel songbooks.

White gospel music in the thirties continued to be dominated by the quartets. Although the publishing houses no longer monopolized the control of such quartets, the V. O. Stamps Company still exerted a leading and innovative role in gospel music. Several quartets were on the road including the name of Stamps in their performing titles, a practice that enhanced both the company's business and the reputations of the quartets. V. O. Stamps further popularized the name of his company and his quartets by having his parent quartet sing at the Texas Centennial in 1936. From the Texas Centennial the quartet moved to a regular spot on 50,000-watt KRLD in Dallas.

The quartets still explained their existence in terms of religious mission, and their singers generally came out of the singing schools. But show business persistently intruded into the styles of the singers alongside the missionary impulse, and newer songs replaced the older hymns. The quartets competed with each other to find the lowest bass singers and the highest tenors. A few quartets, such as the Texas-based Chuck Wagon Gang (D. P. Carter and his children, Anna, Rose, and Jim), sang to guitar accompaniment, but the piano was almost universally used, and many quartets were in fact known by the skill and showmanship of their pianists. Such pianists as Dwight Brock and Marion Snider generally faced their audiences as they played, and with great flourishes they clowned and hammed their way through all but the most serious songs. In a profession that took itself and its mission very seriously, the gospel pianists often provided the only comic relief.

As professional as their performances might be, the gospel quartets were still not sufficiently commercial during the depression years to achieve extensive economic rewards for their talents. By their very nature they were isolated from most of the performing outlets that were open to blues or country musicians. They were still generally confined to concerts in schoolhouses or auditoriums, or to church-related functions where receipts were small and often based on donations. The fundamentalist churches of the South, particularly those of a Pentecostal persuasion, provided the most receptive arenas for the gospel quartets. Energized by their commitment to "making a joyful noise unto the Lord," and showing a democratic receptivity to most musical instruments and even to secular-derived styles, the Pentecostal churches furnished enthusiastic audiences for the touring quartets and were the sources of many of the finest quartet singers. Whatever their denominational affiliations, the churches had little money to contribute to the singers. A quartet could expect warm hospitality, a sumptuous meal at some good church-member's home, and whatever sum the collection brought in. Anything extra came from the diligent hawking of songbooks, records, and photographs.

Because of the desires of their conservative listeners, the quartets always sang many of the old familiar hymns, but within their repertories the newly composed songs always outnumbered the old. The most popular songwriter in the white gospel field, and one of the most beloved musicians in the rural South, was Albert E. Brumley. Brumley, who was born on a tenant farm near Spiro, Oklahoma, in 1905, began writing songs soon after he attended a singing school near his home community in 1922. He worked as a teacher, singer, and writer for E. M. Bartlett's Hartford Music Company in Hartford, Arkansas, one of the leading shape-note publishing houses in the South, and a company which the Brumley family now owns. His first successful composition, one of the most popular gospel songs of all time, was "I'll Fly Away" (1931), with a spirited melody and structure reminiscent of the nineteenth-century camp meeting songs. Brumley songs thereafter entered the repertories of all the gospel quartets, moved into most of the country churches via the shape-note hymnals, appeared frequently on country recordings, and from there came into the permanent possession of the southern folk.

Brumley's compositions, memorable because of their simplicity and melodic beauty, were quintessentially southern in tone and theme. They generally fell into two categories: conventional gospel songs, such as "I'll Meet You in the Morning" and "If We Never Meet Again," which stressed the heavenly joys awaiting the faithful Christian, and nostalgic rural songs, such as "Dreaming of a Little Cabin" and "Cabin in the Valley of the Pines," which reminisced about childhood, mother and father, and the old country home. Brumley's religious songs were widely appealing because they were nondenominational but well within a framework of evangelical Protestantism. They posited a conception of a merciful, benevolent God who waited to gather in His children amidst scenes of pastoral bliss. Brumley's nostalgic songs, on the other hand, breathed with a consciousness of life's evanescence as they affectionately described an abandoned and decaying rural world held together only by the steadfast love of mother and father. In his religious songs, the unfulfilled wishes of this world are projected as being realized in the heavenly world to come.

While the otherworldly message was consoling to many southerners during the depression years, there were those who were not so content to wait for economic security and human justice beyond the grave. Hard times inspired protest, and protest often made its way into the messages of both blues and country songs, secular and religious, as in Big Bill Broonzy's "Black, Brown, and White," Slim Smith's "Breadline Blues," and David McCarn's "Cotton Mill Colic." Professional blues, country, and gospel singers often commented on the social and political events of the day, but the most sustained expression of protest (as opposed to mere commentary) came from humble farmers and workers who poured out their anguish in music.

The textile strikes in the Southern Piedmont (1929), the bloody conflict in the eastern Kentucky coal fields (1931), the organizational efforts made in the Deep South by the Southern Tenant Farmers Union (STFU) (1934–1936), and the southwestern dust storms (late 1930s) all produced their balladeers. As southern labor stirred,[1] organizers and sympathizers came in from the North to lend their support to what basically had been spontaneous uprisings. Communist-dominated unions–the National Textile Workers' Union and the National Miners Union–added an explosive ingredient to the situation while also introducing a revolutionary rhetoric that was totally new to the experiences of southern hill-country and mountain folk. According to folklorist Archie Green, "Piedmont mill villages and Cumberland mine camps became meeting grounds for the ideologies of Andrew Jackson and Karl Marx, Abraham Lincoln and Mikhail Bakunin," as conservative southern workers joined in temporary though unlikely alliance with radical northern organizers. One result was the appearance of a body of topical songs which "fused timeworn melodies with strange, revolutionary lyrics."[2]

The textile, coal, and sharecropper strikes were destined to be tragic exercises in futility, but the northern organizers took back home with them a large body of songs that helped fuel the incipient urban folk music movement of the thirties. The lives of most of these songs were short, but a few of them, such as Florence Reese's rousing "Which Side Are You On?" (inspired by police repression in Harlan County), have endured as major documents of the quest for American social justice. Southern folk balladeers actually became better known than their songs, at least among the literate liberal public of the North. The murder in 1929 of Ella May Wiggins, the balladeer of the Gastonia textile workers, made her a martyr to American radicals, and the names of Aunt Molly Jackson and her half-sister Sara Ogan, from the Kentucky coal fields, and John Handcox, the black preacher and songwriter for the STFU, were soon known and revered among liberals and radicals far afield from the songwriters' southern homes.

The name that eventually came to dominate among protest-song writers, however, was Woodrow Wilson "Woody" Guthrie, born in 1912 in Okemah, Oklahoma. The shaping of Guthrie's social consciousness began in the early thirties during his residence in Pampa, Texas, and in his rambles through the oil towns of the Southwest. His reputation as the poet of the Okie migrants and as the Dust Bowl balladeer, however, did not begin to develop until the end of the thirties, after he had lived among the Okies in California for a few years working as a hillbilly singer on KFVD in Los Angeles. He moved to New York in 1940 in the company of actor Will Geer and became part of that city's labor-radical movement. Guthrie's legitimate working-class credentials, his indomitable courage and good humor, and his facility as a songwriter ("Talking Dust Bowl Blues," "So Long, It's Been Good to Know You," "Philadelphia Lawyer," "This Land Is Your Land"), made him the inspiration for that large body of socially conscious singers who are still active in American life.

The tradition of protest singers which began with Ella May Wiggins, Aunt Molly Jackson, and Woody Guthrie in the thirties has demonstrated its enduring strength in our own day through two vital groups of musicians: the urban-born singers (principally northern) such as Pete Seeger, Phil Ochs, Joan Baez, and Bob Dylan, who fueled the urban folk revival of the sixties, and the rural, southern-born singers such as Nimrod Workman, Billy Edd Wheeler, Anne Romaine, and Hazel Dickens, who sing their protest material within the context of country music. Dickens comes closest to typifying and perpetuating the tradition of Aunt Molly Jackson; she wrote some of the songs and did most of the compelling singing for the sound track of the award-winning documentary film, *Harlan County, USA*. The living tradition of protest song provides dramatic evidence of the way that southern music has affected both the consciousness and the popular culture of the nation at large.

While the Brumley songs evoked images of a vanishing rural South and held out the promise of a blissful home in the sky, the protest singers called for the establishment of economic and social justice in this world. A large body of southerners, and of Americans generally, however, wanted in their music neither heavenly solace nor radical politics; hence the popularity of the thoroughly escapist swing music of the thirties. The big pop bands of the Glenn Miller variety had large followings in the South (and some leading Big Band musicians, such as Tex Beneke and Harry James, were southern-born), but southwestern rural musicians made significant innovations to the swing style and created a form of music, now known as western swing, which effectively combined rural and urban motifs. The westernmost portion of the South (Texas, Louisiana, Oklahoma) was peculiarly situated because of its ethnic and racial diversity, the presence of New Orleans there, the emergence of the oil boom, and the sway of the cowboy culture, to produce grass roots music forms of a hybrid nature. The region was heavily rural until World War II, but the presence of alternative cultures and competing economic systems contributed to the breaking down of traditional patterns earlier than in the southeastern states. Texas, for example, has contributed the largest number of musicians to the country music profession and has always had a vigorous tradition of old-time fiddling which derived from the migrants who came there from the older southern states; nevertheless, rural Anglo musicians learned from the blacks, Cajuns, Mexicans, and Central Europeans with whom they came in contact in the sprawling Southwest, and they were always conscious, too, of the lure of the cowboy myth. Texas fiddlers knew and loved the old-time hoedowns, but they tended to play them with greater melodic variation than elsewhere, and they also included in their repertories waltzes, schottisches, polkas, ragtime, and jazz tunes. One consequence of this musical eclecticism was a style of music which has since been described as western swing.

Western swing was within the country music framework, but was heavily indebted to pop, blues, and jazz. It evolved out of the fiddle-and-guitar bands of the Southwest, but its most crucial development came with the creation in 1931 of the Light Crust Doughboys, a radio band sponsored by the Burrus Mill and Elevator Company in Fort Worth. Two of the original members of the group, singer Milton Brown and fiddler Bob Wills, went on to organize their own influential bands, while their announcer (and Burrus Mill's general manager), W. Lee O'Daniel, later became both governor and United States senator from the state of Texas.

Before his death in an automobile accident in April 1936, Milton Brown led the Musical Brownies, the most popular band in the Southwest. With Fort Worth as their headquarters, the Musical Brownies toured extensively in Texas, performing their hot dance rhythms for appreciative audiences. The Brownies were essentially a fiddle band and played any kind of song that their dance-minded listeners wanted to hear. Although the fiddles usually took the lead, on everything from "St. Louis Blues" to "Sweet Georgia Brown" and "El Rancho Grande," they were supported by a piano and steel guitar, both played in the fashion of jazz instruments. Bob Dunn, the steel guitarist, was one of the seminal musicians of country music history. His technique of guitar improvisation, marked by riffs that sounded like the bursts of a trumpet, was unique in country music, and in 1934 he became the first known country musician to electrify an instrument, an innovation soon copied by other steel guitarists such as Ted Daffan and Leon McAuliffe.

Bob Wills, born in Limestone County, Texas, in 1905 and reared in West Texas near the community of Turkey, was descended from old-time fiddlers on both sides of his family. Wills remained essentially a hoedown fiddler to the end of his life, but he was an eclectic musician with a special affinity for the blues, and as a boy had been a fan of singers as diverse as Bessie Smith, Jimmie Rodgers, and Emmett Miller. The careers of Milton Brown and Bob Wills demonstrate the strong impact that the phonograph recording had on musicians who emerged professionally in the thirties. The performances of Brown and Wills, as well as those of other musicians, were often no more than copies, stage patter and all, of previous recordings. After Wills left the Light Crust Doughboys, he formed the Texas Playboys, played for a short time in Waco, and then moved, first to Oklahoma City, and then, in 1934, to Tulsa where he remained until 1942. According to Charles Townsend, in *San Antonio Rose: The Life and Music of Bob Wills* (one of the best biographies yet written on any American musician), the Tulsa years were the "glory years" for Wills and his

brand of music.³ Wills popularized his music through daily broadcasts over powerful KVOO, dances at Cain's Ballroom, personal appearances throughout the Southwest, and, of course, phonograph
recordings. No band was more revered throughout the Southwest
than the Texas Playboys, and its influence on the whole field of
country music is incalculable.

Beginning as a fiddle band, the Texas Playboys expanded in
personnel as Wills diversified the instrumentation, adding saxophones, trumpets, clarinets, piano, steel guitar, and drums. The
Playboys contributed nothing to the evolution of jazz, and there is
little evidence that the jazz world ever recognized the band's
merits, although it could not have avoided being envious of the
crowds the Playboys drew. This was a band that could play both
country music and the popular swing music of the decade. In style,
size, and repertory it often resembled the swing bands, but its use
of the fiddle planted it squarely in the country music tradition, and
it is there that Wills and his musicians made their most lasting
impact. Tommy Duncan, chief vocalist of the Playboys for many
years, inspired a generation of country singers. Smokey Dacus,
their drummer, seems to have been the first to play such an instrument in country music, and Leon McAuliffe, steel guitarist,
played a major role in making that instrument one of the dominant
sounds in country music. The influence of such Playboy fiddlers
as Jesse Ashlock, and Wills himself, is still strongly felt in country
music today. And a large number of songs—ranging from "San
Antonio Rose" and "Take Me Back to Tulsa" to "Maiden's
Prayer" and "Faded Love"–are known by virtually all country
singers and, in fact, have often moved into the mainstream of
American popular music.

Texas bands as a whole, including those that were only loosely
related to swing music, began to exert a powerful influence on
country music toward the end of the thirties, although the chief
influence of Texas music would not come until after World War II.
The music of the western swing bands was heard far and wide on
recordings, and several of the bands circulated their music through
personal appearances. With his headquarters in Beaumont, Texas,
Cliff Bruner, for example, a one-time fiddler for the Musical
Brownies, worked the southwestern area of Louisiana extensively
with his band, the Wanderers. Bruner is largely responsible, there-

fore, for the dissemination of the swing style among Cajun musicians. Through attending Bruner dances, and hearing swing music broadcast from Texas radio stations, young Cajuns were encouraged to diversify their styles and repertories. Leo Soileau, who had begun his recording career in 1928 as a Cajun fiddler, by the end of the thirties was leading a band called the Four Aces, a group that could shift easily from Cajun to swing. The Rayne-Bo Ramblers and the Hackberry Ramblers were other Louisiana groups that were combining Cajun and country music by the end of the thirties. Since that decade most Cajun bands, while continuing to sing in French, typically have included instruments that readily permit them to shift from one style to another: the fiddle and accordion, electric guitars (both steel and standard), plus bass and drums.

Although Bruner's band showed the strong influence of western swing, particularly in Bruner's own jazzlike fiddling, it was significantly different from the Bob Wills prototype. For one thing it was smaller. Costs of maintaining a large band were high, and now that the growing use of electrical instruments permitted a small band to be heard even in the noisiest of places, most Texas bands tended to be confined to four or five musicians. One of those noisiest of places, the dance hall, proved to be a mighty molder of the type of country music that emerged from Texas.

Particularly after the repeal of prohibition, hundreds of musicians found employment in bars, taverns, and dance halls where they created a subgenre of music that would ultimately be known as honky-tonk music. The honky-tonk musicians established a beat strong enough for dancing, but their music was essentially lyric-oriented and aimed at working-class listeners. While their songs typically dealt with their listeners' values, preoccupations, and fears, including the problems of drink, illicit love, and divorce, many songs dealt specifically with the milieu in which the performers worked: the honky-tonk. Al Dexter, from Troup, Texas, recorded in 1935 one of the first hillbilly songs to carry the word in its title: "Honky Tonk Blues." During World War II Dexter would record a smash hit, "Pistol Packin' Mama," which recalled the turbulent atmosphere of honky-tonk life during the East Texas oil boom of the thirties. He and other Texas cohorts, such as Ted Daffan, Floyd Tillman, Moon Mullican, and, preeminently, Ernest

Tubb, wrote or recorded songs that increasingly made their way into the larger world of country music. Furthermore, the music they created would soon become the sound of national country music, as the styles of the Southwest fused with those of the Southeast in the decade of the forties.

As important as style fusion was in the obliteration of regional differences within country music, a common dress or uniform often seemed to be the most apparent unifying factor. Up until the late fifties virtually every country singer, from the West Virginia hills to the Texas Plains, dressed in some semblance of cowboy costume and called himself something like "Tex," "Slim," "Hank," or "the Lone Cowboy." The cowboy image would have been appealing to country singers even without Hollywood, and the man on horseback was certainly a much more romantic figure to Americans than was the backward hillbilly. But the silver screen of the thirties made the most powerful contribution to the myth of the cowboy and its identification with country music. In 1934 Gene Autry, of Tioga, Texas, sang in a Ken Maynard film and ushered in the era of the singing cowboy. In the following ten years Autry did more to introduce country music to a national audience than did any other country singer. In so doing, he popularized the guitar among American youth and contributed mightily to the identification in the public mind of the image of the cowboy with the country singer. The popularity of the singing cowboy was not lost upon Hollywood moguls, and Autry was soon followed by other cowboy singers. The fan of Saturday afternoon cowboy movies might see Tex Ritter, Roy Rogers, Rex Allen, Jimmie Wakely, Johnny Bond, Eddie Dean, the Sons of the Pioneers, or the Riders of the Purple Sage, all of whom began as country singers and who maintained singing careers along with their professions as actors. Other country singers, such as Ernest Tubb, Jimmie Davis, and Bob Wills, made occasional appearances in cowboy shows, and a few people who became well-known country songwriters, such as Fred Rose and Cindy Walker, contributed songs to the screen cowboys.

The Hollywood singing cowboy disappeared from American popular culture after World War II, but he left his mark upon country music. With the exception of an occasional number like "El Paso," cowboy songs declined in the country repertory, but the cowboy mystique endured as evidenced in the wearing of cowboy costumes and the sporting of cowboy monikers. Along with the emergence in the thirties of other "western" styles such as honky-tonk and western swing, the music of the Hollywood singing cowboys contributed to the shaping of the once-popular term "country and western."

As the United States entered World War II, the grassroots music forms of the South still demonstrated their regional origins and identification. In various ways, however, the music of the South was already being exported to other regions of the nation and moving into the consciousness of Americans generally. Population migrations had played powerful roles in the dissemination of southern music. Blues and black gospel music had traveled north with the black migrations, and although the migration of southern whites had not been as extensive as that of blacks, the Okie exodus to California in the late thirties had done much to transplant hillbilly music to that state's sunny climes. As southerners left the marginal economy of their region to seek employment in other cities, flocking to the automobile plants of Detroit, the rubber plants of Akron, Ohio, the packinghouses or oil refineries of Chicago, or to industrial work in more contiguous cities such as Cincinnati or Saint Louis, they often took their musical preferences with them and permanently implanted them in the new little southern enclaves around the United States.

Even without migration, southern-derived musical forms would have circulated throughout much of the nation via the media. By 1941 radio had made much of the nation aware of the folk-derived music of the South through the broadcasts of the Mexican border stations, such 50,000-watt American stations as WBAP in Fort Worth and WWVA in Wheeling, West Virginia, and the Grand Ole Opry on NBC each Saturday night. The movie industry had given employment to many country singers while also providing them with an audience that might not otherwise have given them a hearing. And, of course, phonograph recordings made by southern-born entertainers might conceivably wind up in any American home. It is difficult to know either the extent of circulation or the sales figures of recordings issued before World War II, but we do know that hillbilly and blues records had been nationally advertised, as in Sears Roebuck and Montgomery Ward catalogs, since the twenties. Popularity or "Hit Parade" charts were not nearly so common in the thirties as they are now, but *Billboard* had begun to run its charts by the end of the decade. Even before the war brought its great changes to American entertainment and exerted its homogenizing effects on our musical tastes, records by such southern-born entertainers as Louis Jordan, Nat "King" Cole, Bob Wills, and Jimmie Davis were already appearing on jukeboxes in areas outside the South. Furthermore, songs from such sources were occasionally being "covered" by pop singers, as in the case of Bing Crosby's hit recording of "San Antonio Rose." The music of the grass roots South was gradually making itself heard in the farthest reaches of the nation, but the explosion of interest in such music, and its metamorphosis into mainstream popular music, was yet to come.

6

The Nationalization of Southern Music

WORLD WAR II wrought revolutionary changes in the social structure of both the South and the nation at large. While promoting major transformations in the habits, employment, and residence of rural southerners, the war also effectively nationalized their music. The war accelerated changes that had long been under way among blacks, and to a lesser extent among whites. Wartime demands promoted a major shift in the South from agriculture to industry, thereby creating alternative opportunities for rural and small-town people, opening up new sources of wealth, and accelerating the move from the country to the city. The establishment of defense centers in the South during the war, and the burgeoning of oil, petrochemical, and space centers in the fifties, also encouraged the arrival of thousands of people from outside the South who did not share the cultural affinities of native southerners. Southerners therefore came into contact with new people as well as new experiences.

As was true everywhere during the forties, southern families confronted social pressures that had never seemed quite so overwhelming in a rural environment. Family solidity was weakened; women were faced with greater breadwinning responsibilities; and children found alternative role models among their new urban peer contacts and among those provided by the media. The new life in the city, especially in an industrial atmosphere, brought both frustration and liberation, and adjustments were made with varying degrees of success. One of the most profound consequences of these social changes was the Black Revolution of the late fifties and early sixties, but the effects of the socioeconomic transformation could also be seen in the striving for cultural identity exhibited among southern youth. Social change had always come slowly in the South, and the effects exerted on the youth would not become readily apparent until ten years or so after the war. Among the results would be the explosion known as rock 'n' roll and the consequent shattering of the older concepts of popular music in the United States.

While important demographic changes took place within the South, the region asserted itself just as dramatically in the nation at large through population migrations. The movement of black people to the North and West, which had been significant since 1914, surged to even greater heights during the war years. Black people generally fled the South as a region of economic and human oppression, but the large white migration of the period, much of it from the Upper South, was generally motivated by the desire for improved economic opportunities. By failing to provide economic security for its people, the South had, in effect, expelled many of its most loyal sons and daughters—rural poor whites.

Lured by wartime prosperity and new defense jobs, thousands of rural and small-town southerners moved to Detroit, Washington, Baltimore, Philadelphia, Cincinnati, and Los Angeles, as well as to the cities of the South. In these cities their children would ultimately lose most of their rural ways, but more immediately much of the rural South was exported to other regions as the migrants took their cultural preferences with them. Storefront, fundamentalist churches, "southern," or "redneck," bars, and southern accents multiplied in those cities where the migrants congregated, and jukeboxes began featuring greater numbers of songs like "San Antonio Rose," "Pistol Packin' Mama," "You Are My Sunshine," and "Born to Lose." The migrants absorbed much from their new environments, but they also implanted much of their own culture. Not only does country music have a strong following today in Detroit, Chicago, Southern California, Pennsylvania, and southern Ohio, but the music preferred—probably reflecting the cultural conservatism of the migrants—tends to be that of a more traditional orientation such as bluegrass.

While southern civilians took their musical preferences all over the United States, their sons and daughters in the military took such music all over the world. Some servicemen merely carried their affinity for music with them; others performed as blues or country musicians in special service units. Northern and southern boys heard (and unwittingly absorbed) each other's musical preferences—from jukebox choices, and from pickin' and singin' in the barracks, on troop ships, and on the battlefield and in other places of imposed fraternal association. Servicemen were starved for anything reminiscent of home and were therefore delighted at the appearance of any kind of musical performer, whether jazz, blues, pop, or country. Many people were therefore exposed to various kinds of music to which they had never before deigned to listen. Some people no doubt recoiled from the experience of listening to country music with the feeling that it was nothing more than one long, atrocious, nasal lament but others developed a liking for it, as did Julian Aberbach, who came home from military service and founded Hill and Range Publishers, one of the most important publishing houses for country music. Musical preferences among servicemen generally reflected their opposing cultural backgrounds, and disputes over radio or jukebox selections, which sometimes descended into fights, were often projections of North-South antagonisms. Military units were not racially integrated until the fifties, but since that time barracks and service clubs have periodically reverberated with violent clashes between black and white servicemen concerning tastes for soul or country music.

The war years also witnessed changes in the music industry which promoted the growth of southern-derived music forms. The number of coin-operated music machines, popularly called jukeboxes, increased as music entrepreneurs moved to satisfy the needs of servicemen and defense workers for a cheap form of entertainment. The jukeboxes obviously expanded the market for the recording industry, but they also encouraged the creation of louder forms of music. Placed in noisy cafes, drugstores, or honky-tonks, the jukeboxes required an amplified sound that would permit the songs to be heard above the din; hence, the increased use of electric instruments.

In addition, two conflicts within the music industry positively affected the airing of grass roots music. The first of these involved the struggle between two music-licensing organizations—the American Society of Composers, Authors, and Publishers (ASCAP) and Broadcast Music, Incorporated (BMI). ASCAP was founded in 1914 by Victor Herbert and others to protect the performance rights of American composers. It remained a tightly knit group of writers of sophisticated popular music, reputedly biased against folk-derived forms. BMI lent active support to all kinds of grass roots music, having been founded in 1939 by broadcasters during their conflict with ASCAP over the use of ASCAP-licensed material on radio. After the expiration of a five-year contract with ASCAP, the broadcasters refused to negotiate an agreement calling for a greatly increased licensing fee and on January 1, 1941, announced a ban on all material controlled by ASCAP. As a new licensing organization, BMI suffered because it had few songs in its catalog and because it had to depend on new and inexperienced songwriters. Gradually, however, publishing firms began to join the organization, some of whom, such as M. M. Cole and Southern Music, had extensive catalogs of country and race material. In 1942 the Nashville-based Acuff-Rose company also joined BMI, an action in which most other new companies followed suit. By the time ASCAP and the radio networks had resolved their differences in October 1941, BMI had become securely established and its stable of grass roots–oriented publishers and writers had gained similar recognition.

Right on the heels of the ASCAP-BMI struggle came the American Federation of Musicians' recording ban of August 1, 1942, occasioned by the fear that jukeboxes and radio stations which used phonograph records were putting musicians out of work. The refusal by the recording companies to establish a fund for unemployed musicians led to the strike. The major record companies, such as Decca, Victor, and Columbia, tried to hold out against the strike, but they began capitulating in September of 1943. Meanwhile, the small and independent labels, many of which specialized in country, Latin, or rhythm and blues music, signed contracts with the musicians' union almost immediately. As a result, such music gained a foothold in American popular culture that it otherwise might not have enjoyed.

Despite the "artificial" advantages gained by southern folk-derived musical forms during World War II, these styles had long been developing under their own steam and without the encouragement enjoyed by mainstream popular music. Millions of people yearned to hear such music, and the small record labels moved to meet the demand. There was a proliferation of such labels during the war and on through the early fifties, and most of them specialized in grass roots music (country, rhythm and blues, gospel, Mexican, Bohemian, Cajun) and served local interests. Many performers who first attained local popularity in a city like Houston, Atlanta, or Memphis later went on to contracts with major companies and to national popularity. Most of the labels eventually disappeared or were bought up by the big companies, but a few of them endured to become major companies themselves. Most important of all, many of the songs that first gained local or regional popularity during this period gradually entered the national consciousness and were subsequently recorded, or "covered," by entertainers on major labels. And the route by which these songs became part of the national consciousness was usually through the young people from middle-class homes who were receptive to music their parents generally ignored.

In the period after 1941 hillbilly music left its regional base in the South, intruded into the national scene, and gained an acceptance that had never before seemed possible. By the end of the fifties the term "hillbilly" was being universally replaced by "country" or "country and western." At the beginning of the era of national expansion, when its rural origins still clung tightly to it, the singer who dominated the music was a mountain boy from East Tennessee named Roy Acuff. Acuff joined the Grand Ole Opry in 1938 after having performed for about three years in his home town of Knoxville. He rode to fame largely on the strength of two songs, "The Wabash Cannon Ball" and "The Great Speckled Bird," both of which he still performs each Saturday night on the Grand Ole Opry. Acuff achieved great fame and commercial success with a singing style that was radically different from those of the western swing performers and other country crooners, such as Eddy Arnold, who were beginning to become prominent in country music. His earnest, almost wailing, style suggested the mountain gospel churches, and his songs were either old-time ballads or songs with an old-time flavor. And his popularity was not confined to the Southeast or the Deep South. He drew large crowds wherever he traveled. For instance, when he performed at the Venice Pier in Los Angeles, local promoters feared that the immense crowd who came to hear him would cause the pier to collapse.

Acuff's rise to fame—he eventually became, in 1963, the first living performer to be elected to the Country Music Hall of Fame —paralleled that of the Grand Ole Opry and was in fact partly responsible for the show's new prominence. The broadcast ran from seven-thirty to midnight each Saturday night and because of its presence on 50,000-watt, clear-channel WSM, the Grand Ole Opry already had a South-wide audience before it blossomed nationally after 1939 on the thirty-minute NBC segment. Acuff hosted the show while he was at the peak of his popularity, but after the war the program was directed by Red Foley, a smooth singer and genial master of ceremonies, who was supported by guest artists and two well-known comedians, Rod Brasfield and Minnie Pearl (Sarah Ophelia Colley).

Acuff was only the first of several "stars" who came to the Opry during and just before the war years: Bill Monroe came in 1939, Ernest Tubb in 1943, and Lloyd "Cowboy" Copas and Eddy Arnold, both in 1944. Each of these entertainers built important and influential careers in country music, but Eddy Arnold, the first great country crooner, won the most widespread acclaim. Born the son of a sharecropper in Chester County, Tennessee, Arnold came to the Opry as a member of PeeWee King's Golden West Cowboys. But by 1945 he had embarked on a solo singing career, and between 1946 and 1949 he became the dominant country entertainer and one of RCA Victor's brightest stars. He has since abandoned the country music field, but in the immediate postwar years he made major contributions to the building of Nashville as a major music center and of country music as an international industry.

Ernest Tubb's affiliation with the Grand Ole Opry in 1943 was the beginning of an association that still persisted as of 1979. Tubb was born in Crisp, Texas, in 1914. When he made his first, largely unnoticed, records for Victor in 1936, he was singing and yodeling in the manner of his idol, Jimmie Rodgers. Tubb sang for about six years on Texas radio stations, ranging from San Antonio to San Angelo to Fort Worth, and in dance halls all over the state. When his first big record, "Walking the Floor over You," was introduced on Decca in 1941, he was living in Fort Worth and singing on KGKO and also touring much of the state in a sound truck as the Gold Chain Troubadour (he was sponsored by Gold Chain Flour). On the strength of "Walking the Floor," "Blue Eyed Elaine," and other songs, he was signed to a Grand Ole Opry contract in late 1942 and joined the show in January 1943. Tubb was the first major performer to take the honky-tonk style to the stage of the Grand Ole Opry. His joining of the show was more than symbolic of the fusion of southwestern and southeastern styles during the war. He was an immensely popular performer, and a large number of country entertainers became singers because of his example or shaped their styles partially in imitation of his. The country music that predominated in the years after 1946 and at least up to 1955 was a composite of styles that drew their strength from Texas musicians.

The commingling of styles that characterized country music's first boom period after the war was nowhere better represented than in the career of Hank Williams. Williams, the greatest country superstar of the postwar years, was a young singer who acknowledged his two chief influences to be Roy Acuff, a mountain singer, and Ernest Tubb, a Texas honky-tonk singer. Hank Williams was born on September 8, 1923, near Georgiana, Alabama. Like most rural southerners who grew to manhood during the war years, Hank was torn between the traditional music he had always heard at home and in church and the newer dynamic, electrified sounds that were beginning to predominate in country music. He was already singing in the honky-tonks of South Alabama by the time he was fourteen. He sang in an earnest, emotional style suggestive of Roy Acuff, but drew his instrumentation from the honky-tonk bands and called himself the Drifting Cowboy. His repertory was broad-ranging, including gospel songs, blues tunes, beer-drinking songs, sentimental numbers, and plenty of lonesome love songs. He was a member of the Louisiana Hayride in Shreveport when his recording of an old blues tune, "Lovesick Blues," became the top country song of 1949. By 1950 he was on the Grand Ole Opry and was the most talked-about performer in country music. The music had reached its highest peak of commercial success yet, and Hank Williams was its acknowledged leader.

In these booming years of country music popularity, songs with country identification began increasingly to be picked up by pop singers. These were the years when the pop music industry began to be cognizant of the small labels and the "ethnic" styles they recorded. For a few years the mainstream pop singers profited from the covering of country and rhythm and blues tunes (as with Patti Page's "Tennessee Waltz," Rosemary Clooney's "Half as Much," and Georgia Gibbs's "Dance With Me, Henry"), but very soon those same singers would find themselves pushed aside by the very singers from whom they had taken material. Hank Williams did most to break the fragile barriers between country and pop music, and his songs were covered by several pop entertainers, such as Tony Bennett, Frankie Laine, and Guy Mitchell. Hank never made the popular charts himself, but his songs crossed into pop territory with great frequency. Williams died of a heart attack on January 1, 1953, and by the time of his death, his life had become much like the tragic songs he often sang. He had been fired from the Grand Ole Opry because of chronic drunkenness and emotional instability and had once again become a rather unsteady member of the Louisiana Hayride. Divorce and remarriage during the same period only added to the personal turmoil that shortened his life.

Country music's emergence as a lucrative industry attracted to it a larger number of entertainers and a consequent realization among the industry leaders that the music's scope and image needed broadening. This broadened perspective, augmented by the liberating social trends of the war, produced a more tolerant attitude toward women performers. Some women entertainers, such as Lulu Belle Wiseman, Maybelle Carter, Patsy Montana, Texas Ruby Owens, Molly O'Day, and Rose Maddox, had won a large degree of earlier recognition, but they had been associated with family groups and only rarely had achieved any kind of individual identity. The first genuine female superstar of country music appeared in 1952 when Kitty Wells (born Muriel Deason in Nashville, Tennessee) recorded "It Wasn't God Who Made Honky

Tonk Angels," the "woman's answer" to Hank Thompson's earlier hit, "The Wild Side of Life." Throughout the fifties Kitty Wells was the acknowledged "Queen of Country Music," and was in fact a performer who consistently outdrew most of the men. Ironically, she remained the most modest and unassuming of people and never adopted even the faintest semblance of "women's liberation." Her husband, Johnny Wright, remained her spokesman and manager. In short, although she opened the door for the success of other women singers, such as Patsy Cline, Loretta Lynn, and Dolly Parton, her own life and values generally conformed to the image of the southern housewife.

Until approximately 1955 country music continued to win commercial success, and its styles remained identifiably rural and southern. Few people suspected that the music would soon be virtually in a state of collapse. Indeed, few people suspected that the whole field of mainstream pop music would soon be obliterated, at least as it had been known for about three decades. The nation was on the threshold of the rock 'n' roll revolution.

In the years following World War II, American youth gained an influence and buying power that no other youthful generation had possessed. Led by urban youth whose values and sensibilities were shaped increasingly by television and other media forms, and personally cut adrift because of the weakening of parental restraints during the war, young people everywhere became acutely conscious of their specialness in a youth-oriented culture. They consequently began looking for symbols, models, and entertainment forms that most closely mirrored their own existences. And, of course, the American entertainment industry was ready, once the youth market was recognized, to shape and satisfy its needs.

As American youth groped for self-understanding, they found little with which to identify in mainstream pop culture. Much of the older popular music was too sophisticated, bland, or repressed to satisfy their cravings, and they sought novel or exciting alternatives in the various kinds of ethnic or grass roots material found on small record labels. By 1952 or 1953 they were listening to rhythm and blues material that their parents scarcely knew existed, and some young, white would-be musicians were already experimenting with these songs. In the meantime, many young people also found cultural heroes among such "method actors" as Marlon

Brando and James Dean whose shrugs, confused postures, inarticulate mumblings, and antiauthoritarian stances paralleled their own gropings. The dress, hairstyles, and demeanor of the method actors, combined with the rocking beat of American grass roots music, provided the volatile ingredients of rock 'n' roll.

The rhythm and blues that predominated during the forties and early fifties was a composite of styles aimed almost exclusively at black audiences. Very little of the older style of country blues remained after World War II. Even such singers as Lightning Hopkins, Muddy Waters, and John Lee Hooker, who adhered to the older ways of singing, generally adopted electrified instruments. The great migration to the cities in the twentieth century had spawned a new generation of blacks who had only a secondhand knowledge of rural conditions or of the South. And many who had come from the South tried to reject those things that reminded them of earlier degradation, so they and the urban, northern-born blacks sought musical forms that corresponded to their own values and aspirations. The electrical amplification of instruments certainly divested their music of many of its rural connotations. Not only was the guitar universally electrified, it came increasingly to be played in the single-string style pioneered by T-Bone Walker and Charlie Christian, with little of the finger style so common in the twenties. Rhythm and blues bands, despite their emphasis on vocals, were basically dance-oriented, so they partly filled the vacuum left by the decline of the big bands after World War II. But as dance bands, and as groups that played in noisy environs, their sound had to get louder; hence the electrification and the addition of basses and drums. Most of the performers who were now described as rhythm and blues gravitated to the cities—some, like T-Bone Walker, to the West Coast, but more of them to Chicago or Memphis. And their music appeared on a large number of small record labels, virtually all of them white-owned: Specialty, Peacock, Duke, Aladdin, Aristocrat, Chess, Vee Jay, King, Apollo, Deluxe, and Savoy.

Many of the black performers lived out their entire performing careers known to only a handful of white listeners who might have stumbled upon their records or heard them perform on black radio shows. The r & b entertainers played for the black masses, whether they lived in the ghettos of Chicago, Detroit, or Los Angeles, or in the cities or small towns of the South. According to Charles Keil's *Urban Blues* (the best analysis yet written of the relationship between bluesmen and their culture), the blues singers of today are "culture heroes" in black communities and are important masculine models for black youth. Keil suggests that the hustler and the entertainer provide "two important value orientations for the lower-class Negro and need not be distinguished from the lower class as a whole."[1] Both the hustler and the entertainer are seen as men who are clever and talented enough to be financially well off without working. Although the bluesmen assume heroic proportions to their listeners and accordingly dress in a manner fitted to their stations—with flashy, well-tailored clothes, processed hair, shiny jewelry—their success derives from the fact that there is no cultural gap between them and their audience. Like the white country singers, the bluesmen share the cultural values of their listeners but have achieved a glamour and aura of power that plain folk can generally admire only from afar.

Several of the blues singers of the postwar period were men whose styles and careers dated from the thirties. Aaron T-Bone Walker was born in Linden, Texas, in 1910 and could point to a strong acquaintance with the country blues tradition of that state. Since it seems almost obligatory for Texas bluesmen to point to an association with Blind Lemon Jefferson, one might respond to Walker's claim to such a connection with some reservations. He seems at least to have heard Jefferson on occasion. Walker's link to the older traditions, and his seminal importance to the new, cannot be questioned. He was one of the first men to play an electric guitar in 1935; he was a pioneer in the employment of a single-string technique; and he was one of the first men to take the blues to the West Coast, playing in Central Avenue clubs in Los Angeles in 1936–1937. After the war he became a fixture on the West Coast blues scene and recorded for several labels. His biggest song, recorded in 1947, was "Stormy Monday."

Chester Burnett (known as Howlin' Wolf) and McKinley Morganfield (Muddy Waters) were also older bluesmen who were able to adjust to the newer urban and electrified style of blues music. Both men were born in the Mississippi Delta, in 1910 and 1915 respectively, but neither gained any real recognition until they moved to Chicago after the war and were discovered by white

Bessie Smith

Above: Louis Armstrong's Hot Five,
ca. 1926. Left to right: Johnny St. Cyr,
Kid Ory, Louis Armstrong, Johnny
Dodds, Lil Hardin Armstrong.
*Courtesy of William Ransom Hogan
Jazz Archive, Tulane University*

At left: Jimmie Rodgers. *Courtesy of
John Edwards Memorial Foundation*

Albert Brumley. *Courtesy of Albert Brumley Music Co.*

Light Crust Doughboys, 1933. Left to right: W. Lee O'Daniel, Bob Wills, Herman Arnspiger, Tommy Duncan, Sleepy Johnson, Henry Steinbarth (driver). *Courtesy of Bob Pinson*

At left: Mahalia Jackson. *Courtesy of Columbia Records*

Below: B. B. King at New Orleans Jazz and Heritage Festival. *Photograph by Mike Smith*

Hank Williams, Sr. *Courtesy of Country Music Foundation*

At left: Bill Monroe.
Courtesy of MCA Records

Below: Balfa Brothers.
Courtesy of Swallow Records

Charlie Daniels

Dolly Parton. *Courtesy of RCA Records*

blues aficionados. As his name suggests Howlin' Wolf groaned
and shouted in a manner reminiscent of the Mississippi field hollers, while Muddy Waters played the French harp and the bottleneck style of guitar. Of all the old-time bluesmen who remained
active during the forties and fifties, Waters seems to have made the
best adjustment to rhythm and blues and to have had the greatest
international impact. He was sufficiently rural in the early forties
to record for folklorist Alan Lomax and the Library of Congress,
but by the late forties he was an active and leading member of the
aggressive Chicago rhythm and blues scene. He did not have a
large white following at the time, but his influence asserted itself
in a strange and unexpected way. One of his recorded songs from
the latter period, "Rollin' Stone," inspired the name of the famous
British rock group. The popularity that such bluesmen as Howlin'
Wolf and Muddy Waters enjoyed among some of the performing
groups in Great Britain was a factor in their discovery in this
country. When the Beatles came to the United States, they brought
with them an appreciation for the southern blues which they passed
on to their American fans.

Among the generation of blues singers which came of age
during World War II, the name of Riley B. (B. B.) King is preeminent. Born in 1925 on a Delta plantation near Indianola, Mississippi, King moved with his guitar to Memphis shortly after the
war and began playing on street corners and in dance halls. He
soon obtained a job on WDIA, a 50,000-watt station, where he sang
and worked as a disc jockey. It was here that he became known
as the Beale Street Blues Boy (abbreviated B. B.), and began
building his reputation as a great blues singer. King refused to
capitulate to rock 'n' roll during the fifties, and stuck to his Delta-
born style through successive changes in music fashions. While he
did not share in the adulation that the black rock 'n' rollers received from American youth at the time, King won the passionate
devotion of the black audience and inspired many people to enter
the music profession, including Bobby Blue Bland. With a schedule
that included a staggering number of one-night stands, extending
all over the South and to the West Coast and then back again,
King traveled with his guitar, Lucille, and built a rapport with his
listeners that any entertainer might envy. Charles Keil, writing in
1966, asserted that King was "the only straight blues singer in

America with a large, adult, nationwide, and almost entirely Negro audience."[2] Since those words were written, B. B. King has become known to a much wider circle of Americans, largely because of the publicity given him and his songs by his British rock admirers.

Although a large number of black singers, such as B. B. King, were almost totally unknown in this country outside of the black community, there were others whose songs gradually began to intrude into the white consciousness in the late forties and early fifties. These singers, whittling away at the edges of mainstream pop music, prepared the way for the coming of rock 'n' roll. Louis Jordan, from Brinkley, Arkansas, was the first black r & b singer to produce songs that were popular with both black and white Americans. Jordan had been a jazz musician in the thirties, but his postwar recording success came with the production of comic and novelty songs: "Choo, Choo Ch' Boogie," "Caldonia," and "Open the Door, Richard." Jordan's songs seem to have been popular with all age groups, but the r & b singers who came after him were more particularly attuned to youth. At any rate, American white youth began to turn on to black music, finding in it a freedom, expressiveness, and sensuality that they did not hear in other forms of music. Between 1952 and 1955 a succession of rhythm and blues songs, recorded on the little 45-rpm discs that had been introduced in 1948, competed for the favor of American youth. These included Lloyd Price's "Lawdy Miss Clawdy" and the Clovers' "One Mint Julep" (1952); Clyde McPhatter's "Money Honey" and Ruth Brown's "Mama, He Treats Your Daughter Mean" (1953); Joe Turner's "Shake, Rattle, and Roll"; Lavern Baker's "Tweedle Dee"; and Hank Ballard's "Annie Had a Baby" and "Work with Me, Annie" (1954); and Fats Domino's "Ain't It a Shame" (1955).

The emergence of Antoine "Fats" Domino, from New Orleans, Little Richard (Penniman), from Macon, Georgia, and Chuck Berry, from Saint Louis, provided the transition from black rhythm and blues to rock 'n' roll. Not only were their songs often copied by white singers, but these black rock 'n' rollers also competed favorably with the white singers and often appeared alongside them on the popular charts. With his exuberant vocal style and chorded, boogie-woogie piano playing, Domino had done much to create the distinctive "New Orleans dance blues" sound. Domino's recordings were made in the studios of Cosimo Matassa; in fact, virtually every r & b record made in New Orleans from the mid-forties until the late sixties was produced in studios owned by Matassa.[3] Some of the great New Orleans musicians, such as pianist Roy Byrd (known as Professor Longhair), regrettably never became known outside of the Crescent City, but Fats Domino became so much a part of mainstream rock 'n' roll that he often turned the tables on white musicians and made successful adaptations of their songs. In 1956, for example, he recorded a very popular version of a song introduced by cowboy singer Gene Autry, "Blueberry Hill."

Rock 'n' roll was not exclusively southern in origin or manifestation, but it first exploded on the national scene with a southern accent, and most of its early southern practitioners were young men who drew upon country, gospel, and rhythm and blues roots. Sam Phillips, the owner of the Memphis Recording Service and the Sun Record Company, had long recognized the commercial potential that lay in the fusion of southern black and white grass roots forms. He had often said that if he could find a white man who could sing in a convincing black style, he would make a million dollars. If Elvis Presley was that man, Phillips seems not to have recognized him immediately, for he ignored his first recording tests. Furthermore, Presley seems to have stumbled upon the idea of recording a rhythm and blues tune only after his attempts with other types of music had not caught fire.

Presley was born on January 8, 1935, to very poor and religious parents in East Tupelo, Mississippi. His first exposure to music came at the First Assembly of God Church, but he also listened to country music on the radio. Although he certainly must have heard such music earlier, his most direct contact with rhythm and blues came after he and his family moved to Memphis in 1948. By the time he made his first records for Sun in 1954, Presley had absorbed both songs and styles from most of the grass roots traditions of the South, but he seemed to have no exclusive commitment to any of them. In fact, when he made his first test records, he was singing some of the bland pop hits of the day. On July 6, 1954, he and two local musicians, guitarist Scotty Moore and string bass player Bill Black, were jamming in the Sun Studios when, purely by chance, they performed a song that excited them and also sparked Phillips's first real interest in their music. This was an old blues tune, learned from Arthur "Big Boy" Crudup, called "That's All Right, Mama." When their first record was released, "That's All Right" was backed with "Blue Moon of Kentucky," a country tune written by Bill Monroe. This choice too was the result of rather aimless jamming. Never was a revolution launched in such a playful and unplanned manner.

"That's All Right, Mama" became a big hit in Memphis soon after it was featured by white disc jockey Dewey Phillips on his rhythm and blues show, "Red Hot, and Blue." Presley and his music were such hybrid phenomena that no one could categorize them. Soon after the record appeared, Presley made guest appearances on the Grand Ole Opry and the Louisiana Hayride and then joined the regular cast of the latter show. Old-time country fans were wary, if not appalled, by the frenzied, sensual style of the singer, but Presley achieved two results that had not occurred among "country" singers before: he mesmerized youthful audiences that had not previously been attracted to country music, and he aroused emotions within them that had heretofore been latent. Presley tapped an enormous reservoir of repressed emotion among American youth, North and South, and the "rebels without a cause" of the fifties began to find a sense of common identity in a music that reflected their values and fears.

As an entertainer, Presley lost his exclusive regional identification forever by 1956. He had come under the astute management of Colonel Tom Parker, a former carnival man and booking agent, and he had signed a recording contract with RCA Victor. Presley went on to experience a national success and international recognition that has seldom been matched by any figure in American popular culture. In the twenty years that preceded his death in 1977, Presley's popularity never really declined from the peak reached in the late fifties. His records did not always dominate the charts, but he successfully adapted to the various changes that came to pop music during those decades, and he maintained an astounding commercial viability through numerous movies, Las Vegas appearances, and television specials. He never lost his original audience, and he picked up a new one among younger people who had never seen him in person. He became so much the property of the American people, and the mythologized projection of their dreams, that he retreated into the isolation of his mansion and the small circle of friends, bodyguards, and relatives who gathered around him.

Even though Elvis became part of the international realm of show business, neither he nor the other young southern singers who followed in his wake could ever escape (even had they desired) the marks of their southern-bred culture. Generally described as "rockabillies" because they supposedly embodied both rock 'n' roll and hillbilly characteristics, such singers as Carl Perkins, Roy Orbison, Jerry Lee Lewis, Charlie Rich, and Conway Twitty carried the dialects and inflections of the Deep South in their speech and singing styles. Their music was also deeply indebted to the varied folk styles of their native region, reflecting an interesting fusion of gospel music (both white and black), country, and rhythm and blues. Growing up in the South, they scarcely could have avoided hearing such music on radio, recordings, or jukeboxes, but they usually could testify to even more personal forms of indebtedness. Charlie Rich, for example, grew up in a family of gospel singers, but he also learned the blues style from an old Negro singer who lived near his home in Arkansas. Carl Perkins, whose recording of "Blue Suede Shoes" was one of the big hits of 1956, had been born into a tenant farm family on a plantation near Lake City, Tennessee. Perkins was a faithful listener to the Grand Ole Opry and was particularly fond of Bill Monroe, but he credits his guitar style to a Negro musician who lived on the plantation.

Jerry Lee Lewis, in many ways the most interesting of the rockabillies, often acted as if he had walked out of the pages of Wilbur J. Cash's *Mind of the South:* he is the prototypical ambivalent southerner, embodying both hedonistic and puritanical traits. Lewis was born in Ferriday, Louisiana, the son of devout Assembly of God parents. He briefly contemplated going into the ministry and did spend some time at a Bible school in Waxahachie, Texas. Religious music, therefore, was very much a part of his life, but "sinful" music exerted a more powerful sway. In Ferriday he spent a considerable portion of his free time, as did his musical cousins, Mickey Gilley and Jimmie Lee Swaggart, at Haney's Big House, a black club that specialized in rhythm and blues music.

While Lewis's piano style, with its flourishes and rolling chords, is reminiscent of white gospel music, it probably owes a good deal to sounds heard at Haney's. Each of the three cousins has built a prominent career as a professional musician; Lewis mixes country with rock 'n' roll; Gilley sings mainstream country music; and Swaggart is a singing Pentecostal evangelist. All play the piano, and in much the same style.

Lewis vaulted into the national music limelight in 1957 with his hit recording of "Whole Lot of Shaking Going On," and with subsequent appearances on Steve Allen's "Tonight" show, where he bowled over the audience while almost wrecking the piano. He was soon thereafter embroiled in controversy when it became known that he had married his thirteen-year-old cousin (Lewis was twenty-three). He now sings mostly country music, but he has never lost the energy, dynamic flair, and swaggering confidence that characterized his early rockabilly days. Neither has he abandoned the life-style that veers from the sanctified to the sinful. Periodically he has announced a recommitment to Christ and an avowal that he will no longer perform where liquor is sold; but before that testimony can sink in, Jerry is back in some dance hall pounding the keyboard or has made the headlines because of some public indiscretion.

The rockabillies were definitely culture heroes to young Americans, and they contributed at least unconsciously to the youth revolution of the sixties. Their music was as popular in Great Britain as it was at home; Charles "Buddy" Holly, the Texas rockabilly who died in a plane crash in 1959, and the Everly Brothers (Phil and Don) from Kentucky, were direct influences on the music and harmony of the Beatles. But if the rockabillies themselves were rebels, their rebellion was in no way political and is hard to document; they certainly exhibited no rebellion toward the South. Presley, Lewis, and their cohorts were a whole world and a culture away from the bizarre, antiauthoritarian hard rockers of the 1960s. When as a Memphis teenager Elvis Presley decked himself out in bright, flamboyant clothing and worked his hair into a ducktail, he was in no sense flouting society's rules but was affirming his identity in a milieu that generally ignored the sons of the working-class poor. Likewise his and the other rockabillies' employment of a sensual performing style was as much an expres-

sion of the macho complex so deeply imbedded in southern working-class culture as it was a violation of conventional middle-class
standards. Presley never intended to antagonize any facet of that
southern lower-class world from which he came. However, his
exhibitionism, his employment of the emotionalism he had picked
up in church (where it was sanctioned and socioculturally "safe")
certainly had other implications when carried to the general public.
Even preachers of his own denomination denounced these antics,
much to Presley's surprise and disappointment. Hell-raisers the
rockabillies could be; but radicals they were not. Although he sang
with a heavy black-tinged style, Presley never questioned the racial
values of his region. His manners, with a profusion of "sirs" and
"ma'ams," epitomized southern courtesy. He willingly served his
country in the military and, alarmed by what he considered to be
scandalous conduct on the part of many hard rockers in the sixties,
reportedly offered his services to the FBI as an informer. If his personal habits did not always meet his public image (stories about
his alleged drug use were widely circulated after his death), his
discretion nevertheless helped maintain both the image and his
privacy.[4]

Yet Elvis Presley, Fats Domino, and their fellow southern
rock 'n' roll performers contributed to a social revolution that
still exerts an influence on the popular music and youth of the
world. As we look back on the period from a perspective of twenty
years and compare it to the rock culture that emerged in the sixties,
rock 'n' roll now seems an innocent and naïve phase of American
cultural history. American youth merely groped in the fifties for
answers that youth in the sixties would assert with fury and finality.
Regardless of the intent behind the music of the fifties, and regardless of the social consequences spawned by its emergence, the
southern rock 'n' rollers effectively implanted much of the culture
of the working-class South in the nation at large. Their visibility
as concert performers and their prominence on the national record
popularity charts were the obvious symbols of their impact; they
had taken their music further into the realm of national popular
culture than any southern grass roots performers before them.

7

The Sixties and Seventies:
Rock, Gospel, Soul

ALTHOUGH native rock 'n' roll's impact on popular music had diminished before 1960, the year 1964 saw a turning point in American music with the coming to the United States of the Beatles —an event that marked the beginning of a full-fledged invasion of the United States by British rock 'n' rollers. In a sense, the arrival of the British groups meant that rock 'n' roll had come full circle— from the recordings of grass roots American entertainers, to Europe, and then back again. But the British musicians also contributed significantly to the American music scene. Through their influence electronics returned to music with a vengeance (this was at the end of the acoustic-dominated urban folk revival in the United States). With their long hair and mod dress, the British rockers contributed directly to a revolution in dress habits among American youth that has not yet really dissipated. The British musicians, and their psychedelic counterparts from San Francisco, introduced the strongest urban tone yet heard in American rock 'n' roll. Their heavy electric instrumentation, their stage costuming, their sex-and-drugs-oriented repertories, and their brash performing styles suggested very little of the earlier rural-tinged music of the southern rockabillies. In short, rock 'n' roll was transformed into rock, and much of the innocence and naïveté of the earlier music disappeared.

Rock was much less derivative of the past than was rock 'n'

roll; conversely, it seemed to be attuned much more to contemporary youth, as a product of their urban experiences. The rock music of the mid-sixties was as powerful a de-regionalizing force as had yet appeared in American popular culture. Young southerners who were drawn to it, either as performers or listeners, were part of a culture that knew no regional bounds. Rock music, in the sixties at least, made its appeal neither to class, to race, or to region; it was an art form that spoke exclusively to youth. The rockabillies of the fifties often recorded in the South, and their southernness was very apparent. The rock singers of the sixties, on the other hand, usually recorded in New York or Los Angeles, and whether they came from Mobile, Des Moines, or Boise, they reflected a culture that was virtually worldwide in its traits: long hair, modish or bizarre costumes, drug-use, emphasis on sexual freedom, and inclination toward radical politics. Rock music's emergence during the turbulent sixties, when all of the nation's institutions were being challenged, further explains the southern rock singers' unwillingness to identify with the South. A hopeful southern rock musician moved to where the action was—to New York, Los Angeles, or San Francisco—and he could scarcely avoid being embarrassed about his southern background (its politics, religion, and racism). His affinity for rock music may have been sharpened, in fact, by a rebellion against the values of the white majority of his region. Whatever the cause, in the sixties when all roads led toward New York or the West Coast, there was little inclination for anyone to create anything that might have become southern rock.

Although they might often recoil against an identification with the South, the southern-born rock musicians could not avoid absorbing many of the region's musical traits. The Winter Brothers, Johnny and Edgar, from Beaumont, Texas, were devotees of black blues, but they remained in obscurity until they left Texas and relocated in New York. Doug Sahm, from San Antonio, Texas, drew upon at least three musical sources—blues, Tex-Mex, and country. He had been a child steel guitarist in local country bands, but later spent much of his time playing with Chicano and black organizations. Shortly after the Beatles' invasion of the American musical scene, Sahm's producer, Huey Meaux, instructed him to grow his hair long, find four other musicians, and prepare to emulate the

Beatles' methods. The result was the Sir Douglas Quintet, the first American rock band to show the direct effects of the British invasion. The quintet made one successful record, "She's about a Mover," and broke up after a marijuana bust in Houston; Sahm left to become part of the San Francisco scene.

The most successful southern rocker during the sixties was Janis Joplin. Her career is indicative of the multiplicity of influences that helped to shape the rock genre, but it also demonstrates how unreceptive the South was, at least initially, to its daughters and sons who would not conform to the prescribed culture of their region. Janis grew up in a middle-class family in Port Arthur, Texas. She was a bright and sensitive child whose liberal attitudes and artistic inclinations (an interest in music, art, and literature) set her apart from most of the city's youth, and she was made to feel self-conscious about her slightly plump physical appearance (although photographs from the time do not bear out her self-conception as an ugly duckling).[1] She sought escape in music and among young people who shared her sympathies.

When Joplin enrolled at the University of Texas in Austin in 1962, the city had not yet become an important music center, but there was an active urban folk scene which she entered immediately. Joplin, however, avoided the polite, Kingston Trio variety of folk music and immersed herself in the earthier forms of blues, gospel, bluegrass, and country, singing often in a hillbilly bar in north Austin called Threadgill's. Although her clear preference was for black blues—her idol was Bessie Smith—Janis had no exclusive style during her Austin days; she generally sang a song in the style of the person from whom she learned it. She and her friends were known in Austin as much for their unconventional dress and life-styles as for their music. Although the term was not yet current in Austin, Janis anticipated the hippie culture, and when she heard that San Francisco might be responsive both to her music and to her life-style, she left for that city in 1963. Joplin found an acceptance in the rock music world that she had never gained in her Texas home, and after her discovery at the Monterey Pop Festival in 1967, her career skyrocketed. With a vocal style partly shaped by her fascination with Otis Redding, and with an aggressive energy that punctuated her stage presence, she was soon touted as the best white blues singer in America.

By the time Janis Joplin died on October 4, 1970, the victim of an accidental overdose of heroin, much of the mood of rebellion and angry protest that had characterized the previous decade had dissipated. As the nation moved to the right and as civil rights legislation brought measurable improvement in the race relations of the southern people, the glare of national publicity moved significantly away from the ills of the South and instead concentrated on the continuing evils of the northern ghettos. The election of a new group of progressive governors, such as Reubin Askew in Florida, Dale Bumpers in Arkansas, and Jimmy Carter in Georgia, inspired a fresh wave of "New South" rhetoric. Carter's election to the presidency in 1976, with its promise of sectional healing and a reunited nation, intensified the feeling that a progressive South would lead the nation to racial justice and human brotherhood. With the disappearance or decline of the evils of southern society, along with the guilt that had accompanied them, young southerners were freed to reaffirm or rediscover the good that lay in their culture. Inevitably, the conceptions of what was "good" in the South, or what was indeed "southern," would vary considerably. The promotion, or "hype" as it is called in the music business, surrounding "southern rock music" in the seventies was largely a reassertion of the mythic South, but in the context of a heightened New South ideology.

The promotion and recording of southern rock musicians had not been entirely absent in the South—as witnessed by Huey Meaux's operations in Houston, and by Bill Lowery's success in Atlanta with the recording of Joe South, Tony Joe White, and Ray Stevens—but until the emergence of Phil Walden and his Capricorn label in 1969, no southern-based company had successfully rivaled those in other regions of the United States. Walden had been the manager of Otis Redding and was one of many southern music entrepreneurs who had long resented the failure of the South to hold on to its rock musicians. His establishment of Capricorn Records in Macon, Georgia, was explained as an effort to make use of the musical wealth of the South while keeping the region's rock performers at home. Walden literally created the Allman Brothers Band in 1969 when he asked Duane Allman, a great sessions guitarist at the recording studios in Muscle Shoals, Alabama, to recruit some other musicians for recording and concert purposes. The Allman Brothers subsequently gained great popularity throughout the United States, made Capricorn a nationally known label (with a gross in 1976 of $43 million), and were largely responsible for the creation of what became known as the Macon Sound. The Allmans used an instrumental format that would be widely copied by other southern rock bands, particularly by those who recorded for Capricorn: two guitars, two drums, keyboards, and bass. Theirs was basically a blues-rock sound given shape by Duane Allman's slide-style guitar and by Greg Allman's white soul singing, but the Allmans also sometimes projected a country feeling through the playing and singing of their other guitarist, Dickie Betts (as in "Rambling Man").

Some of the southern rock bands, such as Lynyrd Skynyrd (from Alabama), Marshall Tucker (from South Carolina), and the Charlie Daniels Band (from Tennessee) have adhered very closely to the Allman Brothers' instrumental format while often differing widely on the type of material performed. Others, such as Wet Willie (from Alabama), Sea Level (a direct offshoot of the Allmans), and ZZ Top (from Texas) diverge greatly from the Allman instrumental pattern. Wet Willie and Sea Level are basically white blues bands with no country admixture at all. The Wet Willie band produced at least one major national hit, "Keep On Smilin'," which recreated the black soul sound for the white youth audience. ZZ Top is essentially a hard-rock band specializing in raunchy lyrics. The lead singer and guitarist, Billy Gibbons, also has a black-tinged voice, and although the band contains only three instruments (guitar, bass, and drums), it produces some of the highest-decibel sounds in American rock music.

The music of the southern rock bands has been merchandised with extensive publicity devoted to their southernness. Capricorn distributed thousands of buttons admonishing record buyers to "Buy Southern." Phil Walden made the most of his personal and political friendship with Jimmy Carter. As governor of Georgia, Carter had supported a bill to control tape piracy whose passage was desired by Walden. Walden, in turn, made contributions to Carter's political campaigns. During the crucial opening stages of Carter's campaign for the presidency, several of the southern rock bands participated in concerts to raise money that was indispensable in the early state primaries. Carter's identification with the rock bands certainly did not hurt him among the nation's youthful voters, and the bands undoubtedly profited from their association with the president (Marshall Tucker and Charlie Daniels were featured bands at the main inaugural ball).

In such rock magazines as *Rolling Stone* and *Crawdaddy*, and in other types of promotional literature, constant allusions were made to the presumed southern qualities of the bands from the South. It was not solely their music, with its indebtedness to blues, soul, and country forms, that was said to be southern; other more intangible qualities concerning attitude, behavior, and life-style were said to denote their southernness and to mark them off from rock musicians from other areas of the country. Sometimes this "style" was projected as nothing more than the reflection in music of an easy-going ambience and an honest, down-to-earth approach to life, but often the emphasis was on the mythical southern machismo: a hedonistic attitude with an underlying hint of violence. One music journalist described southern music as "something more than just rock-and-roll south of the Mason-Dixon line. At best, it's the living image of Southern culture; a fusion of the varied and sometimes antagonistic elements of Southern life. At worst, it's awful, a sort of mindless, shake-your-butt disco music for the smash-the-beer bottle-over-the-waitress'-head set."[2]

Charlie Daniels is probably the most aggressively southern of all the rock musicians, and the South he presumes to represent is that of the hell-raising good old boy who lives only to play music, get drunk, make love, and even fight if someone steps on his toes. The Lynyrd Skynyrd band also built a devil-may-care image which carried more than a hint of potential violence. Ronnie Van Zant, the lead singer of the group who died in an airplane crash in 1977, was the coauthor of "Sweet Home, Alabama," a militant hymn of praise to the state and its famous governor George Wallace. One line in the song is a reply to singer Neil Young's disparaging remarks about Alabama: "A Southern man don't need him around anyhow."

Chet Flippo, a southern-born rock journalist, probably spoke for many southern rock fans when he said that the Allman Brothers "more than anything else, returned a sense of worth to the South." We probably learn more about Flippo's own sense of cultural inferiority, and that of many other southern youth, than we do about southern rock music when he argues that the Allmans had "moved a whole generation of southern kids uptown" and that "kids in the South finally had cultural heroes of their own."[3] Going "uptown," of course, is something that most southern musicians have strived to do. Whether they can make the trip without losing much of their cultural baggage is an arguable question.

Despite all the ballyhoo concerning the distinctive southern spirit or even the southern sound of these rock bands, a statement made by Toy Caldwell, leader of the Marshall Tucker Band, probably comes closest to the mark: "I guess to me, Southern music is just a band from the South playing music."[4] The southern-born rock entertainers have strongly identified with their native region, and as successful musicians they have become personalities southerners can be proud of. But their music is not substantially different from that of a hundred other rock bands heard in every section of the United States. Furthermore, the images that appeal to the southern rockers are often closer to those of the "Austin outlaws" than they are to scenes or symbols in their own home areas. Charlie Daniels, for instance, can speak of his southern origins with a truculent pride and say "Be proud you're a rebel" in his song of praise to his fellow southern musicians ("The South's Gonna Do It Again"), but he dresses like a saddlebum and has a penchant for Louis L'Amour western novels. The members of the Marshall Tucker Band are products of cotton-mill families in Spartanburg, South Carolina, but their hearts are in the Old West. Like Charlie Daniels, they too affect the attire of working cowboys, and their passion, apart from music, is old cowboy movies.

The "little old band from Texas," as ZZ Top calls itself, has carried the cowboy myth (or a Texas version of it) to its greatest lengths yet among rock musicians. As was true of the Allman Brothers Band, ZZ Top was the creation of a music promoter, Bill Ham, a former Houston record distributor. Their concerts have been accompanied by an avalanche of publicity exceeded only by that earlier accorded the Beatles and Rolling Stones. The band travels with seventy-five tons of equipment, including a 40,000-watt sound system, transported in eleven vehicles, seven of which are forty-foot semitrailers (each painted with a Texas scene). They perform on their own stage, which is sixty-three feet across and built in the shape of Texas. As the curtain goes up, the audience is presented with a scene of frontier Texas. Stationed at various locations around the fringe of the stage are a purebred longhorn steer, a black buffalo, two trained vultures, and two Mexican rattlers, and back of the stage is a two-dimensional panorama of Texas painted by a team of sixteen artists.

While they did not universally share the values and preoccupations of rock music, all forms of music in the sixties showed the evidence of heightened commercialization and organization, and all exhibited an awareness of the primacy of youth in contemporary popular culture. Consequently, virtually all entertainers—secular and gospel—understood the importance of displaying a youthful image and vitality, while also keeping abreast of changing fashions and styles. Long hair and modish dress became associated with nearly all musicians, and not solely those with an affinity for rock music. Every variety of American music became deeply immersed in the matrix of big business, and each demonstrated a concern for packaging, promotion, and merchandising that showed how far it had traveled from its folk roots. Furthermore, drums and electric instruments were used in every type of musical approach, and instrumental techniques and even vocal mannerisms borrowed from rock appeared with regularity in other musical genres.

By the beginning of the sixties gospel music had certainly come to terms with the world and had thoroughly appropriated the techniques of show business, while continuing to infuse much of its own spirit into the field of secular music. The sense of religious mission no doubt still burned brightly in the lives of many gospel singers, but an increasing number viewed the music as just another facet of popular music, or as an avenue for entrance into different kinds of performing careers. Singers with rural or downhome flavor still existed, and some of them, both white (the Chuck Wagon Gang, the Sullivan Family, Wendy Bagwell and His Sunlighters) and black (the Consolers), attained great popularity. And almost any night, on a string of radio stations across the country, one could hear the transcribed broadcasts of the Reverend and Mrs. J. Bazzel Mull as they talked to the "neighbors" and hawked their special offers of Chuck Wagon Gang and other gospel quartet albums.

The world of the Mulls and the Chuck Wagon Gang, however,

has been a gradually receding one. No facet of American music has been more competitive or more highly professionalized than gospel music. Black and white gospel singers alike typically have dressed in expensive, elegantly tailored suits and sported processed or styled hair; male singers often have worn mustaches, looking like either morticians or professional gamblers. The days of simple piano accompaniment have gone almost completely, and virtually every quartet has begun performing in front of drums, electric bass, and a retinue of horns or electric guitars. The white gospel groups have leaned toward country and western instrumentation, while the black singers have adhered to the instrumental sounds of rhythm and blues or soul music. The performing styles of black and white singers still differ greatly, with the choreography and the physical prowess of the blacks most obviously marking their style. Black singers dance and strut all over the stage and out into the aisles of the auditoriums and churches. Except for the need to lean into the one microphone that was usually reserved for singing, white quartets traditionally have stood rigidly and formally while their pianist cut up or acted the fool. Although the differences were still very apparent, the gap was narrowed somewhat in the sixties when the white quartets began to use multiple microphones and introduced well-rehearsed physical routines. Often this new concern for coordinated movement meant nothing more than the use of precise and synchronized gestures, but in the case of a few singers, most notably the Oak Ridge Boys, the routines were not far distant from those of the soul singers.

The songs of the gospel entertainers have undergone a similar evolution toward homogeneity and slickness. In an effort to make their music palatable to the largest possible audience, the gospel singers and composers have created a product much like that of the fast-food franchises: generalized, bland, and quickly produced. The songs have little theological or denominational identification, and generally eschew references to death or hellfire-and-damnation. Their general tone is that of an up-tempoed, or soothing, affirmation of life, and seldom does one hear the old-time "blood" songs, or the world-rejection songs (such as "Farther Along" and "I'd Rather Have Jesus"), that were once so dear to the heart of southern Protestants. The devotee of songs like "Lonely Tombs,"

"We'll Understand It Better By and By," "Conversation with Death," or "The Blood That Stained the Old Rugged Cross" will search for them in vain in the repertories of the white quartets; he is most likely to hear them in the performances of the country and bluegrass gospel groups, such as the Sullivan Family, or in the singing of a downhome black group, such as Iola and Sullivan Pugh, who record under the name of the Consolers. Black gospel singers, on the whole, have preserved a stronger traditional feeling in their songs than the white quartets. Although they have exhibited characteristics derived from jazz, rhythm-and-blues, and soul idioms, the black singers in the 1970s are still singing, and making hits, of such songs as "I'm Waiting for My Child to Come Home" and "Don't Drive Your Mother Away" (a best-selling sermonette recorded by Shirley Caesar in 1969).

Whatever the nature of their songs, and regardless of the motives that underlie their singing, the black and white gospel entertainers have included some of the greatest singers that America affords. Men and women of great vitality, with enormous vocal range and remarkable voice control, they generally have performed for audiences composed exclusively of the faithful, and only rarely have become known to mainstream America.

If gospel music has had an international superstar, it would surely be Mahalia Jackson, born in New Orleans in 1911. She grew up in a home of devout Baptists, but absorbed much of the fervor of the Sanctified people who had a church near her home. She also loved the records of Bessie Smith, and this fusion of blues and gospel music was no doubt a major factor in her appeal. When she moved to Chicago in 1927, she entered a community that was already teeming with great solo gospel singers, but she held her own among them even as a teenager. Although she recorded for Decca in 1937, her career did not blossom until after World War II. During the war she had joined forces with Thomas Dorsey with whom she toured the entire United States. She resumed recording in 1946, and her third record, "Move On Up a Little Higher," was one of the best-selling gospel records of all time and the prime force behind her national success. At this stage of her career, Mahalia sang in the free-wheeling style of the southern churches, and her popularity was particularly intense among the black southern mi-

grants. Tony Heilbut maintains that she was "unashamedly Southern, roaming and growling like the down-home congregations, and
skipping and strutting like the Sanctified preachers."[5]

In the early fifties Mahalia began to build a large following in
white America, largely through her appearances on the popular
Studs Terkel radio shows, as many jazz devotees began to notice a
resemblance between her and Bessie Smith. In 1954, amid great
fanfare, she signed with Columbia Records and began appearing
on her own radio and television shows. An appearance at the Newport Jazz Festival in 1958 and a best-selling album recorded with
Percy Faith were continuing examples both of her success and of
how far she had traveled from the downhome churches of the
South. Although her style and choice of songs came to diverge
widely from the music of her childhood—"Silent Night," for example, was her first big international hit—she retained the loyalty
of black people everywhere until her death. Because they had both
done so much, in their own special ways, to liberate and elevate
black Americans, it was only fitting that she should sing in tribute
to Martin Luther King, Jr., at his funeral; she chose Dr. King's
personal favorite, that great hymn written by Thomas Dorsey,
"Precious Lord." When Mahalia died in 1972, she was laid to rest
in New Orleans, in one of the most heavily attended funerals in
that city's history.

No other gospel singer won such acclaim as that accorded to
Mahalia Jackson, but Sister Rosetta Tharpe, from Cotton Plant,
Arkansas, a guitar-playing, Holiness-style singer, did make some
very popular records for Decca during the forties, and saw them
go higher in the *Billboard* charts than any previously recorded by
gospel singers. Her swinging, blues-tinged singing of such songs as
"Strange Things Happening Every Day" and "Up above My Head"
(sung with Marie Knight) won support among a widely diverse
array of listeners; her records, for example, could often be heard
on country deejay shows. Still, Sister Rosetta never became a
major force in American show business, and even though other
singers, such as Bessie Griffin, Alex Bradford, Andrae Crouch,
and the Clara Ward Singers, created sophisticated routines and
carried them even into the nightclubs, they never achieved the
standing in American popular culture attained by Mahalia. The
chief arenas for black gospel music remained the churches where

the robed choirs still hold sway, or the auditoriums in cities around the country which periodically attract package shows featuring the Swan Silvertones, the Five Blind Boys, Shirley Caesar, or James Cleveland.

The white gospel singers similarly never achieved the lionization received by Mahalia, nor did they move with much frequency away from the traditional gospel audience, but occasionally someone like Red Foley, Stuart Hamblen, Martha Carson, Jimmie Davis, or Tennessee Ernie Ford, singers who had built earlier identifications as country singers, recorded religious songs that made the popularity charts. Thomas Dorsey's "Peace in the Valley," in fact, attained its greatest popularity through a Red Foley recording. At least one white quartet, the Jordanaires, gained an entrée into Hollywood during the late fifties and early sixties, as well as considerable recording success, through their role as backup singers for Elvis Presley. The Statler Brothers (none of them are named Statler) won initial exposure as part of Johnny Cash's traveling show, but they soon left the gospel field altogether to win fame as country singers. No quartet, however, took gospel music farther afield from its traditional milieu, nor from its earlier image, than the Oak Ridge Boys. Sporting long hair and mustaches and wearing modish costumes, the Oak Ridge Boys, or "Oaks" as they often have been called, sing up-tempoed, handclapping gospel songs, such as "The Baptism of Jesse Taylor," to the support of electric, rock-style instrumentation. They have carried their supercharged gospel music into the nightclubs of Las Vegas and have profited from high-powered promotional techniques. Although they no doubt have gloried in the hip image that surrounds them, even the Oaks must have been embarrassed when an overzealous adman asserted that they "sing the hell out of a gospel song."

Despite the exceptional success attained by the Oak Ridge Boys, the white quartets, on the whole, have stayed close to the one-night-stand format, playing in churches, courthouses, schoolhouses, auditoriums, and at all-night singing conventions. Performing schedules have been as grueling for the quartets as for the country and rhythm and blues singers, and the big, customized bus with the gospel group's name painted on the side has been as commonplace a sight on the nation's roads and highways as that of the country and western singer. The quartets began making effective use of television during the sixties, with several of the groups, such as the Florida Boys and the Happy Goodman Family, combining to present syndicated shows on Saturday afternoons or Sunday mornings. The connections with the publishing houses have now been severed; the name "Stamps," for example, is now merely a registered name owned by bass singer J. D. Sumner, and has no affiliation with either a business or any member of the Stamps family. The evolution of the gospel business increasingly has paralleled that of the country music industry, not only in the nature of the music performed, but in the techniques used to advertise and merchandise the music as well. The Gospel Music Association in Nashville works to build a popular image for the music while promoting its sale. A Hall of Fame, similar to the one that promotes country music, admits a list of honorees each year, and the GMA annually bestows Dove awards on those performers deemed most deserving in a number of special categories.

If any quartet can be said to have dominated the gospel world during the sixties and seventies, it would be the Blackwood Brothers. And if any one singer in white gospel music can be designated a superstar, that singer would be James Blackwood, born in Choctaw County, Mississippi, on August 4, 1919. James Blackwood has been with the Blackwood Brothers Quartet since it was organized in 1934 and has been a consistent winner of the Dove award as top male gospel singer; he was elected to the Gospel Music Hall of Fame in 1974. The Blackwoods' music grew out of their Pentecostal church experience—James is a devout member of the Church of God in Memphis, Tennessee—and their concerts are religious services in song. Although they had always been greatly admired as singers, their status as the top act in white gospel music came in 1954 when they won first place on the Arthur Godfrey Talent Show and subsequently saw their version of "Have You Talked to the Man Upstairs" climb into the top ten of the *Billboard* popular music charts. Tragedy followed soon thereafter when two of the quartet's members, R. W. Blackwood and Bill Lyles, lost their lives in the crash of their small plane near Clanton, Alabama. The Blackwood Brothers quartet has undergone numerous changes in personnel in the twenty-three years since the disaster, but, with James Blackwood as its enduring nucleus, the quartet has remained at the top of the gospel music business, prospering through the adroit fusion of innovation and tradition. The evangelical fervor and integrity of the Blackwood Brothers' performances evoke the old-time primitivism of the little country church, a quality that most effectively counterbalances their supreme vocal control.

If audience involvement was often an important factor in the performance of both white and black gospel music, it was positively indispensable in the soul music that became such a vital force in American popular culture in the mid-sixties. Soul music is, in part, an extension of rhythm and blues—that is, it was first popularized by singers who had earlier gained identification as r & b singers—but its real power and distinctiveness came from the infusion within it of black gospel music. There are references to the usage of "soul" as a term for black music as early as the nineteenth century, but the term came into wide use in the mid-sixties and was obviously inspired by the emergence of the Black Power movement. The word was susceptible to many definitions, but to most people, at the time, soul was identifiable with and a product of the black experience in the United States. Soul was something that presumably only Negroes had, and it embodied the essence of their survival and life-styles as a people who emerged from slavery, segregation, and rural poverty. Many people would now deny that soul is exclusively confined to blacks, but it came to be widely used, particularly after 1967–1968 when the media seized upon it in the wake of the ghetto riots, to describe a wide range of black musical styles. Those singers designated as "soul" often came out of rhythm and blues experience, but invariably they, and the younger singers who appeared, pointed to some type of gospel music training. And, in fact, much of the style associated with soul music had specific origins in the church or in church-derived music.

Soul music was associated largely with two groups of performers: second-generation blacks living in the North, particularly those who recorded for the Motown label in Detroit; and southern-born blacks, especially those associated with the Memphis Sound. Strangely, many of the singers identified with the Motown Sound had a heavily diluted pop sound, and they presented a style of music that was highly commercial—that is, palatable to the general white audience. Such singers as Diana Ross and the Supremes were sometimes dismissed as "Oreo singers," a term used by some blacks to describe others who were black on the outside and white on the inside. There is no question, however, that such singers had a massive following among blacks too, particularly among black youth who took great pride in the success of their peers.

Another Detroit singer, Aretha Franklin, was, many would argue, the number-one singer among black performers in the late sixties and early seventies; she has unquestionably been a major force in the entire world of American popular music. Although she was not southern-born, Franklin's style was clearly moored in the black church, and she freely admitted the influence of the gospel-singing Clara Ward. Her father is the Reverend C. L. Franklin, the prominent pastor of the Bethel Baptist Church in Detroit, who successfully carried on a tradition introduced by the Reverend J. M. Gates in the twenties, having recorded over fifty best-selling albums of sermons. Despite attempts made by occasional producers to change her style, there is nothing Oreo about Aretha, and even "The Star-Spangled Banner" sounds soul when she sings it.

Southern-born singers usually performed with styles that were considerably more earthy than those of northern performers. But this did not prevent some of the southern singers, such as Ray Charles, from winning wide acclaim among white listeners in areas other than the South. Charles was born Ray Charles Robinson in Albany, Georgia, on September 23, 1932. Blinded by glaucoma at the age of six, Charles turned to music and was playing professionally in Florida by the time he was a teenager. In 1948 he moved to Seattle, where he organized a piano trio in the fashion of Nat "King" Cole's earlier very popular group. Although his rough voice did not permit him to recreate the Nat Cole vocal sound, Charles exhibited a fascination with pop music that has remained with him. By 1952 he was on the Atlantic label as an r & b singer, and he contributed mightily to the popularization of that genre and to the mixing of categories which came in the mid-fifties. In 1954 Charles became one of the first r & b entertainers to record songs that were secular remakes of gospel songs: "I Gotta Woman" had been "I Gotta God," and "This Little Girl of Mine" (1955) had been "This Little Light of Mine." He also began injecting gospel vocal techniques into his music at about the same time: falsetto shouts, groans, extended melisma, and call-and-response (usually between Charles and his female trio, the Raelets). He had never sung in a gospel group; he simply had heard and absorbed the music all his life. But Charles never sang just one type of music exclusively. He also tried to revive traditional jazz and in 1955 recorded "A Bit of Soul" and in 1956, "Houseful of Soul," two of the first usages of the term in the postwar period.

In 1959 Charles's recording of "What'd I Say" made the pop charts, and there have been many such incursions into those charts since that time. In 1959 he joined ABC-Paramount and in 1960 did "Georgia on My Mind," which became number one on the pop music charts. He has since recorded show tunes, pop standards, and some very successful albums of country and western songs (*Modern Sounds in Country and Western Music*, volumes 1 and 2). In his progress toward becoming one of the most successful black musicians of all time, Ray Charles has retained a very large following among black people, although some of his original fans now accuse him of selling out. However, Charles can reply to his detractors that he was an eclectic musician from the time he entered professional music in the mid-forties. In discussing his country albums, for example, Charles noted that as a boy he had often listened to the Grand Ole Opry, and that one of his earliest professional stints was with a white country band called the Florida Playboys.[6]

The fusion of country and western music with rhythm and blues had been a factor in the music coming out of Memphis since the mid-fifties. Memphis's emergence as a recording center had begun about 1954 when Sam Phillips and his Sun label began recording white talent covering r & b tunes. The second stage in that evolution began in 1959 when a local banker and ex–country fiddler named Jim Stewart and his sister, Estelle Axton, opened a studio in a former vaudeville theater in the heart of the black ghetto. Their Stax label achieved national prominence in 1962 when a local band named Booker T. and the MG's recorded a million-seller named "Green Onions." Organist Booker T. Jones and the other MG's served as the house musicians for Stax. The label's success was attributed to the easy-going ambience and biracial character of the people who owned and produced it. Stewart was a white man, but his vice-president was black. The house band was racially mixed, and the company's two principal writers, Isaac Hayes and David Porter, were black men who freely borrowed from many musical sources, including country and western (for its lyrics).

The Memphis Sound, as developed by Stax and several other small companies, was touted as a composite of two southern folk traditions—black r & b and white country. The contrast with Detroit's Motown was obvious. As Arnold Shaw said, "The Memphis Sound has more grit, gravel, and mud in it than the Detroit Sound."[7] By the early seventies, Memphis was described as the fourth-largest recording center in the nation, behind New York, Los Angeles, and Nashville, and some of the most exciting sounds in the soul genre were coming out of its studios.

Many fine musicians were associated with the Memphis soul scene, but the acknowledged superstar of the Memphis Sound was Otis Redding. Redding was born the son of a minister in Dawson, Georgia, in 1941 but grew up in Macon in an active r & b environment that included Little Richard, the singer Redding most admired. Although he had recorded a few songs on small labels in Macon and on the West Coast, Redding's most fruitful recording affiliation came with Stax after November 1962. By 1966 he had taken his music to enthusiastic audiences in Great Britain and France, and a British music magazine, *Melody Maker*, called him the world's number-one male vocalist. Redding was always popular among black fans, but after a critically acclaimed performance at the Monterey Pop Festival in 1967 he seemed on the verge of winning both white and national support. But on December 10, 1967, his private plane crashed, killing him and four of his band members. The posthumously issued "Sitting on the Dock of the Bay" was an award-winning and best-selling record.

Many of the so-called soul singers showed evidence of having absorbed nonblack musical influences or, as in the case of Ray Charles, of having consciously strived to win white support. But James Brown, the "King of Soul," never compromised his musical approach; his has been the "blackest sound" in American popular music, and he has never diluted it even when singing before white audiences. Brown's music, therefore, most closely conforms to the popular image of soul: black music performed for black audiences.

Brown was born in Georgia near the South Carolina line in the early thirties, but he grew up in Augusta where he literally reared himself, dropping out of school in the seventh grade and working at everything from shoeshining and cotton picking to dancing in the streets for nickles and dimes. Fatherless, poor, and black, Brown was led by his frustrations into a short experience with juvenile delinquency, and he served almost four years in a reform school. After his release at the age of nineteen, he began singing in a church in Toccoa, Georgia, in order to support his early marriage. Soon thereafter he took his gospel-tinged style into the dives and honky-tonks of the Deep South, and in 1956 he recorded his first big hit, "Please, Please, Please," for the King label.

Until the mid-sixties, when the emphasis on Black Power encouraged a closer look at authentic black talent, Brown remained almost totally unknown to the white world, while consistently ranking at the top of the r & b list. Brown never tried to cross over into the pop field, neither during the rock 'n' roll period, nor during the Motown era, a resolution that endeared him all the more to his militant black fans. His songs have never been the type that white pop artists could easily cover, and he never modified his approach in order to gain pop appeal. Brown's great reputation in the ghettos was enhanced in the mid-sixties when he began visiting them and communicating directly with the teanagers there. His first publicized trip was to San Francisco in 1966, here he advised black youngsters to remain in school. The visit was soon followed by a recording of "Don't Be a Drop-Out." After the assassination of Martin Luther King, Jr., in April 1968, Brown responded to urgent pleas from the mayors of Boston and Washington, D.C., by appearing for hours on television in both of the cities pleading for ghetto-dwellers to remain orderly and stay off the streets.

Brown's prominence in riot quelling and his adulation by ghetto dwellers contributed to the larger public's discovery of him, and his sociopolitical identification was certainly the major factor that promoted the publicity accorded him by the media. Americans were acutely conscious of Black Power rhetoric and the ghettos in 1968. Brown definitely identified with Black Power, but he alienated some of the black radicals, such as H. Rap Brown and LeRoi Jones, when he opposed the violence of the riots and affirmed his commitment to America, as in "America Is My Home." Along with his emphasis on education, which was almost a religion to him, Brown promoted the idea of black economic self-help. Black capitalism, to Brown, seemed to be the essence of Black Power, and it was this aspect of his career—his fabulous commercial success—that was most intriguing to the media. Magazine accounts invariably stressed his wealth and material acquisitions, as they have always done when discussing any folk-derived musician who has made it big. Admittedly, Brown's earnings and investments were enough to attract anyone's notice. In 1968 his gross from one-nighters was about $2.5 million. He owned two radio stations (including the one in Augusta where he had once shined shoes), a record production company, extensive real estate, a castlelike house, 500 suits, 300 pairs of shoes, a fleet of six cars (including a Rolls-Royce and two Cadillacs), and a $713,000 Lear jet airplane.

Musically, Brown was unique in that his was almost a totally black sound. And he has succeeded with it as no other black performer ever has. By 1968, after leading the r & b field for years, he was named *Cash Box*'s choice as the number-one male vocalist in all of popular music. He achieved this distinction with a style that seemed to come not only from the rural southern black churches but, with its heavy emphasis on beat and rhythm at the expense of lyrics, from the African roots as well. At a time of musical amalgamation, when the leading Motown performers were reaching out toward the middle-class mainstream, Brown reached far back to the very sources of black music. Performance was everything in a James Brown concert. Using grunts, moans, and unearthly screams, repeating words endlessly and bending them to unbelievable lengths, and interacting with his musicians, chorus, and audience in an erotic call-and-response pattern, Brown communicated with his enormous audiences as few performers had ever done. These performances were choreographic experiences, and Brown has had few peers as a dancer. His act was folk in its primitivism and in its indebtedness to older forms and styles, but it was also ultramodern in its organization, polish, and timing. It was the creative tension between the poles of eclectic folk background and contemporary techniques of appeal which yielded Brown such success, the same matter of balance which affected the other "soul" music of the United States—country music.

8

The National Resurgence of Country Music

THE SUCCESS enjoyed by soul music was only one facet of a general flowering experienced by southern-derived grass roots music in the sixties. After suffering temporarily from the rock 'n' roll onslaught after 1955, country music gained a stature in American popular culture that had scarcely been dreamed of during its hillbilly beginnings. Fiddles and steel guitars, the instrumental mainstays of World War II country bands, virtually disappeared from country recordings for a few years, to be replaced by rock 'n' roll-style electric guitars, or by pop-style instrumentation. The accent was now clearly on youth, and record companies energetically searched for new and exciting successors to Elvis Presley. Almost all older country singers tried their hands at either rock 'n' roll or some upbeat style that would be appealing to a youthful audience. Rock 'n' roll left its mark on country music in many ways. Several rockabillies, including Jerry Lee Lewis and Conway Twitty, carved out very successful careers as mainstream country singers. Other rock 'n' roll musicians became sidemen in country bands, taking their instrumental licks with them and thereby permanently altering the sound of country music. Country music as a whole moved into the sixties thoroughly committed to a heavy electronic sound, with only the bluegrass musicians holding against the tide.

Although tradition-minded country fans wept at what appeared to be the disappearance, or betrayal, of old-time country styles, the trends of the period were actually misleading and somewhat short-lived. Tradition-based styles were still flourishing away from the glare of the public limelight, and some of them would command national attention a few years hence. But in American popular culture, transitory phenomena can seem like a lifetime in the intensity with which they seize the public imagination.

By the time country music began its comeback about 1958, the term "hillbilly" had been universally abandoned except by a few scholars who used it to describe the music of pre–World War II days, and by a scattering of fans and performers who, at least privately, liked to refer to themselves and their music as "hillbilly." The word "country" was now universally employed to describe the music, and the acknowledged center of the "industry" (this, too, was now a commonly used word) was Nashville.

Much of country music's commercial regeneration can be attributed to the efforts of a new trade organization, founded in 1958, called the Country Music Association. This organization worked to elevate the image of the music and to demonstrate its commercial potential to advertisers everywhere. One active campaign of the CMA was the encouragement of radio stations that played only country music. The proliferation of such stations contributed to the national popularization of country music, but it also often promoted a blurring of identity within the music. Most of the country stations developed their own versions of the Top Forty formats pioneered by rock or youth-oriented stations. The listener might turn his radio dial all day long and hear nothing but the same handful of songs, and no one could ever be sure how the tight play-list was determined in the first place. Because of the rapid multiplication of country radio stations, a large number of announcers became associated with country music who had had no earlier experience with it. Some of these young deejays were first attracted to music during the rock 'n' roll era, and they carried many of the perceptions of those years into their new affiliations with country music. Characteristically, the disc jockey long associated with country music would have established a personal style with his audience, a folksy rapport that extended the "hayseed" image projected by the music. Then, too, his own biases and predilections would have affected his selection of records so that the music styles themselves were in turn influenced. By the sixties, these deejays had almost totally disappeared, leaving a rare exception here and there such as Gordon Baxter of Beaumont, Texas, who for more than thirty years has uncompromisingly insisted on maintaining his unique "loose board," downhome style of friendly chatter and favorite records. He runs the constant risk of getting fired for his individualized style which runs counter to the homogenized hype of the Top Forty format.

The country music industry reacted to the rock 'n' roll threat by attempting to create a product that would appeal to the broadest possible spectrum of listeners—that is to say, a music shorn of most of its "rural" characteristics. Chet Atkins, RCA's recording director in Nashville and one of the prime forces behind the music innovations taking place there, explained the changes as a "compromise" that made country music more popular while permitting all of its substyles to endure and flourish. The music that emerged from the recording studios of Nashville, called variously the "Nashville Sound," "country-pop," "countrypolitan," or "middle-of-the-road music," de-emphasized or omitted the fiddle and steel guitar and introduced background voices and sedate instrumentation designed to reach new listeners while holding on to the older ones. Country-pop music would preserve the ambience of rural music while adopting some of the sophisticated techniques of popular music.

Chet Atkins and other record producers deliberately sought to create recordings with appeal in all markets. Country songs had been picked up by pop singers with great frequency since the early fifties when songs written by Hank Williams enjoyed great vogue, but country singers themselves almost never appeared on pop charts. Rock 'n' roll, however, had changed all the rules, and in the climate of the sixties "crossovers" became a typical aspect of the music business. In the early part of the decade those country singers with smooth voices and little rural identification had the best chance of gaining acceptance as pop singers. Eddy Arnold, despite his popular designation as the Tennessee Plowboy, had long anticipated the country-pop approach, but Jim Reeves, from Panola County, Texas (often described as the singer with the velvet touch) won the widest acclaim with such songs as "Four Walls" and "He'll Have to Go." The popularity enjoyed in the sixties by such singers as Arnold, Reeves, and Roger Miller was surpassed in the seventies by that of Mac Davis, from Lubbock, Texas, and Glen Campbell, from Delight, Arkansas, both of whom hosted nationally syndicated television shows and built images that were only loosely related to country music.

The emergence of country-pop music was paralleled by Nashville's rise to preeminence as a music center. Culturally pretentious Nashvillians, who had once termed their city the "Athens of the South," and who had been embarrassed by the presence there of the Grand Ole Opry, learned to swallow their pride as money rolled in to feed the burgeoning music industry. Publishing houses, booking offices, and recording studios hummed with such activity that Nashville was now described on billboards and in city-sponsored promotional material as Music City, USA. Country singers appeared on the pop music charts so frequently in the early sixties that a large number of other singers began coming to Nashville to use its recording facilities and versatile session musicians. Nashville has become known far and wide as the country music capital, but the music recorded there actually encompasses the entire spectrum of popular music.

Country music's commercial revival and national surge of popularity have been marked by an accompanying identification with national purpose and identity. This phenomenon has been demonstrated by the music's growing "respectability," by White House endorsement, and by the use of the term "American" by some of the performers to describe their music. In its most extreme form, the equating of "country music" and "Americanism" has ben shown in such lyrics as "when you're running down my country . . . you're walking on the fighting side of me."[1] During the sixties when urban-born folksingers and rock performers were subjecting the government and its domestic and foreign policies to a vigorous critique, the appearance of a spate of such pro-America songs contributed to country music's reputation for 100-percent Americanism and helps to explain why President Nixon would travel to Nashville during the most troubled period of his administration to participate in the formal opening of the new Grand Ole Opry House.

Country music's emergence as an ultrapatriotic and even jingoistic genre during the late stages of the Vietnam war was not simply an extension of southern working-class values into a national setting. It also reflected the polarization of the period at the very time of the country industry's attempts to gain acceptance by identifying with national trends and attitudes and capitalizing on public fears and neuroses. Merle Haggard, the California-born son of Okie migrants, and the singer who is most often, and regrettably, identified with the "reactionary" songs of the period, no doubt would have become a superstar without "Okie from Muskogee" (an attack on the hippie culture and a paean of praise to Middle America), but the song brought him national exposure and media coverage beyond anyone's dreams. His ascent to stardom and country music's rise to national recognition were clearly helped along by the national mood of emotional schizophrenia which accompanied the Vietnam war, the civil rights movement, and the rise of the counterculture. Haggard's compositions struck a responsive chord among audiences far from the South, and he received standing ovations in such cities as Philadelphia and Duluth. Partly because of its identification with "the silent majority," country music was "discovered" by the media, by pop scholars, and even by the national political establishment. Presidents Johnson and Nixon both brought country entertainers into the White House, gestures that no doubt disgusted those who recalled the artistic soirees of the Kennedy years.

As in the chaotic twenties, many people in the turbulent sixties seemed to find something in country music that projected a more stable image than that conveyed by youth music. In the twenties, the cultural disintegrator was jazz; in the sixties, it was rock. But country music allegedly represented 100-percent Americanism, and some people on the left of the political spectrum no doubt found the country music world strangely fascinating if not downright terrifying. An article in *Harper's* blamed everything from working-class alienation to the truckers' strike of 1972 on country music, while in *Mademoiselle* the music was described as "the perfect musical extension of the Nixon administration" and a repository of values that "ought to frighten every longhaired progressive urbanite, and every black man who is not part of it."[2] As in the early days of its commercial history, country music still evoked stereotypically opposed responses: people regarded it either as a music of genuine patriotism and morality, or as a music of unthinking bigotry.

But if one stops to reflect upon country music's identification during the Nixon years with "establishment" values, he must immediately be struck by the incongruity of it all and must wonder at what point history got turned upon its head. How did a music once contemptuously dismissed as "hillbilly" and presumed to be the province of cultural degenerates living in a "benighted" region get to be the exemplar and upholder of national norms? And how did the descendants of rebels, who fought for four bloody years against the nationalizing process and killed 350,000 Yankees while doing it, get to be such apostles of unquestioning patriotism? The relationship between country music and "Americanism" is a tenuous one, but one that is rooted in the South's ambivalent relationship to the nation at large—the sense of being both out of the mainstream and at the same time more "American" than other regions of the nation. The music especially reflects this ambivalence. It is conscious of its "southernness," and therefore presumably of its uniqueness, but it is also convinced that it embodies the best in the American character as a whole.

The country music industry has energetically endeavored since the fifties to broaden the base of the music and to take it "uptown" (to make it respectable, and therefore more marketable). Much of the identification with the Establishment, therefore, comes from the bourgeoisification of the music and is seemingly the product of entrepreneurs who seek to palm the music off as the embodiment of middle-class propriety and law-and-order. But those who would posit a respectable, conformist attitude for country music play havoc with its history and traditions. The music has been much more complex than either its devotees or detractors have recognized. The rural South from which the music sprang remains a complex culture, a "counterculture" if you will.[3] It seems strange indeed for a region and a people that have always taken great pride in their intense individualism to make such a fetish today of national conformity. The tradition of the drifter, the rounder, and even the lawless man, preceded the period of commercialization and has been a continuing thread in the music from Jimmie Rodgers to Waylon Jennings. The "law" was never treated with particular reverence in the old country songs, and personal morality, while often preached as a virtue, was just as often violated in practice. The contemporary endorsement of the status quo in country music, a mood which often assumes rather mindless, bland, and homogenized forms—directed as much toward the pocketbook of Middle America as toward its mind or heart—obscures the facts of the music's historic diversity. Despite the abundance of songs stressing the domestic virtues and the sense of place, country music, as much as anything, has been the music of an uprooted people with an acute consciousness of a world of shifting values. Country music is indeed "American," but its Americanism is broad rather than narrow, deriving from many sources and presumptions.

The quest for legitimacy within country music has not been without its innovative or "liberal" components. The industry has attempted to be all things to all people. That is, while on one hand projecting conservatism, it has also strived to be "with it," to be aware of new trends, and at least to give the impression of broadening its horizons. The music's image as the most male–dominated white Protestant music in America is not quite so monolithic as it once was. The sixties and early seventies, for instance, saw the emergence of the first black country superstar, Charley Pride, from Sledge, Mississippi; the first Chicano superstars, Johnny Rodriguez and Freddy Fender, from Sabinal and Weslaco, Texas, respectively; the first Cajun superstar, Doug Kershaw, from Tiel Ridge, Louisiana; and at least one Jewish country singer, Kinky Friedman, from Austin, Texas, who, if not a superstar, is certainly one of the most colorful and outrageous of the country singers.

Probably more significant, though, than the ethnic breakthrough in country music has been the burgeoning activity of women singers. Until the appearance of Kitty Wells in the early fifties, almost no women had attained independent identities apart from men, and they had seldom won the financial rewards gained by male singers. In the contemporary period, however, women have been competing with men on more than even terms and have won the kind of success that black women singers have commanded for forty years. Tanya Tucker, Tammy Wynette, Crystal Gayle, Melba Montgomery, Emmylou Harris, Loretta Lynn, and Dolly Parton are only a few of the women who have achieved stardom in the modern period. Of these, some built eclectic styles which have attracted followers from outside country music: Crystal Gayle as a middle-of-the-road pop singer, and Tanya Tucker, Emmylou Harris, and Dolly Parton as rock-tinged country singers. Loretta Lynn's style and personality, however, are purebred country, and she has achieved a recognition in American life that none of the other women singers, and few of the men, have attained, appearing frequently on television shows, gracing the front covers of several magazines (including *Newsweek* in June 1973), and writing (along with George Vecsey) a best-selling autobiography called *Coal Miner's Daughter*.

Loretta Lynn has become widely known as much for her wit and open, country honesty and charm, as for her fine singing. Born in Butcher Hollow, Kentucky, the daughter of a coal miner, she began trying her luck at singing in Custer, Washington, in 1961 (she and her husband Mooney Lynn had moved there in the early fifties). When her first song, "Honky Tonk Girl," appeared on a small label in that same year, she and Mooney set out by automobile across the United States, sleeping in the car, dressing in service-station washrooms, and pushing her record to deejays in radio stations everywhere. Since that date her personal appearance schedule has remained almost as rigorous, but she now travels in a luxurious, customized bus and has the deejays clamoring after her and seeking the rare interview which she grants. But she has always remained accessible to her audiences, and women especially identify with her success and her attempts to balance professional and family life. Loretta has long since moved away from the poverty of her humble origins and even from the downhome sounds heard on her early records, but her clear, pure voice and quaint diction still give testimony to her mountain beginnings.

The mountain roots still cling tightly to Dolly Parton also, even though she has moved even farther than Loretta Lynn from the "hard country" repertory. Parton won the readers' poll in *Rolling Stone* as the top country singer of 1977, and by the end of that year was hosting her own television show and was making a determined effort to carve out an identity acceptable to the rock/youth audiences. She was one of eleven children born into a mountain farm family near Sevierville, Tennessee. Her first singing experience came in a Church of God congregation where her grandfather was pastor, but she began appearing on local barn dances and singing on the radio in Knoxville when only a small child. No one was really surprised, therefore, when she set out by bus for Nashville on the day after her high school graduation.

Dolly's entrée to stardom came through her participation in Porter Wagoner's syndicated television show and through her very popular duet recordings with Wagoner. The viewers of Wagoner's television show, or those who attended his many road shows, soon became familiar with a buxom girl with an hourglass figure who dressed in skintight clothing and wore outrageous blonde wigs. Dolly was acting out the fantasies of a poor mountain girl whose family had never been able to buy her the rouge, jewelry, or fine clothes she desired. But those who were turned off by her affectations—and there were many—may also have missed the opportunity to hear one of the great talents in American popular music.

Like Loretta Lynn and several other popular country singers, Parton has excelled both as a singer and as a songwriter. Her soaring soprano voice is one of the most expressive in any field of American popular music, moving easily and convincingly from the tenderest love songs to rousing novelty tunes and even yodels. Although she is considered to be preeminently an entertainer, she is also one of the best writers in country music. Her compositions run the gamut of themes and emotions commonly found in country music, but she invests even the most personal of songs with such a convincing, charismatic integrity that they acquire a universality which is altogether appealing. Some of her best songs deal with her childhood and are bittersweet in their recollections of growing up as a sensitive child in a large, poor, but loving family. No song more effectively describes the ambivalent feelings that she and many people with country origins have when they reflect upon their rural experiences than "In the Good Old Days When Times Were Bad." But her greatest song, and probably the most intimate one in her repertory, is "Coat of Many Colors," a personal childhood narrative that weaves a poignant verbal image of poverty and a mother's love.

Women have made dramatic gains in country music since World War II. They hold positions of power as businesswomen in the industry, and as performers they have competed on increasingly favorable terms with men and often command salaries that are more lucrative than those of the male performers. Their progress constitutes a phase of the liberation of women in the United States and marks an especially dramatic shift in both the status and the image of southern women. Revolutions, however, come very slowly in country music, and the women singers still sing of an older world of values while leading lives as entertainers that often run counter to those values. Most of these women strive diligently to preserve the veneer of domesticity while pursuing careers with an aggressiveness and singleness of purpose that leaves little time or energy for home and family. For the most part, too, the world described in their songs is a man's world, and their lyrics deal chiefly with woman's dependency on man.

Although old attitudes persist, new ones have crept into country music along with a "new breed" of writers and musicians. Consequently, the audience for country music has changed significantly since the sixties. With the defusing of tensions since that decade, country music has ceased to be thought of as solely an expression of Middle America and has gained an audience that cuts across generational, geographic, and socioeconomic lines. In part, the broadened interest in country music reflects a new wave of nostalgia or "back to the roots" urge in American life that has not been confined to old people, transplanted ruralites, or die-hard reactionaries. The mood has been shared by many young people as well, many of whom might have called themselves "radicals" or members of the counterculture back in the sixties. Anyone who has ever attended a bluegrass festival or a "progressive country" concert at the Armadillo World in Austin, Texas, or one of Willie Nelson's giant outdoor picnics, has seen the wide spectrum of humanity which now turns on to the music. Country has become chic among many Americans who once ignored or despised it. The reasons for these reversals of attitude are many and complex, but one important factor must surely be that the music itself has changed. A new generation of songwriters has appeared since the sixties. They have drawn upon the resources of other musical forms for sustenance and have been much influenced by the social currents of their own day. Their music is largely attuned to youth and is largely preoccupied with that everlasting staple of American popular music, romantic love—but the subject is treated with a candor and guiltless sensuality that have been rare in country music.

The writer who has most consistently appealed to the widest spectrum of American listeners is Kris Kristofferson. Kristofferson is a highly untypical hillbilly–an army brat born in Brownsville, Texas, and reared in California, who became a Rhodes scholar preparing for a career as a professor of English literature. After five subsequent years in the army, Kristofferson turned down an appointment as an instructor of English literature at West Point and moved to Nashville. Inspired by an early love for Hank Williams's music, he began writing country songs. "Me and Bobby McGee" (recorded in 1969 by Roger Miller) was the first of a long succession of very successful songs recorded by leading country entertainers: "For the Good Times" (Ray Price), "Come Sundown" (Bobby Bare), "Help Me Make It through the Night" (Sammi Smith), and the song that won him his first CMA award in 1970, "Sunday Mornin' Comin' Down" (Johnny Cash). Kristofferson's own recording career began in 1969 for Monument, and in 1973 he recorded at least one very popular song, "Why Me, Lord," which was inspired by a religious experience he had one evening in a Pentecostal church in Nashville. Kristofferson has since gone on to superstardom as an entertainer and actor, and his production of hit songs has declined substantially. Still, it was his writing that opened all the other commercial doors for him. Pretty, singable melodies, economy of language, aphoristic phrases, basic themes, united with a preoccupation with freedom, honest relationships, and sensual experience, mark his work and constitute the enduring quality of Kristofferson's best songs.

The more explicit of the "new breed" of songs have aroused the indignation of many people both within and without the country music industry; some radio stations refuse to play them, and veteran country songwriter Cindy Walker calls them "skin songs." [4] Old-time country fans may have had some difficulty in adjusting to such songs as Freddy Weller's "Sexy Lady," Charlie Rich's "Behind Closed Doors," and Conway Twitty's "You've Never Been This Far Before," but there has been a sufficient audience to make each of them a superhit. It has been considerably more difficult for fans to accept such songs from a woman, but Linda Hargrove, from Florida, and one of the most candid and sensitive of the new breed of songwriters, wrote such a song–"Just Get Up and Close the Door"–and saw it emerge as a hit for Johnny Rodriguez. Her own recording of "Mexican Love Songs" is even more explicit: the woman picks up a man in a honky-tonk, then regrets waking up the next morning with a cowboy who "takes up three-fourths of the bed."

While the new songwriters contributed to the broadening of perspectives within country music, a group of singers and musicians have done most to introduce alternative styles while also posing a challenge to establishment values. Many of these singers have become strongly identified with the active musical scene in Austin, Texas, one of several southern cities that have become important music centers.[5] Austin's rise to musical prominence was accompanied by a heightened interest in what has been called "progressive country music," an ambiguous term first associated with the eclectic programming pioneered by station KOKE in Austin, a format then copied by several other stations. The KOKE directors announced an intention to play all kinds of country music, from the traditional to the modern, but their selections actually leaned heavily toward rock-influenced material, and particularly toward that produced by Austin-based entertainers. Progressive country music, therefore, became increasingly associated with youth-oriented music–country rock–and of course was presumed to be superior to other forms of country music. KOKE's programming, like the music played in most of the clubs in Austin, was aimed at the city's youthful audience, a rock-reared generation. As the site of a state university with an enrollment of over forty thousand, Austin has a large and annually self-replenishing young audience that seeks musical diversion.

The musicians in Austin, like the deejays at KOKE, affect cowboy dress, and many of the young people who constitute the audiences demonstrate a similar fascination with western motifs. The stereotype associated with Austin music is the hippie in a cowboy costume, the "cosmic cowboy," as Michael Murphey phrased it in one of his songs. The first major locus of activity for these people and their music was the Armadillo World Headquarters, founded in 1970 in an old national guard armory, and a direct outgrowth of the city's counterculture movement. Beginning as a haven for rock music, the Armadillo World soon began to feature country entertainers too, particularly those who, like Waylon

Jennings and Commander Cody and the Lost Planet Airmen, could attract both country and rock audiences.

In the next two or three years the number of similarly oriented clubs multiplied and they, along with the older country and western clubs in the city, such as the Broken Spoke and the Split Rail, soon gave Austin the reputation of being a thriving center of live music. Much of the talent found in the city enjoyed only local or Texas recognition (Frieda and the Firedogs, for example, led by the best singer in Austin—Marcia Ball), but a few musicians with some national reputation, such as Jerry Jeff Walker (the New York urban folkie who had written "Mr. Bojangles") and Doug Sahm (a Texan who had been prominent in the sixties rock scene), made Austin their home base of operations. Austin was already a burgeoning "colony of musicians," therefore, when Willie Nelson moved there from Nashville in 1972.[6] Nelson, a major if long neglected talent of country music, was both a supreme vocal stylist, whose blues-tinged voice was one of the most distinctive since Jimmie Rodgers, and a gifted songwriter, whose finely crafted songs had placed him in the vanguard of Nashville's "new breed" of writers. After he moved to Austin, Nelson demonstrated that he was consummately skilled in still another art, that of image building.

Willie Nelson was born in Fort Worth in 1933, but reared in Abbott, Texas, where he absorbed a heavy diet of gospel, honky-tonk, pop, and western swing music, all of which would later show up in his own highly individualistic style. In Nashville, where he moved in the early sixties, Nelson won immediate success as a songwriter, supplying hit songs for other entertainers: "Crazy," for Patsy Cline, for example, and "Funny How Time Slips Away," for Billy Walker, "Hello Wall," for Faron Young, and "Night Life," for Ray Price. Willie was far from being a failure in Nashville, and although he was at least on the periphery of a small group of musicians known as the "Nashville Rebels" (or "Outlaws"), he was really neither an iconoclast nor a nonconformist. His decision to move to Austin was primarily motivated by the conflagration which destroyed his home, but more generally by his desire to return to the simpler and more familiar pace of his Texas home. Willie deliberately set out to build an audience among the rock-oriented youth of his state, and he succeeded in a way that has been unequaled before or since by any other country singer.

The most intriguing facet of Willie and his updated image is that his singing has remained the same—consistently excellent—and, if anything, his style and choice of songs have become more traditional. Many of the listeners he has attracted to gospel and earlier varieties of country music, including honky-tonk, would not have listened to such music without Willie's sanction. Waylon Jennings, on the other hand—Nelson's comrade and fellow "Outlaw"—capitalizes on the Texas image of expansiveness and easy-living in his songs, especially in his number one hit of 1977, "Luckenbach, Texas," in which he urges his listeners to "get back to the basics of love." It is ironic that Nelson moved to Austin, established his own recording company, and maintained his original musical sound, adjusting his physical image to suit contemporary Texas youth tastes, while Waylon (a native of Littlefield, Texas) remained in Nashville, aligned with the largest record company in America (RCA) and merely sang of being an outlaw, cut free from the constraints of the Nashville scene.

The fusion of country and rock sounds and the consequent gravitation of a youth audience toward country music are owed as much to the experimentation of country-oriented rock musicians as they are to the innovativeness of country musicians. Many young fans admitted an interest in country music only after the music was lent respectability through an endorsement by some rock singer. Bob Dylan, for instance, probably did more than any other individual to break down prejudice against country music when he went to Nashville and recorded with local musicians an album of his own country-flavored songs, *Nashville Skyline*. About nine months before Dylan's album appeared, however, the Byrds' *Sweetheart of the Rodeo* came out, and this was actually the first album by a rock group to be composed exclusively of country songs. The Byrds were well known for their experimentation, having earlier pioneered in the performance of psychedelic rock and folk rock, but at least two of their members, Chris Hillman and Gram Parsons, had experience with and genuine love for country music. Together, they comprised the nucleus of a later and more consistently country group called the Flying Burrito Brothers, the prototype of most of the country-rock groups that were to emerge afterwards.

Gram Parsons was born Cecil Ingram Connors in Waycross, Georgia, on November 5, 1946.[7] Though he came from the right side of the tracks–he was the inheritor of great wealth from his mother's family, the Snivelys, and from her later marriage to Robert Parsons–Parsons brought to rock music a fascination with hard-core, honky-tonk country music. When he left the Burrito Brothers, he set out on a campaign, about three years before Willie Nelson's highly publicized Texas ventures, to fuse more closely the sounds of country and rock and to break down the mutual suspicion between the two audiences. Parsons was destined to fail in his efforts within his own lifetime, but since his death in 1973 he and his music have become objects of cult adulation. The real tragedy in Parsons's personal saga was the compulsion for self-destruction which completely undermined his potential and caused the waste of his young life.

The young rock audience to which Gram Parsons catered has not yet come to terms with country music to the extent that he hoped. But the whole country-rock movement, including such successful entertainers as the Eagles, the Marshall Tucker Band, and Linda Ronstadt, is heavily indebted to the Georgia-born singer because of the inroads he made for country music within the youth audience of America. No one can yet document the number of musicians, obscure and otherwise, who may have been influenced by Parsons. The most direct and important influence, however, was exerted upon his protégé Emmylou Harris.

Harris was a southern girl, born in Birmingham, Alabama, and reared in Virginia, but, as the daughter of a career marine officer she was hardly country. Her first musical experience came as an urban folksinger, but Parsons taught her country phrasing and introduced her to what she calls "root country," and she began adding to her repertory songs from Merle Haggard, George Jones, the Louvin Brothers, and the early Everly Brothers. Her first solo album in 1975, *Pieces of the Sky*, was highly praised, and a single from the recording, an old Louvin Brothers song called "If I Could Only Win Your Love," was one of the most popular country songs of the year. Emmylou brought one of the purest and most refreshingly clear voices heard in country music in a long time, and she was immediately touted as a future superstar. One of the most remarkable aspects of her success has been the fact that she has built strong bases of support within both rock and country audiences by generally adhering to older styles of country music.

Despite all the modernizing trends of the postwar period, and despite the almost irresistible pressures placed on country musicians to modify their performing styles, many of the older forms did persist. Much of the impetus behind the revival of tradition-based styles came from a phenomenon of the late fifties and early sixties called the urban folk movement (folk material, or songs with a folk sound, performed by nonfolk entertainers). From the 1958 popularity of the Kingston Trio's "Tom Dooley" (an adaptation of a North Carolina murder ballad) to the coming in 1964 of the Beatles, there had been a strong flurry of interest in what was loosely termed "folk" music. Urban folk music, thus seen, may have prospered as a reaction against rock 'n' roll, but more likely it represented just one more flirtation with the exotic or innovative. Although urban folk music drew much of its inspiration and repertory from the South (at least indirectly)—from the protest singing of such 1930s radicals as Aunt Molly Jackson and Woody Guthrie, and from the Library of Congress collection of southern field recordings—it was basically a facet of mainstream pop music and was supported by the widest possible spectrum of Americans, most of whom had no identifiable roots in the cultures from which the songs derived. The music became increasingly, and even joyously, liberal after the election of John F. Kennedy and the birth of the civil rights movement, but its tone became more strident and cynical after the death of JFK and as the promise of reform dissipated in the wake of America's deepening involvement in Vietnam. Urban folk music became a vehicle for many young people to express themselves both musically and politically —and to get a start in the music business, especially after rock 'n' roll receded from its first delirious peak. Many an alumnus of the urban folk movement, such as Janis Joplin and Bob Dylan, went on to careers in rock or other forms of pop music.

On the other hand, the folk fad did contribute to an awakening of interest in real grass roots American music. Once their appetites for folk music were whetted, many young people reached

back for the rural roots of such music: blues, cowboy, hillbilly,
Cajun, and other related forms. This interest had important social
and musical consequences. A few of the recording companies released much of the material from the twenties which had long
been buried in their vaults, and devoted collectors produced long-
playing recordings of old-time music taken from their own private
collections of old 78s. Most happily of all, several of the pioneer
performers, such as bluesmen Mississippi John Hurt and Furry
Lewis, and hillbillies Clarence Ashley and Buell Kazee, were re-
discovered and given chances to build second careers they had
never dreamed of. Furthermore, the urban folk audience was receptive to younger performers with a traditional orientation, such
as the Balfa Brothers, Cajun musicians who received a hearing
far beyond the borders of southwest Louisiana. Scholars also for
the first time began to recognize the relationship between folk
music and such commercial forms as blues, gospel, and country.
The most significant result of this interest was the publication in
1965 of the "hillbilly issue" of the *Journal of American Folklore*,
a collection of essays devoted solely to various aspects of commercial country music.[8]

Indeed, even within the evolutionary framework of commercialization, the distinctive musical sounds of the working-class
South have endured. Some country singers, like Marshall Louis
"Grandpa" Jones, from Kentucky, made no compromises at all
with the newer sounds. A few, like the immensely talented Arthel
"Doc" Watson, a blind musician from Deep Gap, North Carolina,
were skillful enough to alternate convincingly between the very
oldest folk styles and the most modern innovations. Watson is a
singer of great subtlety and power, with a repertory that ranges
from sixteenth-century ballads to modern blues tunes, but his
greatest impact has been as a guitarist. Watson set off a vogue for
flat-picking (the use of a flat pick rather than a thumb pick or the
fingers) that has touched scores of young musicians in both country and rock music (most notably, Dan Crary, Norman Blake, and
Clarence White).

Other musicians, like Bill Monroe, created sounds that were
deeply grounded in tradition, but innovative enough to survive
and flourish in the modern period. Born in Rosine, Kentucky, in
1911, Monroe took his mandolin style, his high tenor singing, and

his string band, the Blue Grass Boys, to the Grand Ole Opry in 1939 where they have remained ever since. Through almost forty years of country music evolution, and during a period marked by the almost universal adoption of electric instruments, Monroe preserved the acoustic style of instrumentation and the "high-lonesome" style of singing, and in so doing created a genre of tradition-based music that has spread around the world. Scores of musicians served apprenticeships with Monroe and then moved on to form their own bands. Many others heard his broadcasts, bought his records, or attended his road shows, and subsequently began copying the sounds Monroe popularized. Increasingly after 1950 the term "bluegrass" began to be attached to the proliferating groups who played and sang in the Monroe fashion.

The original bluegrass bands resisted electrical amplification, sang in a high, strident style featuring two and three-part harmony, leaned toward old or "old-fashioned" songs, and generally performed them at up-tempoed speeds. Although other instruments have since been adopted by bluegrass musicians, the "classic" bands (those adhering most closely to the original Monroe pattern) feature the guitar and string bass for back-up rhythm, and the mandolin, fiddle, and five-string banjo as lead instruments. Monroe's chop-style of mandolin chording was crucial in setting the distinctive rhythmic tone of bluegrass music, but other talented musicians made important contributions that made the music both unique and popular. Preeminently, Earl Scruggs, who was born in Flint Hill, North Carolina, on January 6, 1924, and played with the Blue Grass Boys from 1944 to 1948, featured a style that revolutionized the sound of the banjo and did much to make bluegrass music nationally popular. Building upon styles long heard in the hill country of North and South Carolina, Scruggs perfected a highly syncopated, three-finger style that made the banjo a solo instrument of dazzling speed and versatility. Don Reno, from Spartanburg, South Carolina, also knew the style, having learned it from Dewitt "Snuffy" Jenkins, but Reno joined the Blue Grass Boys only after Scruggs had left the group to form, along with Lester Flatt, another very popular bluegrass organization. Otherwise, what is called "Scruggs style" picking might today be called "Reno style."

The bluegrass audience was first concentrated in the small

towns and rural communities of the South among people who resented the pop trends of country and western music. By the early fifties, however, the music began to win adherents in the North, particularly on college campuses. In 1954 the patriarch of urban folk music, Pete Seeger, included a section on "Scruggs picking" in the second edition of his banjo instructor. Three years later the style won further sanction among urban folkies when Folkways Records issued an album edited by Mike Seeger called *American Banjo Scruggs Style*. Because bluegrass resisted electrical amplification and adhered to traditional songs and sounds, and because so many of its prominent musicians came from the southern hills, the music appealed to many young Americans as a form of mountain folk music (it was certainly more folklike than Nashville-dominated country music). Bluegrass music profited, therefore, from its association with the urban folk boom of the late fifties and early sixties. Earl Scruggs appeared to rave reviews at the first Newport Folk Festival in the summer of 1959, and in that same year Alan Lomax, the best-known American folklorist, further popularized the music among academics and avant-gardists when in an *Esquire* article he termed it "folk music with over-drive."[9] As Flatt and Scruggs led the way with appearances all over the United States (they were the busiest of all country groups during those years), bluegrass music gained a respectability in American popular culture that no other form of country music had ever attained.

Curiously, the country music industry was largely indifferent to the bluegrass phenomenon, particularly during the period of the greatest academic interest. Bluegrass groups, such as those led by Bill Monroe, Flatt and Scruggs, Bobby and Sonny Osborne, and Jim and Jesse McReynolds, did appear regularly on the Grand Ole Opry, and a few other bluegrass entertainers, such as Mac Wiseman, the Stanley Brothers, and Don Reno and Red Smiley, attained some commercial recognition during the fifties. But the bluegrass fan has generally encountered little but frustration in the search for his favorite kind of music. The Top Forty country radio stations do not play the music; jukebox vendors do not distribute it; and the major record labels devote little attention to it. No one has yet investigated the reasons for the country music industry's neglect of bluegrass. The mainstream country singers may have been jealous, or even contemptuous, of the acclaim received by bluegrass in the academic community, or industry people may have been embarrassed by bluegrass's rural image at a time when country music was trying to move uptown.

Regardless of the neglect, the number of bluegrass bands has proliferated since the fifties, and the genre has spawned its own substylings, ranging from the traditional to the progressive, and bluegrass has generated its own methods of dissemination. Almost every community of any size now has at least one bluegrass band, although the music performed is often only remotely related to the original Bill Monroe sound. Bluegrass has a particularly strong following among southern migrants in the North, especially in Detroit and in the southern portions of such states as Pennsylvania, Ohio, Indiana, and Illinois; no bluegrass singer, in fact, has a more pronounced rural sound, nor a stronger commitment to tradition, than Larry Sparks, born in Ohio of Kentucky-born parents.

The city with the greatest concentration of bluegrass interest is Washington, D.C. Since the mid-fifties the city and surrounding metropolitan area have had a large number of clubs catering to the mixed assortment of government workers, students, military personnel, and others who have descended upon the nation's capital from all over the United States. As a city with a large population of ex-southerners, many of them from contiguous areas where the music has long thrived, Washington was peculiarly situated to be a bluegrass capital. Several bluegrass bands have worked out of the area, but the two most important have been stellar exemplars of the "progressive" sound–the Country Gentlemen (led by Charlie Waller) and the Seldom Scene (led by John Duffey).

As demonstrated by the mixed audiences of devotees found in Washington, bluegrass music had attained a mating of cultures long before Gram Parsons and Willie Nelson attempted their respective experiments with country and rock. The chief vehicle for the popularization of bluegrass has been the festival. The first bluegrass festival, organized by Bill Clifton and held near Luray, Virginia, in 1962, was sparsely attended, and the festivals did not become annual events until after 1965. Today, if the bluegrass fan has enough time and money, he can attend a festival somewhere each week in the United States from May until November.

Even the larger festivals (such as those at Bean Blossom,

Indiana; Camp Springs, North Carolina; and Hugo, Oklahoma), which are attended by thousands of people, still retain the brush arbor feeling of the old-time camp meetings. People camp out for days, listen to the music of the visiting professional bands, and stay up all night jamming with each other on fiddles, guitars, banjos, and mandolins. The festivals have been meeting grounds for the young and old, the liberal and conservative, and the hippie and redneck. Truck drivers, coal miners, and farmers share benches with college students, professors, engineers, and hippies and stand by campers hour after hour trading instrumental licks and harmonizing on "Salty Dog Blues" or "Roll in My Sweet Baby's Arms." Nowhere else in the polarized sixties could one find a similar forum where such disparate groups so peacefully communed with each other. The McGovern and Wallace supporters who attended the festivals may not have reconciled their political differences as a result of their similar musical preferences, but their shared liking for bluegrass suggests a common aesthetic based upon a genuine search for sources and a reaction against the plasticized offerings of pop culture.

Bluegrass music definitely represents an impulse toward tradition, but its directions have often been shaped by people and forces outside the South—by the urban folk music movement and by folklorists and others who cling to the romantic myth of the southern mountains as the sole repository of American folk music. Honky-tonk music also experienced a revival in the sixties, but it has never been endorsed by the intellectuals or the folklorists; neither has it really ever become chic among the urban middle classes. Its evolution, therefore, has been a more honest reflection of the organic changes in southern white working-class life than can be seen in the development of any other form of music. Since honky-tonk music generally reflects no particular ideology, it is uninteresting to liberal intellectuals, and because it rarely sings of mountain streams or cabins or little country churches, but instead concentrates on the private concerns of today, with a heavily electrified beat, it has little appeal to the academic folklorists or to those whose conceptions of folk music remain shaped by the vision of a pastoral and nontechnological society.

During the heyday of rock 'n' roll interest, the honky-tonk style was affected more adversely than any other form of country music. Only two major singers, Ray Price and George Jones, both from Texas, remained true to the honky-tonk sound; Price, in fact, gained great success with the form during the very peak years of the rock 'n' roll boom. Jones's rise as a singer in the early sixties paralleled the general resurgence of the honky-tonk style. During these years Jones built his reputation as one of the supreme stylists of country music, singing his cheating and drinking songs to the accompaniment of a bluesy fiddle and wailing steel guitar. The honky-tonk revival was made possible partly by the revitalization of these two instruments which had declined in use so drastically during the late fifties. They, like virtually all instruments in the honky-tonk bands, were now electrified, and pedals had been universally attached to the steel guitars, permitting the musicians to stretch and bend the strings in order to achieve a more sustained and flexible vibrato. By the end of the sixties innovative steel guitarists such as Pete Drake, Buddy Emmons, Ralph Mooney, and Lloyd Green were appearing regularly on Nashville recording sessions. Similarly, the fiddle regained much of the prominence it had once enjoyed. The CMA's choice as instrumentalist of the year in 1976 was the most popular session fiddler in Nashville—Johnny Gimble, from Tyler, Texas.

Honky-tonk music withdrew from its encounter with rock 'n' roll bearing some of the characteristics of its adversary. Rock-derived instrumental licks showed up in every form of country music, and much of the energy of rock 'n' roll suffused the performances of some of the honky-tonk singers. Buck Owens, for instance, born in Sherman, Texas, became the top-rated male country singer of the mid-sixties with a style that ranged from rockabilly to honky-tonk. In the seventies Gary Stewart, born in Kentucky, and now a resident of Florida, has won acclaim among country fans because of his pleading, husky-vibrato honky-tonk-style voice, but he also has received critical praise in *Rolling Stone* for his rollicking rockabilly style. Several singers began their careers as rockabillies and later shifted with great effectiveness to the honky-tonk style. Ronnie Milsap, a blind pianist from North Carolina, brought an approach to country music that is much more eclectic than that of the ex-rockabillies, since he has had classical training as well as an experience with jazz and rock. His expressive voice, probably the most versatile in country music, permitted him to perform creditably in each of the genre's many styles, and his overall showmanship won for him the title of entertainer of the year in 1977. Milsap has never been exclusively committed to the honky-tonk style, but when he devotes his attention to a song such as "Play Born to Lose Again" or "Linda on My Mind," he is at his best.

The honky-tonk genre has had a tenuous existence in country music. The industry as a whole has been biased against this "hard country" sound, and singers are easily tempted into the financially more rewarding area of "country pop" where the possibilities for crossovers exist. Honky-tonk fans are continually hoping that Ray Price will return to his original sound, or that someone will restore the old George Jones style to country music (maybe even George himself). Consequently, singers or recordings are periodically seized upon by hopeful fans as the harbingers of genuine and full-scale honky-tonk revivals: Mel Street's "Borrowed Angel," Wayne Kemp's "Who'll Turn Out the Lights," Ronnie Milsap's "I Hate You," Johnny Rodriguez's "Pass Me By," John Conlee's "Rose Colored Glasses," and Norman Wade's "Close Every Honky Tonk." The promise usually remains unfulfilled. Rodriguez's first album was consistently honky-tonk in style and repertory, a worthy reflection of his Texas inheritance, but his succeeding albums have persistently moved away from that original sound toward the more lucrative field of country-pop.

The most faithful exponents of the honky-tonk sound (although both of them prefer the term "hard country") have been Vernon Oxford and Moe Bandy, born in Arkansas and Mississippi respectively. Oxford's pure country sound has remained unknown to most American country fans, but he has built a remarkable popularity among music devotees in Great Britain. Of all the singers performing today (1979), Moe Bandy (born in Meridian, Mississippi, but a long-time resident of San Antonio, Texas) conforms most closely to the classic mold of the honky-tonk singer: the singer with his guitar in front of a band with a fiddle, pedal steel guitar, and electric walking bass (the essence of the Texas shuffle beat)—singing songs about cheating, hurting, and drinking to a noisy audience shuffling across a crowded dance floor. Here, too, is a man totally at peace with his music: honky-tonk and Moe Bandy are made for each other, and because Bandy instinctively appreciates this, he conveys the messages of songs like "I Just Started Hating Cheating Songs Today," "Don't Anyone Make Love at Home Anymore?" and "Hank Williams, You Wrote My Life" with unabashed sincerity and great personal appeal.

Honky-tonk music's spirited cousin, western swing, had never totally died away after World War II, even though the large bands of the Bob Wills variety had become rare. Among active musicians, Hoyle Nix of Big Spring, Texas, and Hank Thompson, born in Waco, Texas, but now living in Oklahoma, remained closest to the swing pattern during the fifties and sixties, playing for dances all over the Southwest. Their bands, though, were typically small, and Thompson was best known for his interpretation of such honky-tonk songs as "The Wild Side of Life." The memory of Bob Wills's exciting bands, however, was still vivid throughout the Southwest, and songs introduced by him and the Texas Playboys remained in the repertories even of those musicians who were far removed from the western swing format. Well before he died in 1975, a western swing renaissance was under way, and Wills— admitted to the Country Music Hall of Fame in 1968—was becoming a cult figure.

A new generation of western swing enthusiasts came into existence who knew Wills, Milton Brown, and other swing pioneers only through their recordings, or secondhand through the performances of a Merle Haggard or a Willie Nelson. Much of the renewed interest in Wills and western swing came through young "revivalists," such as Asleep at the Wheel, Cooder Browne, and Alvin Crow and his Pleasant Valley Boys, each of whom made their headquarters in Austin, Texas. While these young bands appealed chiefly to the youthful, rockoriented audiences, Red Steagall and the Coleman County Cowboys worked more directly within the country music mainstream and found their most loyal listeners among traditional country music fans. Born in Gainesville, Texas, Steagall carried on the tradition of western swing, but became also the leading performer of rodeo music in the United States. He sang for rodeo dances all over the country and, as an ex–bull rider, has succeeded in writing some very sensitive material about a sport and way of life with which he strongly identifies. With his performance of "Lone Star Beer and Bob Wills' Music," Steagall has also paid tribute to two institutions cherished by country music fans in the Southwest. The popularity of such musicians as Steagall and Asleep at the Wheel suggests that western swing will continue to exert an influence in American music for a long time. Country music fans can find additional satisfaction in the fact that through the revival inspired by the younger performers many of the pioneers of western swing have won a new hearing among country and rock audiences. Several of Wills's original musicians, such as Leon McAuliffe, Smokey Dacus, Al Stricklin, Jesse Ashlock, Keith Coleman, and Leon Rausch, reconstituted themselves as the Texas Playboys and have won an ardent following among young people who never heard the original music.

The resurgence of western swing is in part a tribute to the mythmaking quality of regionalism, in this case the allegedly liberated and expansive Southwest, and to the man, Bob Wills, who put this freedom to the service of music. Western swing appeals both to an older audience appreciative of the past and to those too young to have experienced the music's earlier blossoming but hungry for something that has endured—an original and rare prize in the midst of the ever-shifting patterns of popular culture.

Conclusion

THE SOUTH of imagery endures even as its performers and musical forms gradually become absorbed in the national mainstream. The lure of the South for American musicians remains as strong today as it was in the days of Stephen Foster. Foster and his cohorts did much to create public conceptions of the South; the musicians of today are keeping those conceptions alive. Though a long procession of Yankee poets has contributed to the mythologizing of Dixie and its inhabitants, southern musicians are now playing active roles in keeping their own special versions of the southern myth alive. They remind us that there is not one South but many.

The undying American urge to play cowboy exhibited by the Texas-obsessed ZZ Top, the Marshall Tucker Band, and the Austin musicians, along with the rebel posturing of such rock-oriented musicians as Hank Williams, Jr., Charlie Daniels, and Lynyrd Skynyrd are facets of a more general preoccupation with the South now seen so often in American music. The musical conceptions of the South are as diverse as are the public attitudes toward the region. No one else has carried his obsession with the South quite so far as Steve Young, a "progressive" country singer and a professional southerner (born in Beaumont, Texas, and reared in Gadsden, Alabama), whose southern-flavored songs are shaped by his conviction that he is the reincarnation of a Confederate officer killed during the Civil War. Oklahoma-born James Talley shares Young's fascination with southern scenes and musical genres, but he writes from the perspective of a neo-Populist—a latter-day Woody Guthrie—who identifies with and sings about the poor people, black and white, of the South. Talley gained immediate recognition when Rosalynn Carter announced that he was her favorite country singer. Randy Newman, born in New Orleans, presents an ambivalent view of the South and of its loyal son, the redneck, in his much-publicized and controversial album *Good Old Boys*. The best-known selection from the album, "Rednecks," begins with what seems to be a conventional Yankee (and southern middle-class) put-down of rednecks, but Newman ends with a blast at white northerners, too, who have caged Negroes in the ghettos of the North.

Ironically, the most affectionate descriptions of the South in recent years (apart from the large number of country songs, such as Dolly Parton's "Tennessee Mountain Home") have come in the music of a Negro, Allen Toussaint, and of a white southern expatriate, Jesse Winchester. As a producer, musician, and composer, Toussaint has been at the center of New Orleans music since the early sixties but has never gained the national success that might have been his had he moved to New York or Detroit. Remaining in New Orleans, Toussaint has done much to create the joyous, "carnival sound" of that city's music. His award-winning song "Southern Nights" (made a national hit in 1977 by Glen Campbell) was no doubt inspired by Toussaint's experiences in New Orleans, but it presents a picture of the South that has long been appealing to Americans: that of a sensuous and exotic dreamland.

Jesse Winchester's South is more pastoral than that of Toussaint, but the image is no less sensual in its evocation of balmy summer days, "fields specked with dirty cotton lint," and "cool green leaves of mint." Winchester spent his early days on a Mississippi farm and his teen years in Memphis, but he left his southern, and American, home behind in 1967 when he moved to Canada to avoid the draft. He subsequently obtained Canadian citizenship in 1973, but as an active part of the musical scene in Montreal he produced a number of songs like "Delta Lady," "Brand New Tennessee Waltz," and "Mississippi, You're on My Mind," which were richly suggestive of his native South. Despite his departure from his homeland, Winchester's views of the South have few traces of ambivalence. They reflect his genuine love for the region that nurtured both him and his music. "Mississippi, You're on My Mind" is one of the most unequivocally affectionate portraits of the rural South ever penned by an American composer. The irony of its success is further compounded by the fact that its most popular recorded version is that of Stoney Edwards, a black country singer from Oklahoma who now lives in San Antonio.

Winchester now divides his loyalties between his adopted home and his birthplace, and it is not surprising that his most evocative and poignant tributes to the South should have come after his flight from the region. Texas writer Larry King was speaking of his native state when he said that "it is somehow easier to conjure up the Texas I once knew from Manhattan," but he was actually voicing an attitude felt by many southern expatriates, whether intellectuals like himself seeking fame and fortune in New York, or factory workers on assembly lines in Detroit or Akron.[1] And Winchester spoke for them too in a line from one of his songs, "I want to live with my feet in Dixie, and my head in the cool, blue North."

For a century and a half the South has left its imprint on American music, not only as a source of images, but as an exporter of musicians and styles. Beginning with the spirituals in the late nineteenth century and exploding into the national consciousness after World War II, southern music forms have done more than merely contribute to the revitalization of American popular music; they have virtually become pop music itself. Forms born in cotton fields, timber mills, shacks, honky-tonks, and churches of the South moved on to the television networks, Carnegie Hall, and the nightclubs of Las Vegas. Music became one dramatic avenue through which poor southern boys and girls attained glamour and wealth and escaped the ghettos, coal camps, textile villages, and tenant farms that had for so long held their forebears in bondage.

But in a sense, at the hour of their victory the southern-born musical forms also suffered defeat. Commercial acclaim, general popularity, and international recognition have been won at the price of the loss of distinctiveness and individuality. The world has been enriched by the periodic infusions of southern-derived music, but southern musicians have absorbed much from that wider world to which they have been introduced. Southern styles have become so enmeshed in American popular culture that it is now impossible to determine where their southernness ends and their Americanism begins. Gospel and secular styles are so closely intertwined that only their lyrics differentiate them; black and white musicians borrow freely from each other; country and pop move closer to each other; and musicians in all genres strive for the magic formula that will win them a universal audience. The homogenization of American popular music is not yet complete, but it is well on the way.

Nevertheless, away from the beaten and jaded paths of professional entertainment, older expressions of the folk South still persist. And there is an expanding audience for them, too large to be dismissed as nothing more than old people engaged in a quaint pursuit of nostalgia. It is basically an audience of the young. The enthusiasm for folk music is vividly demonstrated by the immense throngs that attend the fiddlers' contest each year in Union Grove, North Carolina, and seek out other fiddlers' meets in such places as Huntsville, Alabama, or Crockett, Texas. The proliferating blue grass festivals provide further documentation of the back-to-the-roots urge which runs so strong in contemporary America, and the folk-life festivals, such as the Texas Folk-Life Festival and the New Orleans Jazz and Heritage Festival—the best music shows for the money now available in the United States—and the various state-sponsored affairs inspired by the giant festival held each July on the Mall in front of the Smithsonian Institution, provide samplings of the whole wide range of southern music, food, crafts, and customs to ever-increasing audiences.

The folk music vogue is far from being solely a spectator sport. The United States is now largely given over to the processed, the prefabricated, and the franchised, but there is also a great hunger for the homemade, as the interest in the *Foxfire* books would suggest. The craving for homemade music is again leading people to the folk resources of the South. The immense popularity of the guitar was inspired primarily by the example of rock musicians, but an increasing number of young people are taking up such folky instruments as the fiddle, banjo, autoharp, and dobro steel guitar. Bluegrass music, which has long drawn upon the resources of tradition, is becoming increasingly a haven for young musicians, and the performances of musicians who have not yet entered their teen years repeatedly thrill festival audiences. The old forms of music may one day die, but there is a tremendous amount of vitality left in them yet.

Strange and wondrous things are occurring even within the context of commercialization. The pop music world may encourage the homogenization of styles, but homogenization can also breed rebellion. The repetition and uniformity of the Top Forty concept can indeed inspire a search for the novel and fresh. Dissatisfaction with mainstream pop music can encourage experimentation with new forms, and it can also lead to a reaching back for the old. To young listeners who never heard the music during its first appearance, the old can seem new and innovative, as did rhythm and blues, urban folk music, bluegrass, and western swing during their respective "revivals" since World War II. The interest in the older forms of music has often been fueled by "outsiders" who have made use of southern materials (Joan Baez and Appalachian ballads, Tony Glover and blues, Asleep at the Wheel and western swing, the Red Clay Ramblers and old-timey fiddle band music), and much patronage has come from northern audiences. But native southerners are responsible for much of the utilization of older southern music. Some of these southern musicians are conscious revivalists who merely recreate what they have heard; others are eclectic artists who build new forms out of the varied ingredients of the music, both traditional and contemporary, that surrounds them. The Cooder Browne band, for instance, reveals not only the possibilities inherent in the fusion of tradition and modernity – it demonstrates what is actually taking place in the swirling currents of southern music.

As the best band to emerge from the Austin musical environment, the Cooder Browne band is not solely country, nor western, nor rock, nor blues, but a composite of all these influences. Its manufactured name which refers to no living person, along with its cowboy costumes, places it at least partially in the southern rock camp along with groups like Marshall Tucker. But for all its eclecticism and experimentation, the band is centered around the virtuoso fiddling of Larry Franklin, a descendant of old-time fiddlers whose prowess has been recognized in Texas since the nineteenth century. The Cooder Browne band effectively combines, as few other bands do, both the very oldest and newest strains in the music of the South, suggesting that a vigorous and organic regional music can still be produced through the absorption and transmission of a variety of styles and the equal investment of authentic soul.

NOTES

INTRODUCTION

1. George B. Tindall, "Mythology: A New Frontier in Southern History," in Patrick Gerster and Nicholas Cords, eds., *Myth and Southern History* (Chicago: Rand McNally, 1974), 1:1–15.

2. David Potter, "The Enigma of the South," in his *The South and the Sectional Conflict* (Baton Rouge: Louisiana State University Press, 1968), p. 15.

CHAPTER 1

1. Alan Lomax, *The Folk Songs of North America* (Garden City, N.Y.: Doubleday, 1960), p. 155.

2. Dena J. Epstein, *Sinful Tunes and Spirituals: Black Folk Music to the Civil War* (Urbana: University of Illinois Press, 1977), pp. 22, 80–100.

3. This is a central concern, for example, of both Eugene Genovese, *Roll Jordan Roll: The World the Slaves Made* (New York: Random House, 1972) and Lawrence Levine, *Black Culture and Black Consciousness* (New York: Oxford University Press, 1977).

Dickson D. Bruce, Jr., *And They All Sang Hallelujah: Plain-Folk Camp-Meeting Religion, 1800–45* (Knoxville: University of Tennessee Press, 1974), pp. 96–122.

5. George Pullen Jackson, *White Spirituals in the Southern Uplands* (Chapel Hill: University of North Carolina Press, 1933), pp. 31–34.

6. Ibid., pp. 408–9; Joe Dan Boyd, "Judge Jackson: Black Giant of White Spirituals," *Journal of American Folklore* 83 (October–December 1970):446–51; and Boyd, "Negro Sacred Harp Songsters in Mississippi," *Mississippi Folklore Register 5*, no. 3 (Fall 1971): 60–83.

7. David Evans, "Afro-American One-Stringed Instruments," *Western Folklore* 29 (October 1970):229–45.

8. Epstein, *Sinful Tunes and Spirituals*, p. 36. Epstein has written a more complete study of the instrument in "The Folk Banjo: A Documentary History," *Ethnomusicology* 19 (September 1975):347–71. The principal challenge to the Sweeney legend is Jay Bailey, "Historical Origin and Stylistic Development of the Five-String Banjo," *Journal of American Folklore* 85 (1972):58–65.

9. D. K. Wilgus, *Anglo-American Folksong Scholarship since 1898* (New Brunswick, N.J.: Rutgers University Press, 1959), pp. 3–123.

10. Ronald L. Davis, *A History of Opera in the American West* (Englewood Cliffs, N.J.: Prentice-Hall, 1965), pp. 6, 20–21. Henry A. Kmen, *Music in New Orleans: The Formative Years, 1791–1841* (Baton Rouge: Louisiana State University Press, 1966), pp. 229, 232–33, 245.

11. Vernon Loggins, *Where the Word Ends: The Life of Louis Moreau Gottschalk* (Baton Rouge: Louisiana State University Press, 1958).

12. Ibid., p. 141.

13. Carl Bode, *Antebellum Culture* (Carbondale: Southern Illinois University Press, 1959).

CHAPTER 2

1. See Earl F. Bargainneer, "Tin Pan Alley and Dixie: The South in Popular Song," *Mississippi Quarterly* 30 (Fall 1977):527–65.

2. Kmen, *Music in New Orleans*, pp. 237–45.

3. Robert C. Toll, *Blacking Up: The Minstrel Show in Nineteenth-Century America* (New York: Oxford University Press, 1974), pp. 40–48.

4. Ibid., p. 57.

5. William W. Austin, *Susanna, Jeanie, and the Old Folks at Home: The Songs of Stephen C. Foster from His Time to Ours* (New York: Macmillan, 1975), pp. xx, 18, 123–35, 279–80.

6. Ibid., pp. xi, 293.

7. Epstein, *Sinful Tunes and Spirituals*, p. 290.

8. Dvořák, for instance, stressed the importance of "plantation melodies" in an 1895 issue of *Harper's New Monthly Magazine* and called them "the most striking and appealing melodies that have yet been found on this side of the water." Reprinted in Bruce Jackson, ed., *The Negro and His Folklore in Nineteenth-Century Periodicals* (Austin: University of Texas Press, 1967), pp. 428–34.

9. Jackson, *White Spirituals*, pp. 242–302.

10. Henry D. Shapiro, *Appalachia on Our Mind: The Southern Mountains and Mountaineers in the American Consciousness, 1870–1920* (Chapel Hill: University of North Carolina Press, 1978), pp. 260, 261.

11. John Powell, "In the Lowlands Low," *Southern Folklore Quarterly* 1, no. 1 (March 1937):1–12.

12. Annabel Morris Buchanan, "The Function of a Folk Festival," ibid., pp. 29–34.

13. The railroads, timber interests, and textile, coal, and petroleum industries were only a few of the phenomena which were already transforming the lives and culture of the plain people of the South in the thirties. Archie Green has investigated some of the music inspired by industrial innovation in "Born on Picketlines, Textile Workers' Songs Are Woven into History," *Textile Labor* 22, no. 4 (April 1961): 3–5; and in *Only a Miner: Studies in Recorded Coal-Mining Songs* (Urbana: University of Illinois Press, 1972).

CHAPTER 3

1. Eileen Southern, *The Music of Black Americans* (New York: W. W. Norton, 1971), p. 312.

2. William J. Schafer and Johannes Riedel, *The Art of Ragtime* (Baton Rouge: Louisiana State University Press, 1973), p. 5.

3. Ibid., p. 19.

4. Levine, *Black Culture and Black Consciousness*, p. 221.

5. Ibid., p. 237.

6. Samuel Charters, *The Legacy of the Blues: Lives of Twelve Great Bluesmen* (New York: Da Capo, 1977), p. 85.

7. Samuel Charters, *The Bluesmen* (New York: Oak Publications, 1967), p. 32.

8. Jeff Todd Titon, *Early Downhome Blues: A Musical and Cultural Analysis* (Urbana: University of Illinois Press, 1977), p. 29.

9. Charters, *The Bluesmen*, p. 32

10. Titon, *Early Downhome Blues*, p. 47.

11. See "Enigmatic Folksongs of the Southern Underworld," *Current Opinion* 67 (September 1919):165–66.

12. William C. Handy, *Father of the Blues* (New York: Macmillan, 1944).

13. Chris Albertson, *Bessie* (New York: Stein and Day, 1972), p. 34.

14. Perry Bradford, *Born with the Blues* (New York: Oak Publications, 1965), p. 117.

15. Albertson, *Bessie*, pp. 34–36.

16. Titon, *Early Downhome Blues*, p. 23.

17. Ibid., pp. xiii, xiv.

18. William J. Schafer, with the assistance of Richard B. Allen, *Brass Bands and New Orleans Jazz* (Baton Rouge: Louisiana State University Press, 1977), p. 94.

19. Rudi Blesh, *Shining Trumpets: A History of Jazz*, 2d rev. ed. (New York: Da Capo, 1976), pp. 183–84.

20. Donald M. Marquis, *In Search of Buddy Bolden* (Baton Rouge: Louisiana State University Press, 1978).

21. Al Rose, *Storyville, New Orleans* (University: University of Alabama Press, 1974), pp. 106, 123.

22. Blesh, *Shining Trumpets*, p. 212.

23. Marquis, *Buddy Bolden*, p. 2.

24. *Dearborn Independent*, August 6, August 13, 1921.

25. Blesh, *Shining Trumpets*, p. 225.

CHAPTER 4

1. Charles K. Wolfe, *Tennessee Strings: The Story of Country Music in Tennessee* (Knoxville: University of Tennessee Press, 1977), pp. 27–54. See also Wolfe, *Grand Ole Opry: The Early Years, 1925–1935* (London: Old Time Music, 1975).

2. Joe Nick Patoski, "Little Joe," *Texas Monthly* 6, Issue 5 (May 1978):135.

3. Les Blank and Chris Strachwitz are independent film and record producers respectively who often collaborate on ventures dealing with folk and ethnic musicians (Blues, Cajun, Tex-Mex, etc.). Strachwitz's Tex-Mex reissues are on his own Folklyric label.

4. Lauren C. Post, *Cajun Sketches* (Baton Rouge: Louisiana State University Press, 1962), p. 36.

5. Houston folklorist Mack McCormick is credited with the coin-

ing of the term zydeco. Accordionist Clifton Chenier, from Opelousas, Louisiana, is today the most famous of all the zydeco musicians.

6. George B. Tindall, *The Emergence of the New South, 1913–1945* (Baton Rouge: Louisiana State University Press, 1967), pp. 184–218; and "The Benighted South: Origins of a Modern Image," *Virginia Quarterly Review* 40 (Spring 1964): 281–94.

7. There are challenges to the theory that hillbilly music was solely a southern phenomenon: Roderick J. Roberts, "An Introduction to the Study of Northern Country Music," *Journal of Country Music* 6, no. 4 (January 1978):22–29; Simon J. Bronner, "The Country Music Tradition in Western New York State," ibid., pp. 29–60.

8. Wolfe, *Tennessee Strings*, p. 52.

CHAPTER 5

1. The phrase is inspired by Thomas Tippett, *When Southern Labor Stirs* (New York: Cape and Smith, 1931). See also Tindall, *Emergence of the New South*, pp. 318–54.

2. Archie Green, notes to Sarah Ogan Gunning, *Girl of Constant Sorrow*, Folk-Legacy Records, FSA-26. This phenomenon is also discussed in R. Serge Denisoff, *Great Day Coming: Folk Music and the American Left* (Urbana: University of Illinois Press, 1971), pp. 15–37.

3. Charles R. Townsend, *San Antonio Rose: The Life and Music of Bob Wills* (Urbana: University of Illinois Press, 1976).

CHAPTER 6

1. Charles Keil, *Urban Blues* (Chicago: University of Chicago Press, 1966), p. 20.

2. Ibid., p. 102.

3. John Broven, *Walking to New Orleans: The Story of New Orleans Rhythm and Blues* (Sussex, England: Blues Unlimited, 1974), pp. 13–17, 64–72.

4. Immediately after his death, several books appeared which purported to have the "inside" and "hidden" story of Elvis's life. The most sensational is a book by three of his ex-bodyguards—Red West, Sonny West, and Dave Hebler—as told to Steve Dunleavy, *Elvis, What Happened?* (New York, Ballantine Books, 1977). For a review essay on this and four other books on Elvis, see Mark Crispin Miller, "The King," *New York Review of Books*, December 8, 1977, pp. 38–42.

CHAPTER 7

1. The best biography of Joplin, and one that contains a wide assortment of photographs, is Myra Friedman, *Buried Alive* (New York: William Morrow, 1973).

2. Michael Bane, "Hillbilly Band," *Country Music* 5, no. 6 (March 1977):51.

3. Chet Flippo, "Getting By without the Allmans," *Creem* 6, no. 6 (November 1974):34–37, 75.

4. Martha Hume, "Marshall Tucker at Home," *Rolling Stone*, no. 244 (July 28, 1977):20.

5. Tony Heilbut, *The Gospel Sound: Good News and Bad Times* (New York: Simon and Schuster, 1971), p. 94.

6. Don Rhodes, "Lest We Forget: Ray Charles Reflects," *Country Music* 3, no. 4 (January 1975):19.

7. Arnold Shaw, *The World of Soul* (New York: Paperback Library Edition, 1971), p. 219.

CHAPTER 8

1. Much of this discussion was published earlier in Bill C. Malone, "Country Music, The South, and Americanism," *Mississippi Folklore Register* 10 (Spring 1976):54–66.

2. Florence King, "Red Necks, White Socks, and Blue Ribbon Fear," *Harper's* 249, no. 1490 (July 1974):30–34; Richard Goldstein, "My Country Music Problem—and Yours," *Mademoiselle* 77, no. 2 (June 1973):114–15, 185.

3. Sheldon Hackney, "The South as a Counterculture," *American Scholar* 42 (Spring 1973):283–93.

4. The term is also attributed to Grandpa Jones, but Cindy Walker says he got the phrase from her. Interview with Cindy Walker, Mexia, Texas, August 12, 1976.

5. These include Muscle Shoals, Alabama; Macon, Georgia; Bogalusa, Louisiana; Atlanta, Georgia; New Orleans, Louisiana; and Memphis, Tennessee. The Austin story has been told in Jan Reid, *The Improbable Rise of Redneck Rock* (Austin, Texas: Heidelberg Publishers, 1974).

6. It was Townsend Miller, country music columnist for the Austin *American-Statesman*, who first gave Austin the sobriquet "colony of musicians."

7. The only extended account of Gram Parsons thus far is Judson Klinger and Greg Mitchell, "Gram Finale," *Crawdaddy*, October 1976, 43–58.

8. *Journal of American Folklore* 78 (July–September, 1965).

9. Alan Lomax, "Bluegrass Background: Folk Music with Overdrive," *Esquire* 52, no. 4 (October 1959):108.

CONCLUSION

1. Larry L. King, "Playing Cowboy: The Expatriates," *Atlantic* 235, no. 3 (March 1975):44.

BIBLIOGRAPHICAL NOTES

FOLK ORIGINS OF SOUTHERN MUSIC

My interpretation of southern folk music has been much influenced by
Alan Lomax. His *Folk Songs of North America* (New York: Doubleday and Co., 1960) remains the best one-volume collection of American folk songs and is a repository of provocative theories about the
conservatism of folk styles and their relationship to culture. A more
concentrated exposition of his theories is "Folk Song Style," *American
Anthropologist* 61, no. 6 (December 1959), pp. 927–55. The most useful study limited exclusively to white style is Roger Abrahams and
George Foss, *Anglo-American Folksong Style* (Englewood Cliffs, N.J.:
Prentice-Hall, 1968).

There are numerous studies of black folk styles, and most of them
stress African origins. Melville Herskovits stresses African survivals
among black people throughout the Western Hemisphere in his *Myth
of the Negro Past* (Boston: Beacon Press, 1958). Richard Waterman
limits his study to music but makes the same general point as Herskovits in "African Influence on the Music of the Americas," in Sol
Tax, ed., *Acculturation in the Americas* (Chicago: University of Chicago Press, 1952). Works which are more appealing to the general
reader include Marshall Stearns, *The Story of Jazz* (New York: Oxford University Press, 1970) and Paul Oliver, *Savannah Syncopators:
African Retentions in the Blues* (New York: Stein and Day, 1970).
Both writers argue that *all* American black music shares traits that
were retained from the African experience.

The student who wishes to explore a serious scholarly interest in black music should begin with the important collection edited by Roger Abrahams and John F. Szwed, *Afro-American Folk Culture: An Annotated Bibliography of Materials from North, Central, and South America and the West Indies*, 2 vols. (Philadelphia: Institute for the Study of Human Issues, 1977). The complicated question of black-white folk interaction, and the degree of cultural borrowing on either side, has inspired some of the finest American scholarship of the last two decades. Neither John Blassingame nor Eugene Genovese, to cite only two examples of a large group of historians who have grappled with the problems of a slave society, has concerned himself with music as such, but both have perceptively discussed the mechanisms by which black slaves preserved a sense of community: Blassingame, *The Slave Community* (New York: Oxford University Press, 1972); and Genovese, *Roll Jordan Roll* (New York: Pantheon Books, 1974). Dena Epstein's focus, on the other hand, is totally on music in her impressively researched *Sinful Tunes and Spirituals: Black Folk Music to the Civil War* (Urbana: University of Illinois Press, 1977). Lawrence Levine, *Black Culture and Black Consciousness* (New York: Oxford University Press, 1977), already becoming one of the indispensable books in black history, uses folklore and oral history as tools for perceiving black consciousness. Levine demonstrates the continuity in black music from the slave songs to rhythm and blues.

Although Frank Owsley and his students attempted to delineate the lives of southern rural whites in the antebellum era (see Owsley, *Plain Folk of the Old South* [Baton Rouge: Louisiana State University Press, 1949]), there have been no studies of poor whites comparable to what Genovese, Levine, and others have done for blacks. Neither is there anything comparable to the interviews with ex-slaves collected during the Great Depression by the Federal Writers Project: George Rawick has edited 19 volumes under the title *The American Slave: a Composite Autobiography* (Westport, Conn.: Greenwood, 1972–). The Federal Writers Project, however, did compile a massive amount of material about white farmers and workers, but it has been used only rarely, as in *These Are Our Lives* (Chapel Hill: University of North Carolina Press, 1939). When historians explore "white culture and white consciousness," they will find a large number of ballads and folk songs already collected and published, as well as a storehouse of field recordings in the Library of Congress Archive of Folk Song and in other repositories.

D. K. Wilgus discusses folk song collections and collectors in *Anglo-American Folksong Scholarship since 1898* (New Brunswick, N.J.: Rutgers University Press, 1959). The serious researcher should familiarize himself with Francis James Child, *The English and Scottish*

Popular Ballads, 5 vols. (Boston: Houghton, Mifflin, 1882–1898) because, for good or ill, Child has left his imprint on virtually all collectors who came after him. Tristram P. Coffin surveys and describes the Child ballads that have survived in America in *The British Traditional Ballad in North America*, rev. ed. (Philadelphia: American Folklore Society, 1963), while G. Malcolm Laws, Jr., concentrates on other types of British survivals in *American Balladry from British Broadsides* (Philadelphia: American Folklore Society, 1957) and on indigenous American products in *Native American Balladry* (Philadelphia: American Folklore Society, 1964).

Sociocultural studies of southern rural whites (yeomen and non-slaveholders) may be lacking, but religious investigations are not. And two of the great nineteenth-century molders of musical reportory and style, the camp meeting and the shape-note singing school, have inspired extensive scholarship. Charles A. Johnson, *The Frontier Camp Meeting: Religious Harvest Time* (Dallas, Tex.: Southern Methodist University Press, 1955), and Bernard Weisberger, *They Gathered at the River: The Story of the Great Revivalists and their Impact upon Religion in America* (Boston: Little, Brown, 1958), can still be read with great profit, but the most significant study of the early-nineteenth-century revivals in the South is John Boles, *The Great Revival, 1787–1805: The Origins of the Southern Evangelical Mind* (Lexington: University Press of Kentucky, 1972). Both Boles and Dickson Bruce, Jr., in his *And They All Sang Hallelujah: Plain-Folk Camp Meeting Religion, 1800–1845* (Knoxville: University of Tennessee Press, 1974), see the revivals as appealing essentially to the poorer classes of the South. Bruce's book describes the camp meeting songs as important sources for understanding the world-rejection philosophy of the "plain people." His conclusions should be compared with those of James C. Downey, "The Music of American Revivalism" (Ph.D diss., Tulane University, 1968), a study which deserves to be better known.

The ground-breaking study of southern shape-note music from which all other related works have drawn is George Pullen Jackson, *White Spirituals in the Southern Uplands* (Chapel Hill: University of North Carolina Press, 1933). Although Jackson was indifferent if not hostile to secular rural music, and even to other types of religious folk music, he made many acute observations about urban-rural antagonisms which are still relevant to an understanding of southern music. Jackson's conclusions about shape-note singers, writers, and publishers have been amplified and extended by several scholars. Joe Dan Boyd, for instance, found the tradition alive in some black communities, as he reports in "Judge Jackson: Black Giant of White Spirituals," *Journal of American Folklore* 83, no. 330 (October–December 1970):446–51;

and in "Negro Sacred Harp Songsters in Mississippi," *Mississippi Folklore Register 5*, no. 3 (Fall 1971):60–83. Harry Eskew concentrates on the area of first shape-note activity in the South in "Shape-Note Hymnody in the Shenandoah Valley, 1816–1860" (Ph.D diss., Tulane University, 1966); Rachel Augusta Harley writes about the first southern shape-note publisher in "Ananias Davisson: Southern Tunebook Compiler" (Ph.D diss., University of Michigan, 1972); and Charles Linwood Ellington discusses the most famous songbook to emerge from the shape-note movement in "The Sacred Harp Tradition of the South: Its Origin and Evolution" (Ph.D diss., Florida State University, 1969).

The most neglected area of southern religious music is that dealing with the Holiness-Pentecostal-Sanctified movement. As a folk phenomenon of itinerant preachers and musicians who left few written or published recollections of their work, the movement is difficult to document through conventional historical methods. It will require researchers skilled in oral history and folklore to recreate this important musical tradition. Studies of both white and black music make constant allusions to its influence, but no scholar has made a major effort to document the relationship. A good beginning which makes a few suggestive comments about music is Robert Mapes Anderson, "A Social History of the Early Twentieth Century Pentecostal Movement" (Ph.D diss., Columbia University, 1969).

The folk interchange with art and popular music in the nineteenth century and earlier has not been much studied. The presence in folklore of popular-derived forms, as well as of songs and dances from cultivated sources, is well recognized, but just how such music moved into the possession of the folk is not quite so clear. The roles played in this process by itinerant musicians and traveling shows in the nineteenth century will be discussed in the bibliographic notes for the next chapter. Here I will only suggest that the phenomenon is very old (see Carl Bridenbaugh, *Vexed and Troubled Englishmen, 1590–1642* [New York, Oxford University Press, 1968]), and evidence of it can be found in studies of dance masters and concert musicians, traveling actors, equestrian shows, circuses, and puppet shows.

For the purposes of this book, I have found O. G. Sonneck, *Early Concert-Life in America* (Leipzig: Breitkopf and Hartel, 1907), to be the indispensable source for high-art music in the early period. For a study of the music of an individual city no work has surpassed that of Henry Kmen, *Music in New Orleans: The Formative Years, 1791–1841* (Baton Rouge: Louisiana State University Press, 1966). Both he and Ronald Davis, who included New Orleans in his purview in *A History of Opera in the American West* (Englewood Cliffs, N.J.:

Prentice-Hall, 1965), allude to the pervasive interest in opera among all the social classes in the city. The most celebrated product of the New Orleans antebellum musical scene, Louis Moreau Gottschalk, recorded his observations of the United States during his concert tours: *Notes of a Pianist* (Philadelphia: J. B. Lippincott, 1881). His principal biography though is Vernon Loggins, *Where the Word Ends: The Life of Louis M. Gottschalk* (Baton Rouge: Louisiana State University Press, 1958), which shows Gottschalk's indebtedness to the folk resources around him. Although Loggins does not stress it, Gottschalk may also have absorbed material from the popular traveling shows that came to the city, or from people who heard the music of the shows. As Carl Bode has reminded us in *Antebellum Culture* (Carbondale: Southern Illinois University Press, 1959), the boundaries between folk and popular culture were very thin.

NATIONAL DISCOVERY

The literature of black-face minstrelsy is extensive, although there is little that deals with the phenomenon's effects on southern musicians. Carl Wittke, *Tambo and Bones* (Durham, N.C.: Duke University Press, 1930), though old, remains a solid factual history of minstrelsy. Edward LeRoy Rice, *Monarchs of Minstrelsy* (New York: Kenny, 1911) is a mine of biographical information by an ex-minstrel entertainer. Constance Rourke, *American Humor* (New York: Harcourt, Brace, 1931), is the best analysis of the kind of comedy projected by the minstrel shows. The standard interpretation of minstrelsy is Robert C. Toll, *Blacking Up: The Minstrel Show in Nineteenth-Century America* (New York: Oxford University Press, 1974) which comments perceptively on the folk origins of minstrel material and shows how the form contributed to racial stereotyping in the United States. Toll's *On with the Show: The First Century of Show Business in America* (New York: Oxford University Press, 1976) also treats minstrelsy but within the framework of a larger survey of American entertainment.

There still are very few biographies of nineteenth-century popular musicians, but Hans Nathan, *Dan Emmett and the Rise of Early Negro Minstrelsy* (Norman: University of Oklahoma Press, 1962), is a fine study of the composer of "Dixie" and other enduring songs. It is to be hoped that it will be a model for other students to follow. Considerable attention has been devoted to Stephen Foster; John Tasker Howard, *Stephen Foster, America's Troubadour*, rev. ed. (New York: Crowell, 1962), is an admiring biography written by a man with a high-art perspective. Of major importance is William W. Austin, *Susanna, Jeanie, and the Old Folks at Home: The Songs of Stephen C. Foster from His Time to Ours* (New York: Macmillan, 1975) which strips much of the romantic claptrap away from Foster and places his music in the context of Anglo-American popular song and hymnody. While the New York popular music scene in the Gay Nineties is the central concern of Edward B. Marks, *They All Sang* (New York: Viking Press, 1934), Marks saw some of his songs, such as "Mother Was a Lady," become standards in the repertories of southern singers. This is a delightful memoir which deserves to be reissued.

There is no serious study of William Shakespeare Hays, but his songs still endure in the popular culture of the South. Folklorists have seldom mentioned his name, even while printing his songs. Pop music historian Sigmund Spaeth made a few comments about Hays in *A History of Popular Music in America* (New York: Random House, 1948) and quotes some of his songs there and in his witty *Read 'em and Weep* (New York: Doubleday, Page, 1926) and *Weep Some More My Lady* (New York: Doubleday, Page, 1927), two of the few collections of nineteenth-century sentimental songs available.

The study of the popular song as both a reflector and shaper of public attitudes is still in its infancy. Earl Bargainneer, "Tin Pan Alley: The South in Popular Song," *Mississippi Quarterly* 30, no. 4 (Fall 1977):527–65, has discussed the fascination that songwriters have felt for the South. His essay, however, provides only a listing of songs. Now someone needs to seize upon Bargainneer's insights and explore more deeply the effects that pop songwriters have exerted on the shaping of popular conceptions of the South. Jack Temple Kirby, in *Media-Made Dixie* (Baton Rouge: Louisiana State University Press, 1978), comments on country music's South-molding role but neglects the larger and crucial pop music scene.

Many writers have commented on the presence of nineteenth-century pop songs in the repertories of twentieth-century folk and country musicians. Norman Cohen has centered directly on the subject in "Tin Pan Alley's Contributions to Folk Music," *Western Folklore* 29 (1970): 9–20. An indication that at least some folklorists are beginning to overcome the prejudice against the parlor songs is Bill Ellis, "The Blind Girl and the Rhetoric of Sentimental Heroism," *Journal of American Folklore* 91, no. 360 (April–June 1978):657–74, one of the first studies to treat such material without scorn or condescension.

Future students who are interested in preradio popular music and the complex manner in which it moved into the possession of the southern folk should be aware of the vast copyright holdings of the Library of Congress and of the collections of sheet music, pocket songsters, and the like in the New York Public Library and other repositories. Magazines and newspapers often contained song pages. The *Dallas Semi-Weekly Farm News*, for instance, contained a "young people's page" that printed song lyrics at the request of correspondents. With piano rolls, cylinder recordings, and the various kinds of printed musical material available, rural and small-town southerners had ample exposure to the nation's popular music.

The books about minstrelsy demonstrate one important way that popular music forms ventured even into some of the more remote backcountry regions of the South. Studies of other traveling shows will provide additional hints. Carl Bode, *The American Lyceum* (New York: Oxford University Press, 1956), and Joseph E. Gould, *The Chautauqua Movement* (New York: State University of New York Press, 1961), discuss two of the more high-toned purveyors of culture, while Gilbert Douglas, *American Vaudeville* (New York: Dover Publications, 1963), and Albert F. McLean, Jr., *American Vaudeville as Ritual* (Lexington: University of Kentucky Press, 1965), discuss the most popular form of organized show business in the early twentieth century. Country people saw vaudeville routines when they went to the city, but a type of vaudeville came to the villages in the form of the tent repertory shows. There are at least two published studies of the tent-rep shows. One was written by a man who played a prominent role in their dissemination: Neil E. Schaffner, with Vance Johnson, *The Fabulous Toby and Me* (Englewood Cliffs, N.J.: Prentice-Hall, 1968). The other is William Lawrence Slout, *Theatre in a Tent* (Bowling Green, Ohio: Bowling Green Popular Press, 1972). Other studies of the phenomenon include: Larry Clark, "Toby Shows: A Form of American Popular Theatre" (Ph.D diss. University of Illinois Press, 1963; Robert Dean Klassen, "The Tent-Repertoire Theatre: A Rural American Institution" (Ph.D diss., Michigan State University, 1979); and Sherwood Snyder III, "The Toby Shows" (Ph.D diss. University of Minnesota, 1966). Despite the ubiquity of the medicine show in rural America, surprisingly little has been written about it. The best study thus far is Brooks McNamara, *Step Right Up: An Illustrated History of the Medicine Show* (Garden City, N.Y.: Doubleday, 1976). McNamara found much material in issues of *Billboard* magazine, a source that other scholars have insufficiently utilized.

To investigate the discovery of black music in the late nineteenth century one should go directly to the publications that first introduced the material to the literate northern public. Bruce Jackson, ed., *The Negro and His Folklore in Nineteenth-Century Periodicals* (Austin: University of Texas Press, 1967) contains reprints of the most relevant journal articles dealing with the subject. Of course, the real awakening of interest in the spirituals began with William Francis Allen, Charles P. Ware, and Lucy M. Garrison, *Slave Songs of the United States* (New York: A. Simpson, 1867). Dena Epstein, in *Sinful Tunes and Spirituals*, has commented on the book's reception and on its seminal importance to folk scholarship. J. B. T. Marsh, *The Story of the Jubilee Singers with Their Songs* (Boston: Houghton, Osgood, 1880), is an old study of the pioneering black group, but it has not yet been superseded. The vogue for the spirituals which followed the tours of the Jubilee Singers is discussed by several writers, most notably Eileen Southern in *The Music of Black Americans: A History* (New York, W. W. Norton, 1971) and Gilbert Chase in *America's Music from the Pilgrims to the Present*, 2d rev. ed. (New York, McGraw-Hill, 1966). My own information has come principally from such music journals as *Etude*, *Musical Quarterly*, and *Musical Observer*.

As yet there has been no adequate study of musical nationalism at the turn of the century nor of its relationship to folk music. The interested student would be well advised to explore the "high-art" music journals mentioned above in addition to other contemporary popular and scholarly journals where people such as John Powell sometimes expressed their opinions. D. K. Wilgus, *Anglo-American Folksong Scholarship since 1898*, provides the best discussion of the motivations that underlay the collecting exploits of American folklorists, Anglo-Saxonist or otherwise. John A. Lomax, *Cowboy Songs and Other Frontier Ballads* (New York: Sturgis and Walton, 1910), is still the indispensable introduction to that genre, but the conclusions of this book should be balanced with those of John White, *Git Along, Little Dogies: Songs and Songmakers of the American West* (Urbana: University of Illinois Press, 1975), which has done much to divest cowboy song scholarship of the myths of anonymous or communal origins.

The sources of the preoccupation with the southern mountains are discussed most perceptively in Henry Shapiro, *Appalachia on Our Mind: The Southern Mountains and Mountaineers in the American Consciousness, 1890–1920* (Chapel Hill: University of North Carolina Press, 1978). Shapiro's excellent discussion of ballad scholarship and of the settlement schools can be supplemented by material delineated in Robert F. Munn, *The Southern Appalachians: A Bibliography and Guide to Studies* (Morgantown: West Virginia University Library, 1961).

Very little attention has been devoted to our first urban folk movement, that vogue for the concert singing of folk songs which flourished in the World War I period and in the early years of the twenties. There is a very fine essay on Ethel Park Richardson in the *JEMF Quarterly*, written by her grandson: Jon G. Smith, "She Kept On a-Goin': Ethel Park Richardson," *JEMF Quarterly* 13, no. 47 (Autumn 1977):105–15; but, to my knowledge, I am the only scholar who has dug extensively into the music journals and other periodical literature to track down information on the singers of folk songs and costume recitalists.

EARLY COMMERCIALIZATION: RAGTIME, BLUES, JAZZ

Eileen Southern, *The Music of Black Americans*, is the only general survey of black music in all its ramifications and is richly detailed and documented. There are two comprehensive accounts of ragtime. The most recent, William J. Schaefer and Johannes Riedel, *The Art of Ragtime* (Baton Rouge: Louisiana State University Press, 1973), is a competent, interpretive survey, but Rudi Blesh and Harriet Janis, *They All Played Ragtime*, 4th ed. (New York: Oak Publications, 1971) is still the best general history.

The Negro's breakaway from black-face minstrelsy into an independent expression of show business is discussed in Tom Fletcher, *100 Years of the Negro in Show Business* (New York: Burdge, 1954), a detailed but undisciplined account. James Weldon Johnson, in *Black Manhattan* (New York: Knopf, 1930), discusses the black show business scene in New York in the 1890s and tells the story of some southern musicians, such as himself and his brother J. Rosamond.

The American people's awakening consciousness of the blues in the early years of the twentieth century is discussed by the man who was largely responsible for it: William C. Handy, *Father of the Blues: An Autobiography* (New York: Macmillan, 1941). In *Born with the Blues* (Westport, Conn.: Hyperion Press, 1973), Perry Bradford discusses his role in the discovery of Mamie Smith and in the recording industry's decision to exploit the blues.

The blues genre has attracted a great wealth of scholarship, much of the best by English fans and collectors. Derrick Stewart-Baxter, for example, in *Ma Rainey and the Classic Blues Singers* (New York: Stein and Day, 1970), provides a good introduction to the style of blues first presented to the American public. There are at least three biographies of Bessie Smith: Paul Oliver, *Bessie Smith* (London: Cassell, 1959); Carman Moore, *Somebody's Angel Child: The Story of Bessie Smith* (New York: Crowell, 1969); and Chris Albertson, *Bessie* (New York: Stein and Day, 1972). I have found the Albertson book the most helpful.

The first study of the country blues was Samuel Charters, *The*

Country Blues (New York: Rinehart, 1959). In that book and in his *The Bluesmen* (New York: Oak Publications, 1967) Charters relates the musicians to their sociocultural contexts, a method that regrettably is not always followed by other music historians. Paul Oliver's studies of the blues, from the African roots through the era of recording, have been of generally high quality; *Blues Fell This Morning* (London: Cassell, 1960) and *The Story of the Blues* (New York: Barrie, 1969) are excellent analyses as are Oliver's notes to the Columbia anthology, *The Story of the Blues*, Columbia G30008 (intended as a supplement to the book of the same name). Jeff Titon, *Early Downhome Blues: A Musical and Cultural Analysis* (Urbana: University of Illinois Press, 1977), is an impressive multidisciplinary treatment of the blues. William Ferris, Jr., *Blues from the Delta* (Garden City, N.Y.: Doubleday, 1978), is an excellent study of the formative Mississippi blues scene which also has a useful annotated bibliography and discography that are relevant to the larger blues picture.

Among the small number of biographies of country bluesmen, two are of high quality: David Evans, *Tommy Johnson* (London: Studio Vista, 1971), and John Fahey, *Charley Patton* (London: Studio Vista, 1970). Unfortunately, there is no biography of Blind Lemon Jefferson and no full-scale study of the important Texas blues scene. Mack McCormick, one of the most knowledgeable of all the blues scholars and a folklorist of the highest competence, has long been conducting research on Texas blues music. But until his research assumes the form of a book, we will have to be content with the occasional record liner notes that carry a McCormick byline.

The blues are susceptible to varying interpretations. Lawrence Levine, for example, in *Black Culture and Black Consciousness*, sees in blues singing a simultaneous expression of a personalized, individualistic ethos and an urge to retain the old communal roots. LeRoi Jones, in *Blues People: Negro Music in White America* (New York: Morrow, 1963), interprets the music in the context of black nationalism. Tony Russell, on the other hand, sees a vigorous cultural interchange between Negroes and whites in *Blacks, Whites, and Blues* (New York: Stein and Day, 1970).

The literature on jazz is voluminous. There is no definitive bibliography, but a good start has been made by Alan P. Merriam and Robert J. Branford, *A Bibliography of Jazz* (Philadelphia: American Folklore Society, 1954) and by Robert George Reisner, *The Literature of Jazz: A Selective Bibliography* (New York: New York Public Library, 1959). The bibliography compiled by Frank Tirro in *Jazz: A History* (New York: W. W. Norton & Co., 1977), can also be consulted with great profit. There are several good book-length studies of jazz, including Rudi Blesh, *Shining Trumpets: A History of Jazz*, 4th ed. (London: Cassell, 1958); Barry Ulanov, *A History of Jazz in America* (New York: Viking Press, 1955); Rex Harris, *Jazz*, 5th ed. (Harmondsworth, England: Penguin Books, 1957); Marshall Stearns, *The Story of Jazz* (New York: Oxford University Press, 1970); and the 1977 book by Frank Tirro.

Among the biographies and autobiographies of jazz personalities the most important are Alan Lomax, *Mister Jelly Roll: The Fortunes of Jelly Roll Morton* (Berkeley and Los Angeles: University of California Press, 1973), Louis Armstrong's own story, *Satchmo: My Life in New Orleans* (New York: Prentice-Hall, 1954), Larry Gara, *The Baby Dodds Story* (Los Angeles: Contemporary, 1959), and Don Marquis's superb piece of detective work on "the first man of jazz," *In Search of Buddy Bolden* (Baton Rouge: Louisiana State University Press, 1978).

The era of New Orleans music which preceded the first jazz recordings in 1917 is, despite endless speculation, a period still murky and bathed in romance. No one has really done the kind of digging necessary to document the pre-1900 origins of jazz in the city. Henry Kmen told the story down to 1841 in *Music in New Orleans*, but his death in 1978 cut short the efforts which he had begun for the later period. A student at Tulane University, Curt Jerde, is now involved in research on the music of the period from 1841 to 1900. William J. Schaefer has made a significant contribution to our understanding of early jazz history in *Brass Bands and New Orleans Jazz* (Baton Rouge: Louisiana State University Press, 1977). Schaefer was assisted in his efforts by Richard B. Allen, the learned curator of the William Ransom Hogan Jazz Archive at Tulane University, one of the most impressive repositories of jazz lore in the United States. Al Rose, in *Storyville, New Orleans* (University: University of Alabama Press, 1974), provides an illuminating account of early ragtime and jazz musicians in the city and puts the relationship between the emerging music and the red-light district in the proper perspective. As previously noted, Marquis's book on Buddy Bolden fills in some of the missing gaps between the marching bands and the early recordings, and Harry O. Brunn, *The Story of the Original Dixieland Jazz Band* (Baton Rouge: Louisiana State University, 1960), comments on the oft-neglected contributions of white musicians to the developing art form while discussing the band of young white musicians who put the first jazz sounds on records. The inquiring reader would find it instructive to compare Brunn's white-oriented interpretation of jazz origins with the black perspective of someone like Rudi Blesh.

Expanding Markets: Hillbilly, Cajun, Gospel

Compared to the abundant material available on blues and jazz, the publications devoted to country and other rural-derived white musical forms are recent and sparse. There are no bibliographies of country music, for example, analogous to those available for blues and jazz, but Bill C. Malone, *Country Music, USA* (Austin: University of Texas Press, 1968) and Malone and Judy McCulloh, eds., *Stars of Country Music* (Urbana: University of Illinois Press, 1975) are good places to begin.

Two important repositories for country and other grass roots forms of music have come into existence since the fifties: the John Edwards Memorial Foundation in Los Angeles, and the Country Music Hall of Fame and Museum in Nashville. These organizations issue, respectively, the *JEMF Quarterly* and the *Journal of Country Music*. With these, and with *Old Time Music* (published by Tony Russell in England) and *Devil's Box* (a fiddle-oriented journal edited by Bill Harrison in Huntsville, Alabama), the student of early country music now has ample outlets for his scholarly or popular interests.

Before the dawning of academic interest, research and writing on country music was generally confined to dedicated fans and collectors who wrote for fan club journals, song magazines, or collectors' newsletters. Occasionally, there would appear an in-house publication such as George D. Hay, *A Story of the Grand Ole Opry* (Nashville, Tenn.: George D. Hay, 1953), or, even more rarely, a relative's loving memoir of a musician such as Carrie Rodgers, *My Husband, Jimmie Rodgers* (San Antonio, Tex.: Southern Literary Institute, 1935). The first book-length work devoted to country music was compiled by a fan in 1961. Linnell Gentry, *A History and Encyclopedia of Country, Western, and Gospel Music* (Nashville, Tenn.: McQuiddy Press, 1961), is an anthology of essays on country music extracted from magazines and a collection of biographical sketches compiled from questionnaires. It has since been republished by the Clairmont Corporation in Nashville in 1969 and is still a useful and oft-quoted compendium of material.

Much of the scholarly interest in country music of the last twenty years was inspired by the urban folk revival of the late fifties and early sixties. One of the stimulating sparks actually occurred a few years earlier, in 1952, with the issuance of the Folkways recording, *Anthology of American Folk Music*, FA 2951–2953. The six long-playing records included songs taken from hillbilly, Cajun, gospel, and country blues recordings made between 1927 and 1933 (from the private collection of Harry Smith). Packaged under the respectable label of "folk music," the anthology introduced grass roots music to an urban audience that had never heard it before.

In 1965 the *Journal of American Folklore*, after decades of neglect, devoted an entire issue (78, no. 309 [July–Sept. 1965]) to early country music. The "Hillbilly Issue," as it was called, contained important essays on the history of country music and pointed the way toward further research. A few years later *Western Folklore* published an issue (30 [July 1971]) called the JEMF issue, on the sources and resources of country music.

Robert Shelton was not an academician, but as folk music editor of the *New York Times* during the urban folk enthusiasm he became quite aware of the relationship between commercial country music and folk music. The result was *The Country Music Story* (New York: Bobbs-Merrill, 1966), an entertaining survey of country music history marked by a vast array of photographs gathered by Burt Goldblatt.

Bill C. Malone's *Country Music, USA* was based on his doctoral dissertation written at the University of Texas in Austin in 1965. The book was the first full-scale scholarly treatment of the subject (the dissertation, in fact, was the basis for much of Shelton's work). Like Gentry's book, Malone's was the product of a southern country boy who wrote from within the culture which he discussed.

Archie Green, in contrast, came to country music from a preoccupation with labor lore. His search for labor-related materials led him naturally to phonograph recordings, and that in turn led to an exhaustive interest in all types of grass roots music found on commercial recordings, radio transcriptions, song folios, and so forth. Green, *Only a Miner: Studies in Recorded Coal-Mining Songs* (Urbana: University of Illinois Press, 1972), is distinguished not only by its coverage of coal-mining songs, but also by the exhaustive knowledge it reflects of early hillbilly music. Like all of Green's work, it is indispensable.

The seventies have seen a proliferation of works on country music. Of special relevance to the early period of recording history are Douglas B. Green, *Country Roots: The Origins of Country Music* (New York: Hawthorn, 1976), an informal but fact-filled survey of country music history, and Charles Wolfe, *Grand Ole Opry: The Early Years, 1925–1935* (London: Old Time Music, 1975), and *Tennessee Strings: The Story of Country Music in Tennessee* (Knoxville: University of Tennessee Press, 1977). Wolfe's work can also be found in numerous journals and on liner notes of phonograph recordings; he is easily the best scholar now working in the field of early commercial country music.

Biographies of early country performers are not plentiful, but a few are quite good. There is regrettably nothing in country music comparable to the series of blues-oriented books edited by Paul Oliver for Studio Vista in London, but the University of Illinois Press, with its Music in American Life Series, is rapidly filling much of the gap. One of the University of Illinois publications, *Stars of Country Music*, contains essays on some of the early performers (Walter Haden on Vernon Dalhart, Charles Wolfe on Uncle Dave Macon, John Atkins on the Carter Family, D. K. Wilgus on Bradley Kincaid, Chris Comber and Mike Paris on Jimmie Rodgers, and Norman Cohen on an assemblage of performers he calls "early pioneers"). The Comber and Paris essay was extracted from their subsequently published book on the life and career of Jimmie Rodgers: *Jimmie the Kid* (London: Eddison Press, 1976). Nolan Porterfield has completed his impressively researched study, *Jimmie Rodgers*, to be published in the fall of 1979 by the University of Illinois Press. I am convinced that it will be the definitive work on Rodgers and an invaluable interpretation of the early commercial period of country music.

The literature on white gospel music is much sparser than that on country music, and the gospel "industry" has been much slower than the country industry to recognize the need for historical documentation. Ottis J. Knippers, *Who's Who among Southern Singers and Composers* (Lawrenceburg, Tenn.: J. D. Vaughan, 1937) is a good introduction to the gospel personnel of the early commercial period, but it is rare and out of print. Mrs. J. R. Baxter and Videt Polk produced a similar work, *Gospel Song Writers Biography* (Dallas: Stamps-Baxter Music Company, 1971), but it contains little information on the quartets. Jo Lee Fleming, "James D. Vaughan, Music Publisher" (S.M.D. diss., Union Theological Seminary, 1972) is a first-rate work that deserves to be better known and is almost the only scholarly piece available on the post-1920 gospel period. Jesse Burt and Duane Allen, *The History of Gospel Music* (Nashville, Tenn.: K & S Press, 1971), contains very little information on gospel music's early period, and it went out of print soon after its publication. Lois Blackwell, *The Wings of the Dove: The Story of Gospel Music in America* (Norfolk, Va.: Donning Co., 1978), is the first real attempt at a historical overview of the music, but it has only 154 pages of text, about 30 of which are devoted to the 1920s. Charles Wolfe is now overseeing the production of a book of essays on gospel music for the University of Illinois Press which will include work by such scholars as Douglas Green, Neil Rosenberg, Bill C. Malone, Stanley Brobston, and Harlan Daniel. Daniel has provided assistance to many writers, but his wide knowledge of country and gospel music has seldom made its way into print.

Cajun and Chicano styles of music have been similarly neglected by writers and researchers. The preservation and documentation of

Cajun culture were given a decided boost, though, with the establishment in 1974 of the Center for Acadian and Creole Folklore at the University of Southwestern Louisiana in Lafayette. A number of academic theses have shed some light on Cajun culture, but have said little about the music. However, Nicholas Spitzer is currently engaged in a major research project as part of his doctoral program at the University of Texas. One result of his labors is the impressive "Cajuns and Creoles: The French Gulf Coast," in Allen Tullos, ed., *Long Journey Home: Folklife in the South* (Chapel Hill, N.C.: Southern Exposure, 1977), pp. 140–55. A very valuable introduction to Cajun history and culture is Lauren C. Post, *Cajun Sketches* (Baton Rouge: Louisiana State University Press, 1962). It can be supplemented by Pierre Daigle, *Tears, Love, and Laughter: The Story of the Acadians* (Church Point, La.: Acadian Publishing Enterprise, 1972), which contains a number of good biographical sketches and vignettes of Cajun musicians, and by William Faulkner Rushton, *The Cajuns: From Acadia to Louisiana* (New York: Farrar, Straus & Giroux, 1979). Another useful, short introduction to Cajun music can be found in *Acadiana Profile* 4, no. 3 (October–November 1974): 4–7, written by Revon Reed, a leading authority on Cajun music. The varied styles of precommercial Cajun music can be sampled on an album produced for the Louisiana Folklore Society, "Folksongs of the Louisiana Acadians," collected, edited, and annotated by Harry Oster. The best introduction to early recorded Cajun music is the recordings themselves. They can be heard to best advantage on a series produced and edited by Chris Strachwitz on the Old-Timey label (especially vol. 1, "First Recordings, the 1920s"; and vol. 5, "The Early Years, 1928–1938").

Tex-Mex, or Chicano, music is as old as any other form of American folk music, and its recording came about as early (i.e., in the mid-twenties) as any Anglo genre. Nevertheless, there are virtually no published discussions of it, and no theses or dissertations documenting its commercial evolution. Two good discussions of its folk roots, however, are Americo Paredes, *A Texas-Mexican Cancionero: Folksongs of the Lower Border* (Urbana: University of Illinois Press, 1975) and Paredes, *With His Pistol in His Hand: A Border Ballad and Its Hero* (Austin: University of Texas Press, 1958). Some background is provided by Claes of Geijerstam, *Popular Music in Mexico* (Albuquerque: University of New Mexico Press, 1976), but, aside from a brief appendix by Elizabeth H. Heist on border music of the 1970s, the book says nothing about the early period of commercialization. In his review of Les Blank's movie about Chicano music, "Chulas Fronteras," *JEMF Quarterly* 7, no. 43 (Autumn 1976):138–46, Archie Green makes a few discerning comments about early recorded Chicano music and suggests the need for further exploration. The beginning student of Chicano music would be well advised to listen to a series of albums produced by Chris Strachwitz on his Folklyric label (reviewed in the *JEMFQ* issue mentioned above). These volumes, under the title *Texas-Mexican Border Music*, are accompanied by brochures and discographies. They are the products of Strachwitz's own indefatigable collecting of old 78-rpm records in the Chicano communities of the Southwest. Without his labors students of American folk music would be infinitely poorer.

THE GREAT DEPRESSION AND NEW TECHNOLOGIES

The Great Depression was a crucial period for American music, when folk simplicity began to give way to greater commercial awareness, but little has been done to treat the era's music in a comprehensive manner. Bob Coltman, in "Across the Chasm: How the Depression Changed Country Music," *Old Time Music* 23 (Winter 1976–1977):6–12, follows a line of inquiry that should be instructive for students of other types of music.

There is no major study of the Mexican border stations, but Gerald Carson discusses the man who inaugurated border radio programming in *The Roguish World of Dr. Brinkley* (New York: Rinehart & Co., 1960), and Ed Kahn analyzes the x-stations' roles in the dissemination of folk music in "International Relations, Dr. Brinkley, and Hillbilly Music," *JEMF Quarterly* 9, part 2 (Summer 1973):47–55. Another great purveyor of country music in the thirties is discussed by Pat Ahrens in "The Role of the Crazy Water Crystals Company in Promoting Hillbilly Music," *JEMF Quarterly* 6 (Autumn 1970):107–9.

Students of both country music and the blues often focus on one end or the other of the historical period of their subjects, concentrating on the early quasi-folk period of the twenties or on the modern era of commercial growth, thereby neglecting the important interim period. Ivan Tribe, however, is an exception. His area of concentration has been the decades of the thirties and forties, and his prolific research, based principally on interviews, has borne fruit in many articles in such magazines as *Bluegrass Unlimited* and *Old Time Music*.

A few publications convey the feeling of what it was like to be a country musician during a period of hard times. *My Husband, Jimmie Rodgers* and a very rare account of Bob Wills—Ruth Sheldon, *Hubbin' It: The Life of Bob Wills* (Tulsa, Okla.: privately printed, 1938)—both treat their subjects during the depression years. In 1977 the Country Music Foundation Press published the posthumous autobiography of Alton Delmore of the influential Delmore Brothers duet:

Alton Delmore, *Truth is Stranger than Publicity* (Nashville, Tenn.: Country Music Foundation Press, 1977). Edited by Charles K. Wolfe, the book recreates the atmosphere of hillbilly barnstorming during the thirties, and in subsequent decades, as the Delmore Brothers became one of the most popular acts in country music.

The best account of black gospel music during the thirties is Tony Heilbut's pioneering *The Gospel Sound: Good News and Bad Times* (New York: Simon and Schuster, 1971). Actually it is a general survey of the total black gospel scene and is marked by the enthusiasm and affection of a devoted fan. Heilbut's discussion of Georgia Tom Dorsey is perceptive, but along with the remarks made by George Robinson Ricks in "Some Aspects of the Religious Music of the United States Negro" (Ph.D diss. Northwestern University, 1960, and those of Levine in *Black Culture and Black Consciousness*, they are almost the only published assessments of the great black composer. Biographies of both Dorsey and Charles H. Tindley are badly needed.

Few studies of white gospel music in the thirties are available. The books by Ottis Knippers and Mrs. J. R. Baxter mentioned in the preceding section make useful references to musicians who performed during the period, and two books on the Blackwood Brothers discuss the experiences of struggling quartets during the depression: Kree Jack Racine, *Above All: The Blackwood Brothers Quartet* (Memphis, Tenn.: Jarodoce Publications, 1967) and James Blackwood, with Dan Martin, *The James Blackwood Story* (Monroeville, Pa.: Whitaker House, 1975). There is no adequate biography of Albert E. Brumley, but I am now preparing an essay on him which will be included in Charles Wolfe's edited book on white gospel music.

Books have been written on the various cultural projects of the Works Progress Administration, and some scholars have used the material collected by the government-sponsored researchers. But no one has attempted to draw together in one study the disparate ventures in the folk music field undertaken by the W.P.A. or by other agencies such as the Resettlement Administration. One can envision a doctoral dissertation assaying "folk music and the federal government."

Samplings of songs about the depression can be found in several good sources. The New Lost City Ramblers recorded an album, *Songs of the Depression*, Folkways FH5264, which contained selections taken mainly from commercial hillbilly recordings. There has not been a similar utilization of commercial blues or gospel music, but Levine includes a valuable discussion of black depression material in *Black Culture and Black Consciousness*, and Lawrence Gellert collected a vast amount of noncommercial folk material in the thirties, much of the best of which is recorded on *Negro Songs of Protest*, Rounder 4004.

The awakening of southern labor is discussed by Thomas Tippett, *When Southern Labor Stirs* (New York: Jonathan Cape and Harrison Smith, 1931); George B. Tindall, *The Emergence of the New South, 1913–1945* (Baton Rouge: Louisiana State University Press, 1967), and most vividly by Irving Bernstein, *The Lean Years: A History of the American Worker, 1920–33* (Boston: Houghton, Mifflin, 1960). Liston Pope, *Millhands and Preachers: A Study of Gastonia* (New Haven, Conn.: Yale University Press, 1942), provides a cultural explanation as to why unionism, particularly of the radical variety, floundered in the South. It is still the best study of the textile upheavals. Archie Green concentrates more directly on the music of the textile workers in "Born on Picketlines, Textile Workers' Songs Are Woven into History," *Textile Labor* 21, no. 4 (April 1961):3–5, in his notes to the Dorsey Dixon recording *Babies in the Mill*, Testament T-3301, and in "Dorsey Dixon: Minstrel of the Mills," *Sing Out: The Folk Song Magazine* 16, no. 3 (July 1966):10–13. John Greenway has a short section on the minstrel of Gastonia, Ella May Wiggins, in *American Folksongs of Protest* (Philadelphia, University of Pennsylvania Press, 1953), but the reader can get a better inkling of Ella May's emergence as a labor martyr in articles contemporaneous with her death: Jessie Lloyd, "Ella May, Murdered, Lives in Her Songs of Class Strife," *Daily Worker*, September 20, 1929; and Margaret Larkin, "Story of Ella May," *New Masses*, November 1929.

Coal-mining songs that wound up on commercial hillbilly recordings are the subjects of Archie Green's *Only a Miner: Studies in Recorded Coal-Mining Songs*, but in the notes to Sara Ogan Gunning, *Girl of Constant Sorrow*, Folk-Legacy FSA-26, Green takes as his topic the songs of a woman who was an active participant in the labor conflicts of eastern Kentucky. His remarks about the mating of northern radical rhetoric and southern conservative balladry have often been quoted. Gunning's half-sister, Aunt Molly Jackson, one of the most famous of the southern protest singers, has been memorialized in the entire issue of *Kentucky Folklore Record* 7, no. 4 (October–December 1961). Her singing style can be heard on *Aunt Molly Jackson*, Rounder 1002, a collection of songs originally recorded for the Library of Congress in 1939. Her story, as well as that of the other balladeers who struggled for economic justice in the eastern Kentucky coal fields, is discussed by John Hevener in his long-awaited *Which Side Are You On? The Harlan County Coal Miners, 1931–1939* (Urbana: University of Illinois Press, 1979).

Other regions of southern economic turmoil have interested scholars also, but few writers have concentrated on the music that arose from them. The Southern Tenant Farmers Union Papers (Southern

Historical Collection, University of North Carolina, Chapel Hill) have been explored by several writers, but no one has really dug through them to determine the role that music played in the union's organizing efforts. Likewise, insufficient effort has been expended to interview surviving union members who may have some recollections of musical activities, although John Greenway did discuss John Handcox, a leading STFU poet, in *American Folksongs of Protest*.

There are a few sound analyses of the Dust Bowl migration and of its effects on California society. Walter S. Stein, *California and the Dust Bowl Migration* (Westport, Conn.: Greenwood Press, 1973) is the most comprehensive history, while Jacqueline Gordon Sherman concentrates on one specific group of migrants in "The Oklahomans in California during the Depression Decade, 1931–1941" (Ph.D diss., University of California, Los Angeles, 1970). All students of Okie music should, like Stein and Sherman, draw upon the music collection of Charles Todd and Robert Sonkin, now deposited in the Library of Congress Archive of Folk Song. Todd and Sonkin wrote a short account of their field research in "Ballads of the Okies," *New York Times Magazine*, November 17, 1940, pp. 6–7, 18. Someone should now write a history of country music in California.

The poet of the Okies, Woody Guthrie, has been much written about, but often from a romanticized, polemical, or distorted perspective. John Greenway's writings on Guthrie, in *American Folksongs of Protest* and in both popular and academic publications (such as the obituary in the *Journal of American Folklore* 81, no. 319 [January–March 1969], pp. 62–64), are generally both admiring and sensible. The most accurate and unbiased Guthrie scholar, although in sympathy with his subject, is Richard A. Reuss, who compiled *A Woody Guthrie Bibliography* (New York: Guthrie Children's Trust Fund, 1968) and has written the most balanced assessment of the man in "Woody Guthrie and His Folk Tradition," *Journal of American Folklore* 83, no. 329 (July–September 1970):273–304. R. Serge Denisoff has done most to explain the relationship between southern protest singers and northern radical activists, as well as the urban folk music movement which resulted from this fusion, in "The Proletarian Renascence: The Folkness of the Ideological Folk," *Journal of American Folklore* 82, no. 323 (January–March 1969):51–65, and in more extended fashion in *Great Day Coming: Folk Music and the American Left* (Urbana: University of Illinois Press, 1971).

Despite the revival of western swing in our own time, there has been little published material on the genre, scholarly or otherwise. In fact, Ruth Sheldon's 1938 biography of Bob Wills, *Hubbin' It*, was about the only kind of work (outside of collectors' and fan club journals) available until 1976 when Wills's piano player, Al Stricklin, along with Jon McConal, contributed *My Years with Bob Wills* (San Antonio, Tex.: Naylor Company, 1976), and Charles Townsend completed his biography of Wills. Townsend's *San Antonio Rose: The Life and Music of Bob Wills* (Urbana: University of Illinois Press, 1976) is a fascinating account of the man who dominated the country music of the Southwest during the thirties and who has left his imprint on thousands of musicians who came after him. Townsend has expressed an intention to write a biography of that other influential western swing pioneer, Milton Brown, but thus far no other studies of the music nor of its performers have appeared. Neither is there a substantial study of W. Lee O'Daniel, except for Seth McKay's outdated *W. Lee O'Daniel and Texas Politics, 1938–1942* (Lubbock: Texas Tech Press, 1944). If future researchers decide to delve more deeply into western swing history, they will find their tasks greatly eased by the establishment of the Western Swing Collection (composed primarily of records) at Tulsa University. The collection is under the direction of western swing authority Guy Logsdon, who wrote a good survey of the genre for the Texas Folklore Society: "Western Swing," in Francis Edward Abernethy, ed., *What's Going On?* Publications of the Texas Folklore Society, no. 40 (Austin, Tex.: Encino Press, 1976).

Those other dynamic forms of "western" country music–honky-tonk and singing cowboy–have also had few chroniclers. Except for scattered references to the music in popular magazines, my doctoral dissertation of 1965, and the book which proceeded from it (*Country Music, USA*) contain the only extended discussions of the honky-tonk style.

The music of the singing cowboys has received a much fuller literary treatment than that extended to the honky-tonk musicians. Douglas B. Green's essay on Gene Autry in *Stars of Country Music* is a competent assessment of the first great singing cowboy's career, but Autry has always been stingy with interviews; therefore much of his story has always been out of the reach of researchers. An indication that he may have been waiting to tell his own story came in 1978 when Autry, with the assistance of Mickey Herskowitz, published an autobiography called *Back in the Saddle Again* (Garden City, N.Y.: Doubleday, 1978).

Another great singing cowboy, Tex Ritter, is the subject of an affectionate biography by country singer and cowboy actor, Johnny Bond: *The Tex Ritter Story* (New York: Chappell, 1976). Despite his very close personal and business association with Ritter, Bond writes a reasonably objective, and always entertaining, account of "America's Most Beloved Cowboy." The total effect of the singing cowboys upon American popular culture and country music has not been deeply explored, but a good beginning was made by Stephen Ray Tucker, in "The Western Image in Country Music" (M.A. thesis, Southern Methodist University, 1976).

THE NATIONALIZATION OF SOUTHERN MUSIC

Although World War II was a watershed in the social history of the United States, writers on American music have devoted little attention specifically to the period from 1941 to 1945. My *Country Music, USA*, however, explores the relationship between the war and the music's international expansion. All writers on rhythm and blues comment on the Negro's migration north, but few make references to the changed consciousness that the war might have promoted among blacks.

The best discussion of southern white migration to the North is Lewis Killian, *White Southerners* (New York: Random House, 1970). Killian's discussion of "hillbilly bars" and "storefront churches" should stimulate other writers to investigate southern white communities in such cities as Detroit, Cincinnati, and Dayton. (For that matter, no one has really studied the effects of the movement of rural southerners into southern cities during the war.) John Hevener has long been working on a study of southern white migrants in Akron, Ohio, but his research has thus far been conveyed only in an unpublished paper read at the Northern Great Plains History Conference in October 1975: "Appalachians in Akron, 1914–1945: The Transfer of Southern Folk Culture."

The national burgeoning of country music created new "stars," some of whom have inspired biographical accounts. Townsend's biography of Bob Wills recreates much of the atmosphere of wartime America, and Elizabeth Schlappi, in *Roy Acuff, the Smoky Mountain Boy* (Gretna, La.: Pelican Publishing Co., 1978), explains how a mountain boy managed to become the symbol of American country music around the world. Ernest Tubb, the man who took the honky-tonk style to the Grand Ole Opry, has not received a full, published biographical treatment, even though he has been a professional, and highly influential, musician for forty-two years. Townsend Miller's essay on Tubb in *Stars of Country Music* is a competent, though brief, summary, but the most extensive treatment of the singer is Ronnie Floyd Pugh, "The Texas Troubadour: Selected Aspects of the Career of Ernest Tubb" (M.A. thesis, Stephen F. Austin State University, 1978). Another singer whose career began during the war years, but who did not attain superstardom until the early fifties, was Hank Williams. Williams has evoked considerable attention from writers, mostly in popular magazines, but Henry Pleasants included a chapter on him in *The Great American Popular Singers* (New York: Simon and Schuster, 1974) and Roger M. Williams wrote a serious biography called *Sing a Sad Song: The Life of Hank Williams* (Garden City, N.J.: Doubleday, 1970).

The evolution of the blues into an aggressive, electrified, urban art form came at the end of the thirties and during the war years. The story of the emergence of rhythm and blues has generally been buried away in music periodicals or in larger works devoted to the development of soul or rock 'n' roll. Too often, rhythm and blues is treated merely as the precursor of more modern forms of black music and is insufficiently valued for its own sake. Arnold Shaw's The *World of Soul* (New York: Paperback Library, 1971), however, provides a good discussion of rhythm and blues, though in the context of a larger historical discussion of black music. In *Honkers and Shouters: The Golden Years of Rhythm and Blues* (New York: Macmillan Publishing Co., 1978), Shaw concentrates more directly on the important decades of the forties and fifties. Both books are highly detailed accounts by a man who was a long-time producer of rhythm and blues records.

A good short overview of rhythm and blues has been provided by Tony Glover, a white musician who had done much to introduce blues music to young white audiences: "R & B," *Sing Out* 15, no. 2 (May 1965):7–13. The most brilliant study of the modern blues, though, and one that should serve as a model for the study of other forms of music, is Charles Keil, *Urban Blues* (Chicago, University of Chicago Press, 1966). Keil contributes an appendix designed to help the reader/listener distinguish among the varied styles of the blues, and discusses some of the major blues singers such as Bobby Blue Bland and B. B. King.

Other good discussions of B. B. King can be found in Arnold Shaw's two books and especially in a two-part article by Pete Welding, "B. B. King: The Mississippi Giant," *Downbeat* 45, no. 16 (October 5, 1978) and no. 17 (October 19, 1978). The second installment contains material on T-Bone Walker who, despite his seminal importance, has had little of substance written about him. Muddy Waters, one of the prime forces behind the transition of the Delta blues into urban blues, is the subject of two excellent studies: Jim Rooney, *Bossmen: Bill Monroe and Muddy Waters* (New York: Dial Press, 1971) and Robert Palmer, "Muddy Waters: The Delta Son Never Sets," *Rolling Stone*, issue 275 (October 5, 1978), pp. 53–56.

All of the general histories of rock 'n' roll include information on Elvis Presley and the other southern rockabillies. The most complete histories are Carl Belz, *The Story of Rock* (New York: Oxford University Press, 1969) and Charles Gillett, *The Sound of the City: The Rise of Rock 'n' Roll* (New York, Dell, 1972). The most entertaining book on the subject is the coffee table–style volume produced by *Rolling Stone* magazine: Jim Miller, ed., *The Rolling Stone Illustrated History of Rock and Roll* (New York: Random House, 1976). The important contributions made by New Orleans musicians (mostly black) to rock 'n' roll are discussed in John Broven, *Walking to New Orleans: The Story of New Orleans Rhythm and Blues* (Sussex, England: Blues Unlimited, 1974).

There are numerous scattered articles on individual rockabillies. Among the best are Chet Flippo, "The Buddy Holly Story," *Rolling Stone*, no. 274 (September 21, 1978), pp. 49–51; Dennis E. Hensley's interview with Carl Perkins in *Guitar Player* 9, no. 3 (March 1975): 18, 39–40; and Nick Tosches's discussion of Jerry Lee Lewis in *Country: The Biggest Music in America* (New York: Stein and Day, 1977). Collectively, many of the rockabillies are discussed in John Pugh, "The Rise and Fall of Sun Records," *Country Music* 2, no. 3 (November 1973): 26–32.

The literature on Elvis Presley is vast and proliferating. The best book-length biography remains Jerry Hopkins, *Elvis: A Biography* (New York: Warner Books, 1972). A shorter interpretation makes up part of Greil Marcus, *Mystery Train: Images of America in Rock 'n' Roll* (New York: E. P. Dutton & Co., 1976), a brilliant and critically acclaimed attempt to say something about the flawed American promise through the lives and careers of a few blues and rock 'n' roll entertainers. A side of Elvis that was generally kept hidden from the public is presented in Red and Sonny West and Dave Hebler, as told to Steve Dunleavy, *Elvis, What Happened?* (New York: Ballantine Books, 1977). For a review of this and other Elvis-inspired material, see Mark Crispin Miller, "The King," *New York Review of Books* 24, no. 20 (December 8, 1977):38–42.

THE SIXTIES AND SEVENTIES: ROCK, GOSPEL, SOUL

Aside from listening to the music, one can best comprehend modern rock culture by reading the magazines devoted to the phenomenon. As Richard Robinson and Andy Zwerling note in *The Rock Scene* (New York: Pyramid Books, 1971), where a long list of English and American rock periodicals appears, rock music has been a graveyard for magazines. Of those that have endured for any length of time, *Creem*, *Crawdaddy*, and *Rolling Stone* have presented the widest coverage of music. *Rolling Stone* has also had pretensions of being a journal of politics and ideas, and its lengthy essays and interviews are not solely concerned with music. Many of its best articles have been anthologized in *The Rolling Stone Record Review* and *The Rolling Stone Rock 'n' Roll Reader*. Another excellent anthology of articles taken from a wide variety of publications is Jonathan Eisen, ed., *The Age of Rock: Sounds of the American Cultural Revolution* (New York: Random House, 1969).

Among the general histories or interpretations of rock, the three mentioned earlier by Belz, Gillett, and Marcus each have information that helps to illuminate rock 'n' roll's evolution to rock, as do Richard Meltzer, *The Aesthetics of Rock* (New York: Something Else Press, 1970); Stephanie Spinner, *Rock is Beautiful: An Anthology of American Lyrics, 1953–1968* (New York: Dell, 1970); and Stewart Goldstein and Alan Jacobson, *Oldies But Goodies: The Rock 'n' Roll Years* (New York: Mason/Charter, 1977). None of these books has much to say about the Macon Sound or the southern rockers of the seventies. There are, however, three or four books on Janis Joplin, the best being Myra Friedman's *Buried Alive* (New York, Morrow, 1973).

For contemporary black gospel music Tony Heilbut, *The Gospel Sound*, is still the best general reference, while Lois Blackwell, *The Wings of the Dove*, is about the only overview available for the white gospel scene. No one, however, should overlook William C. Martin's fine assessment of contemporary white gospel music: "At the Corner of Glory Avenue and Hallelujah Street," *Harper's* 244 (January 1972):95–99. Biographies and autobiographies of any gospel singers are scarce, but something can be learned about Mahalia Jackson in Laurraine Goreau, *Just Mahalia Baby* (Waco, Tex.: Word Books, 1975) or in Mahalia's autobiography, *Movin' On Up* (New York: Hawthorn Books, 1966). James Blackwood has told his own story, with the assistance of Dan Martin, in *The James Blackwood Story* (Monroeville, Pa.: Whitaker House, 1975), and has been the subject of a biography by Kree Jack Racine: *Above All: The Blackwood Brothers Quartet* (Memphis, Tenn.: Jarodoce Publications, 1967). Another useful autobiography is John Daniel Sumner, *Gospel Music Is My Life* (Nashville, Tenn.: Impact Books, 1971).

The commercial burgeoning of soul music in the mid-sixties, along with the emergence of the Black Power movement, provoked extensive media coverage and popular writing. Along with the material carried in the major music publications such as *Billboard*, *Cashbox*, *Melody Maker*, and *Rolling Stone*, one can find an extensive number of articles on soul entertainers in the popular press. James Brown, for example, received lengthy treatment in *Time*, April 1, 1966; *Newsweek*, July 1, 1968; and *Look*, February 18, 1969.

Books discussing soul music exclusively or in part include Ian Hoare, *The Soul Book* (New York: Dell, 1975); David Morse, *Motown and the Arrival of Black Music* (London: Studio Vista, 1971); Phyl Garland, *The Sound of Soul* (Chicago: Regnery, 1969); and Arnold Shaw's two books, *The World of Soul* and *Honkers and Shouters*.

THE NATIONAL RESURGENCE OF COUNTRY MUSIC

Country music's commercial resurgence in the sixties and seventies was the context for a rash of publications, both scholarly and popular. The joint role played by the Grand Ole Opry and its owner, the National Life and Accident Insurance Company, in promoting Nashville's growth as a music center is discussed by Richard A. Peterson in "Single-Industry Firm to Conglomerate Synergistics: Alternative Strategies for Selling Insurance and Country Music," in James Blumstein and Benjamin Walter, eds., *Growing Metropolis: Aspects of Development in Nashville* (Nashville, Tenn.: Vanderbilt University Press, 1975), pp. 341–57.

The identification of country music with conservative politics was another factor that promoted media, journalistic, and scholarly interest. Florence King, in "Red Necks, White Socks, and Blue Ribbon Fear," *Harper's* 249 (July 1974): 30–34, and Richard Goldstein, "My Country Music Problem—and Yours," *Mademoiselle* 77, no. 2 (June 1973): 114–15, 185, saw only ominous implications in country music's burgeoning popularity. On the other hand, Paul DiMaggio, Richard A. Peterson, and Jack Esco, Jr., presented a more balanced picture of the music's political stance in "Country Music: Ballad of the Silent Majority," in R. Serge Denisoff and Richard A. Peterson, ed., *The Sounds of Social Change* (Chicago: Rand McNally, 1972), pp. 38–55.

In the multitude of magazine articles that accompanied country music's success, writers generally treated the art form seriously and without the sarcasm or condescension it had formerly received. Seldom does one encounter a title such as "Thar's Gold in Them Thar Hillbillies." Among the better magazine issues dealing with country music are *Newsweek*, June 18, 1973; *Time*, May 5, 1974; *Newsweek*, August 14, 1978; and *Playboy*, October 1978 (this last an interview with Dolly Parton).

Several country entertainers such as Chet Atkins, Johnny Cash, Eddy Arnold, Glen Campbell, and Dolly Parton have received book-length treatment, but the best is Loretta Lynn's autobiography, written with the aid of George Vecsey, *Coal Miner's Daughter* (New York:

Warner Books, 1976). A movie based on the book and starring Cissy Spacek is scheduled for a 1979 release.

General histories or interpretations of country music continue to appear. John Grissim, *Country Music: White Man's Blues* (New York: Coronet Communications, 1970) and Nick Tosches, *Country: The Biggest Music in America* (New York: Stein and Day, 1977), are both products of rock journalists who seem drawn to country music because of what they consider to be its bizarre or macho characteristics. Paul Hemphill, on the other hand, stresses the music's working-man image in *The Nashville Sound: Bright Lights and Country Music* (New York: Simon and Schuster, 1970), a series of vignettes about country music personalities. Jack Hurst, *Nashville's Grand Ole Opry* (New York: Abrams, 1975) is a lavishly illustrated, coffee table treatment of that institution. Dorothy Horstman, *Sing Your Heart Out, Country Boy* (New York: E. P. Dutton, 1975), is the most unusual, and in many ways the best, of the books on country music. It is a collection of songs arranged by category (songs of home, prison songs, cowboy songs, etc.) and introduced by commentary, often by the composers themselves, about why the song was written.

There are a few short articles and reviews about Gram Parsons and the Flying Burrito Brothers in the rock journals, but the only extended essay is that by Judson Klinger and Greg Mitchell: "Gram Finale," *Crawdaddy*, October 1976, pp. 43–58. The fullest discussion of Austin music is Jan Reid, *The Improbable Rise of Redneck Rock* (Austin, Tex.: Heidelberg Publishers, 1974). Michael Bane also discusses some of the Austin country singers singers in *The Outlaws* (New York: Country Music Magazine Press, 1978).

The urban folk revival is documented in the various magazines that promoted the phenomenon, most notably *Sing Out, Broadside,* and *Little Sandy Review,* and in the liner notes which accompanied the recordings. Oscar Brand, *The Ballad Mongers: Rise of the Modern Folk Song* (New York: Funk and Wagnalls, 1962), is a good overview of the subject, while R. Serge Denisoff provides analyses of the movement's left-wing origins and contemporary significance in *Great Day Coming: Folk Music and the American Left* (Urbana: University of Illinois Press, 1971).

Bluegrass has inspired several good articles and books. Alan Lomax did much to make the music academically respectable with "Bluegrass Background: Folk Music With Overdrive," *Esquire* 52, no 4 (October 1959):103–9; but L. Mayne Smith, "An Introduction to Bluegrass," *Journal of American Folklore* 78 (July–September 1965):245–56; and Neil V. Rosenberg, "From Sound to Style: The Emergence of

Bluegrass," *Journal of American Folklore* 80 (April–June 1967):143–50, were the first scholarly accounts. The best book on bluegrass music is Bob Artis, *Bluegrass* (New York: Hawthorn Books, 1975), but it may well be superseded when Neil Rosenberg and Ralph Rinzler complete their studies of, respectively, bluegrass music and Bill Monroe (both for the University of Illinois Press).

INDEX

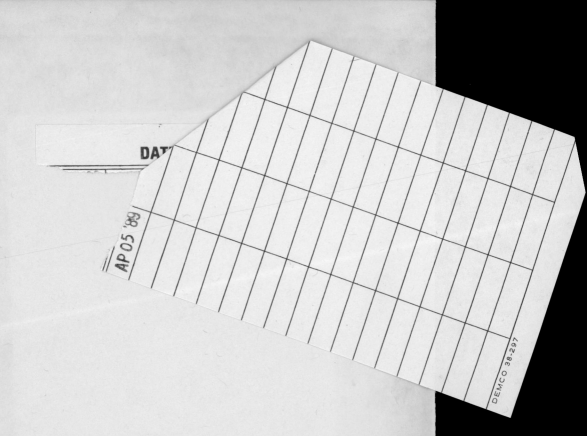